The ACTFL Foreign Language Education Series

D1536986

Modern Media in Foreign Language Education:

Theory and Implementation

Wm. Flint Smith
Editor

James P. Pusack
Robert Ariew
David M. Weible
David H. Wyatt
Kathleen Marshall Pederson
Catherine Doughty
Nina Garrett
John H. Underwood
Philip Hubbard
Constance O. Curtin
Stanley L. Shinall

Published by National Textbook Company
in conjunction with the American Council on the Teaching of Foreign Languages

DUQUESNE UNIVERSITY LIBRARY

Modern Media in Foreign Language Education: Theory and Implementation

Edited by Wm. Flint Smith

In conjunction with the American Council on the Teaching of Foreign Languages

National Textbook Company, *Lincolnwood, Illinois U.S.A.*

P 10
B 7
vol. 18

1988 Printing

Copyright © 1987 by National Textbook Company
4255 West Touhy Avenue
Lincolnwood (Chicago), Illinois 60646-1975 U.S.A.
All rights reserved. No part of this book may
be reproduced, stored in a retrieval system, or
transmitted in any form or by any means, electronic,
mechanical, photocopying, recording or otherwise,
without the prior permission of National Textbook Company.
Manufactured in the United States of America.
Library of Congress Catalog Card Number: 87-62037

8 9 0 ML 9 8 7 6 5 4 3 2

Contents

AUG 22 1991

Foreword

Modern Media in Foreign Language Education is the first volume in the ACTFL Foreign Language Education series devoted exclusively to educational technology in language teaching. Conceived (and advertised) as a single book on a broad range of media-related topics, the original publication effort was quickly redefined to encompass two volumes, the first of which contains writings dealing primarily with CALL (computer-assisted language learning). *Modern Media* provides up-to-date information to language teachers at all levels, as well as to administrators, authors, and researchers on the interaction between computer technology and second-language learning. The second volume will incorporate previously announced chapters on the language laboratory, television, and interactive video, along with reports on CALL or other media-based projects and research.

The contributors to this volume represent an impressive breadth of experience and background. All are applied linguists who have wrestled with the task of achieving better teaching and more efficient learning via CALL. Three teach or have taught German; three teach French (two of them in high school); three are in ESL; and one each teaches Russian or Spanish. Half of them hold important administrative responsibilities in their parent institutions, in addition to teaching assignments. No less significant is the fact that five of the authors have published courseware in their own right; four have been software editors or have written computer columns for major journals or newsletters; three have authored monographs on the topic; and three are teacher trainers. All have carried out extensive research on some aspect of CALL.

The writings in *Modern Media* are essays that represent a broad survey of CALL theory, research, and implementation in the mid-1980s. Throughout its pages, the authors have attempted to suggest the principles that, in the future, should guide CALL in curriculum, methodology, and research efforts, in the design and evaluation of software, and in teacher training. Some acquaintance with the thrust and purpose of media-aided language teaching will be useful in reading this collection, but no previous knowledge of computers or computing as such is assumed.

Modern Media is the result of the collective efforts of many individuals (not only the authors), whose frequent interchanges have helped to shape the scope and content of this book. The Advisory Board to the Editor

(Robert Ariew, Pennsylvania State University; Col. Ruben Cubero, United States Air Force Academy [USAFA]; Charles P. Richardson, Ohio University; C. Edward Scebold, American Council for the Teaching of Foreign Languages [ACTFL]; David Weible, University of Illinois at Chicago) provided invaluable guidance. Grateful appreciation for support and encouragement is accorded to the United States Air Force Academy and associated Defense agencies, as well as to the Department of Foreign Languages at Purdue University. A special thanks is given to Carolyn McDonald (USAFA) and to Terri Hope (Purdue) for extensive typing and word processing throughout this project, and to Kuan-Yi Rose Chang (Purdue) for her intensive effort in preparing the index.

Modern Media in Foreign Language Education: A Synopsis

Wm. Flint Smith
Purdue University

Introduction

Keeping abreast of progress in the rapidly expanding field of computer-assisted instruction is as important as relating these advances to their logical and efficient use. Computers in language learning enjoy less than three decades of history and the microcomputer's entry into language instruction is barely ten years old. Yet their presence is notable. That computer-assisted instruction has found its way into language teaching is no mystery; more surprising, perhaps, is the fact that it has taken so long to be considered seriously despite an increasing attention to quality and relevance in software for foreign languages and recent lower prices for smaller, portable, easier-to-use, and much more powerful machines than their older counterparts. The growth of computer-assisted language learning (CALL) has marched steadily forward since the pioneering efforts that developed strategies and courseware for language learning on PLATO (Programmed Logic for Automated Teaching Options) at the University of Illinois in the 1960s. In fact, there is considerable evidence that CALL in all of its dimensions has progressed beyond the curiosity and skepticism that always accompany innovation:

1. At least one monograph or book on CALL has been published each year since 1982 (Ahmad et al., 1; Brumfit et al., 2; Davies and Higgins, 3; Higgins and Johns, 4; Hope et al., 5; Kenning and Kenning, 6; Last, 7; Underwood, 9; Wyatt 10, 11), and *Dissertation Abstracts*

Wm. Flint Smith (Ph.D., Purdue University) is Professor of Spanish and Coordinator for instruction in the Beginning Spanish curriculum at Purdue, where he also teaches topics in foreign-language education and second-language learning. A former recipient of the Paul Pimsluer Award for Research in Foreign Language Education (1979), he was the 1985-86 Distinguished Visiting Professor in Languages at the United States Air Force Academy. He serves on the Editorial Board for *The Modern Language Journal* and is a member of ACTFL, AATSP, IFLTA (Indiana), and IALLD (The International Association of Learning Laboratory Directors).

International lists more than a dozen doctoral studies on CALL in second-language teaching and ESL completed since 1980.

2. A consortium for Computer-Assisted Language Learning and Instruction (CALICO) was formed early in this decade as a forum for the discussion of CALL-related topics. CALICO (based at Brigham Young University) publishes a journal of the same name, sponsors an annual conference and regional workshops on the entire spectrum of computing in second-language learning, and offers an extensive database to its membership and other interested professionals.

3. A recent and extensive bibliography on CALL (Stevens et al., 8) identifies more than 1700 articles, monographs, and other writings on the subject. Each entry is cross-referenced according to sixteen categories that hold citations to general applications of computers in education and/or to nineteen additional headings specific to foreign languages.

4. All of the major journals in foreign language education (*Canadian Modern Language Review, Foreign Language Annals, French Review, Hispania, Modern Language Journal, Journal of Educational Techniques and Technologies [formerly NALLD Journal], System, TESOL Quarterly, Die Unterrichtspraxis*) devote space to issues related to hardware and software and their use, as does *CALICO Journal* and *Computers and the Humanities (CHum)*. These same publications, in the main, also offer substantive reviews of courseware for second-language learning and ESL, as does the semiannual *Newsletter* of the Northeast Conference.

5. Professional organizations devoted to practical aspects of second-language learning (ACTFL, the AAT's, IALL, TESOL) have formulated CAI interest groups that sponsor sessions or workshops at state, regional, and national meetings and publish relevant articles as reports in their newsletters or journals.

6. Institution-based conferences on CALL—such as the one entitled "Computers in Language Research and Language Learning" held in October of 1986 at the University of Illinois, Urbana-Champaign Campus—are increasingly commonplace.

7. Publishers' catalogs list a growing number of CALL materials for a wide variety of purposes in the commonly taught languages and ESL. The software generally ranges from "stand alone" programs for drill and practice in a variety of skill areas to extensive courseware designed to accompany integrated materials packages (text, workbook, lab manual, testing program, etc.).

Still, Stevens et al. (8, pp. xi–xv) suggest that CALL has not flourished on a larger scale owing to: (1) substandard exemplars, (2) insufficient teacher training, and (3) conflicting ideologies. To the above can be added yet a fourth reason for the relatively minor impact CALL has had on second-language teaching to date: an insufficient drive among experienced language teachers toward both "computer literacy" and "pedagogical literacy using CALL."

Stevens et al. (8) note that almost none of the materials published for CALL suggests a standard for the industry, despite examples of considerable creativity in some of the more recent software. A majority of extant programs still reflect what might be termed primitive exercises or games associated with "becoming acquainted with the medium." Although there are admirable exceptions, far too few programs of the stand-alone variety offer genuine tutorials or simulations to help the student develop insights and uncover strategies that make learning a second language easier, more efficient, and more enjoyable. Other CALL materials (perhaps happily so) tend to be local, unpublished, and quickly obsolete. Although there are notable exceptions, teachers who produce them are largely self-taught in CALL. Typically, they have no programming knowledge or formal training in computers and have had little or no exposure to CALL in teacher training. Their software represents a herculean investment of time for little return. In a similar vein, few professional programmers are also language teachers, and their software, which may even be elegant from a programming perspective, may lack a sound pedagogy or may even present models of language that are simply wrong. Teacher training programs that include training in CALL, along with some introduction to authoring languages and programming techniques, may help to resolve this dilemma, but the combination of factors that produce a knowledgeable and successful author of pedagogically sound foreign language software remains beyond the reach of a large majority of teachers. Nevertheless, until language teachers learn to recognize good software and to use it intelligently, the gap between hardware and software, and between teacher and programmer, will continue to demonstrate the "pedagogical offset" that has plagued the use of media in language teaching almost from the start.

Stevens et al. (8) also observe that CALL has appeared at a time when there was in the profession considerable backlash against the behavioral tenets of audiolingualism in favor of cognitive or functional-communicative approaches to language teaching. Consequently, there has been a tendency for teachers to view drill-and-practice software (which the computer can engage par excellence) as representative of the *limitations* of the medium rather than as the *least complex* (but viable in its own right) of an entire range of routines that are uniquely available to the knowledgeable and creative CALL author. This tunnel vision, in turn, seems to be a function of insufficient knowledge of the literature on second-language acquisition and applied linguistics in a general sense, and a similar ignorance of specific yet revealing writings on CALL. For example, how many teachers are familiar with the summary of advantages and disadvantages of the computer listed by Ahmad et al. (1, pp. 4–9), who note that experience has shown that students enjoy learning with a computer and like its novelty and challenge. Consequently, they drop out less and achieve as well as or better than students not using CALL; they have longer attention spans and learn the material equally well but more quickly. And through CALL, students have the potential for more intensive, concentrated, and individualized interaction with the material than a teacher could possibly offer, except in face-to-face, one-on-one instruction.

These reasons are compelling in themselves to make becoming "pedagogically literate in CALL" a worthy first step toward being "computer literate." In short, teachers need to be able to judge what CALL can and cannot do for them, but that judgment must be based on an integrated knowledge of (1) the student and those variables that influence him or her from within, (2) the principles that organize a course of instruction for a curriculum, (3) the medium and its characteristics, (4) the importance of the instructional milieu, and (5) desirable qualities of CALL for a given approach to teaching. Volume I of *Modern Media* is an attempt to help teachers achieve some degree of literacy in the pedagogy of CALL. To this end, chapter authors endeavor to lead the reader toward an understanding of CALL by describing its attributes, interpreting current thinking or research, and suggesting areas for response in application, in training, in research and evaluation, and in materials design.

An Overview

Basic concepts in foreign language computing are defined and described in Chapter 1 by Pusack, who elucidates common typologies and terms used to characterize the medium and its hardware and software. Pusack also sketches three levels of projects—implementation, development, research—in order of increasing complexity that teachers might undertake as they become familiar with CALL (topics also discussed by Ariew, Chapter 2; Hubbard, Chapter 9; and Curtin and Shinall, Chapter 10). Implementation projects are those that involve the imaginative use of existing self-contained courseware (which, by definition, involves the evaluation of software potential against standards of an organizing principle). Development projects entail a greater degree of effort and expertise. At base, they require some involvement in writing software and decisions related to instructional design, content material, authoring languages, hardware, and program evaluation. Research projects encompass a variety of undertakings including tutorials, animation, the creation of authoring tools and databases, simulations, computer-adaptive testing, and large-scale multimedia studies or experiments. Aside from the informational content in Chapter 1, Pusack underscores that providing CALL means engaging in a long-term process whose success, ultimately, depends on teachers, who must either articulate their needs to those who publish commercial software or be prepared to author courseware themselves.

The role of the ACTFL *Guidelines* as organizer for integrating CALL (and video) as a tool in the curriculum is the focus of Chapter 2 by Ariew, who first examines the breadth of media use in language teaching, paying specific attention to the advantages and disadvantages that the new media bring to the learner and to the instructional environment in comparison with the textbook. The relative strengths of each "tool" are clarified with respect to their integrated use in teaching the four skills. In particular, Ariew examines the "fit" of media vis à vis the *Guidelines* for teaching listening, reading, and writing in order to determine what behaviors may be addressed specifically by CALL or by video, and which medium is most likely to make an impact on learner proficiency in a given skill level. Ariew argues that CALL and video are important pedagogical tools to aid in skill development but that neither medium can by itself shoulder all of the responsibility for teaching one specific skill. The decisions about which media to bring to bear for given skill levels as described in the *Guidelines* reside in an understanding of what CALL and video can accomplish realistically with specific learners at specific moments in time. Thus, teachers must learn how to integrate media, methods, and materials in accordance with a knowledgeable understanding of the role of each tool in the language-learning process and the larger goals carried by a specific approach to a curriculum. Ariew also takes a brief look at technologies of the future and the probable impact of two of them (an all-purpose work station, and compact disk information storage) on foreign language teaching.

Determining what strategies and methods are appropriate for CALL on the basis of its media characteristics is the focus of Chapter 3 by Weible, who contends that inappropriate use of the medium is a major reason that CALL's potential has not been realized, despite the fact that the computer is probably the most radically new information medium ever invented. Comparing the rise of the computer in education to the history of cinema (and more recently video and the teaching machine), Weible suggests that since CAI (computer-assisted instruction) is in a discovery phase, there is a good deal of "sorting out" to do in order to define the medium for CALL in its most logical and efficient way. Part of the discovery process according to Weible includes consciously dissociating the hardware from the earlier and disappointing teaching machine, then realizing that the value of CAI is different from the drill-and-practice role characteristic of what some see as its predecessor, programmed learning. Part of the definition process thus involves not allowing perceptions of the present capabilities of the medium to limit expectations; yet another part is to use the computer to suggest by example a wide variety of strategies the learner can bring to bear in order to comprehend an equally wide range of language stimuli. Examples of the above are found in three unique characteristics of the medium, according to Weible: (1) the ability to structure interactions programmatically, thereby defining the nature of the student's approach to and interaction with the subject matter; (2) the ability to focus on process as well as product, and thereby also simulate processes for the learner or display them as exemplars; (3) the ability to individualize instruction automatically, thereby providing maximally efficient use of specific software by students with a wide range of ability. There are many factors that affect how the computer's potential is used in CALL. First among them must be a continued realization that "the medium *is* the message," and second that strategies for its use derive from its characteristics in concert with the *reasons* for bringing the medium to bear on an educational problem in the first place.

The need to apply pedagogical principles to CALL courseware development is the subject of Chapter 4 by Wyatt, who examines the degree of concordance between currently accepted pedagogical principles in language teaching and computer technology as a basis for challenging the commonly held belief that computers are limited to but a single pedagogical approach (a notion discussed in depth by Hubbard in Chapter 9). In turn, Wyatt proposes using the relative degree of interaction between the learner and the medium as a basis for classifying (and evaluating) software as instructional, collaborative, or facilitative. This tripartite classification allows important insights into the probable success or failure of much of the extant CALL software while offering clear guidelines for correlating future courseware development and its use with the new and emerging approaches to language teaching. Wyatt's schema clarifies the type of student involvement for each category of software; the extent of machine (program) intervention in accordance with the characteristics of typical courseware; and the number, type, and relative cost of equipment to carry forth given programs. Finally, Wyatt discusses three methods of producing CALL—educational authoring systems (templates), educational programming languages (e.g., PILOT), and general-purpose programming languages (e.g., BASIC)—in terms of (1) their relative ease of access to the full range of the computer's capabilities, (2) the type of courseware that can be represented through them under the instructional, collaborative, and facilitative rubrics, and (3) the degree of expertise that is necessary to use (or author) them. Juxtaposing Wyatt's classification scheme of software with typical methods of producing CALL suggests an important dimension for teacher training, as discussed in detail by Curtin and Shinall in Chapter 10.

The research on CALL that has attempted to provide the instructional designer with information that affects courseware design and content or curricular decisions is the focus of Chapter 5 by Pederson, who counsels that the paucity of appropriately conceived and correctly executed studies on CALL lesson delivery is a function of not having asked the right questions. While there is evidence that the *way the medium is used* rather than the medium itself determines how learning is affected by CALL, more research is needed on how to use the computer's coding options to improve learning. Pederson defines and analyzes the purposes and limitations of three types of research that can be brought to bear on these issues (basic, comparative, and evaluative) and discusses the merits or limitations of each along with representative CALL studies and their results (many of which are found wanting in purpose, execution, and interpretation). According to Pederson, cogently designed basic research on the computer's coding options and their interaction with the learner variables known to play a crucial role in language acquisition is the most fruitful means to arrive at truly generalizable conclusions about what CALL can and cannot accomplish for the student in given learning environments. Pederson describes three research models for this purpose: (1) experimental (identification of the effects of learning style, aptitude, task, and coding option on achievement or attitude); (2) ethnographic (identification of hypotheses through observation and interview that might be tested empirically); and (3) formal survey (identification of special needs, trends, and other useful information). The chapter concludes with a summary of reasonably clear tenets that are emerging in CALL and that are supported by other research in second-language education vis à vis the nature of the learner, the learning task, the way materials are designed toward affecting learning outcomes, and the context in which they are applied. Included too are recommendations for less comparative and more cost-effective evaluative research employing software that has a predictable long half-life. No less important, according to Pederson, is for teachers (1) to become critical consumers of the research literature on CALL, (2) to support research through participation in research efforts by investigators who would use their classrooms and their students as subjects, and (3) to require evaluative reports from software distributors before investing in major software packages.

Chapter 6 by Doughty focuses on the unique capabilities of the computer to aid in the analysis of data collected during observation of the second-language learning processes. In the first portion of her chapter, Doughty describes major components of several theoretical models of second-language acquisition: Monitor Theory (and its Explicit/Implicit Representation), Information-Processing Theory, and Interaction Theory. Doughty analyzes these models according to the way each considers five constructs taken as fundamental in second-language acquisition (SLA): input, processing, storage, access and use, and output. Doughty's analysis shows clearly the importance of (1) reconnecting theory and research to classroom application, (2) making the classroom a logical experimental milieu, and (3) using the computer as facilitator in the research process. Doughty also focuses on elements in CALL research on which computers have been or can be brought to bear to study (1) the learner's psycholinguistic processing of the various constituents defined by the theoretical models of second-language acquisition, (2) the relative contribution of these constructs to the learner's developing interlanguage, and (3) the process and degree to which language data are accessed and used by the second-language learner (topics also developed by Garrett in Chapter 7). Doughty underscores the unique role and advantage that the computer offers in making research manageable and accessible to the classroom teacher (who is also seen as a primary source of research questions), and for examining the contribution of the learning process, the influence of learner characteristics, and their respective interaction with learning conditions on the product of second-language learning mediated by CALL. Numerous representative studies are cited as fulfilling (or missing) the bill. Doughty also comments on the application of the computer to track individual learner responses to a range of choices so as to understand preferential strategies and processes students use while completing various language-learning tasks. Equally interesting according to Doughty is the use of the computer's unique computational abilities to generate a model of language production by a learner, or to analyze learner input and understanding of it, or even to study the context in which a given input is embedded. No less important in SLA research is the use of the computer to examine the learning process through learner–computer interaction. The results of investigation into these areas are just beginning to be felt at the experimental level; nevertheless, they are important to pursue, since their impact on curriculum and software can be ultimately large and direct.

In Chapter 7, Garrett argues that the computer and CALL-based activities are ideally suited to help the learner develop a psycholinguistic notion of grammar and to acquire facility in using it where this psycholinguistic processing is taken to mean the ability to recognize a relationship between form and semantic and syntactic meaning. But Garrett, like Doughty, insists that the potential of the computer to interact with the student cannot be exploited fully until decisions about its use are based on insights from theory and research into the language-learning process rather than on traditional ideas of teaching. Garrett distinguishes between conventional foreign language CAI, which incorporates computer-mediated materials to extend the role of the teacher or workbook, and CALL, which uses the computer to help derive hypotheses in order to study how students come to be able to communicate grammatically (as opposed to "learning grammar" in its traditional sense). According to Garrett, CALL should be "learner driven" rather than "teacher driven." Learner-driven software pays particular attention to the interlanguage rules underlying student responses and supplies feedback and error correction based on a careful analysis of them; similarly, it indicates the psycholinguistic rather than the linguistic reason that student input may be erroneous or inadequate. Garrett notes that focusing on the psycholinguistic notion of grammar to encode ideas rather than on its surface representation (as commonly found in foreign language textbooks) is the key to generating CALL courseware with the potential for a substantive and long-lasting impact on learning. Designing software in this way underscores the multiple roles the computer can play in the instructional process: (1) it is a research tool for discovering and documenting how the learner processes the rules of language in order to give meaning to form, and vice versa; (2) the data it provides about learner processes form the basis for designing CALL materials using the notion of processing as an organizing principle; (3) it can be programmed to guide practice with surface linguistic forms and with different kinds of grammatical markings that express meaning; (4) it can provide truly individualized instruction by observing the learner's psycholinguistic processing and adjusting lesson content, flow, difficulty, and feedback accordingly; (5) it can analyze this idiosyncratic processing in order to control the choices of subsequent instructional materials and to contribute to the development of classroom second-language acquisition theory. Garrett provides guidance on how to implement this "processing approach" via CALL and suggests four categories of content as topics for CALL grammar lessons—consciousness-raising activities, lessons on major categories of grammar (case, aspect), particular structures, and surface grammar—along with a general description of their format (tutorial, drill and practice, etc.) and the corresponding role of feedback and error analysis. The implications for materials design, teaching, and research are straightforward.

Artificial Intelligence (AI) and CALL is the subject of Chapter 8 by Underwood, who describes AI as a science that touches on and draws from psychology and computer programming to solve intellectual problems via the medium. The application of AI to CALL, generally, has followed two interest areas: knowledge representation and natural-language processing. Knowledge representation involves the coding of routines that direct an operation based on the observation of a human expert's reasoning process to resolve a narrowly defined problem and the transfer of those observations into some machine-readable format that can then interact with anyone "consulting" this "expert system" within its parameters of knowledge. On the other hand, natural-language processing, according to Underwood, attempts to find ways for computers to understand natural language (print and speech), where "natural" is taken to mean human language in its broadest sense, and involves the analysis of discourse at multiple levels—lexical, morphological, syntactic, semantic, and pragmatic (in addition to "real world knowledge")—in order to achieve a comprehensible interaction between man and machine. Mechanical parsing of speech, machine translation, speech recognition, and speech synthesis represent four different domains of interest. As examples, Underwood offers brief descriptions of ELIZA and SHRDLU, both well-known and early attempts at meaningful conversation with a computer, and then discusses the application of artificial intelligence to language learning as yet another means to study how students learn a second idiom and how language teaching may be most efficiently accomplished.

Underwood categorizes AI research efforts in CALL under three headings (key word matching, parsing, intelligent games) and characterizes several CALL/AI programs—LIESL, Juegos Communicativos, Spion—for each. The chapter concludes with a brief description of major projects using artificial intelligence in CALL (Athena, TALK, Alexis, Grammar Tutor) and offers advice for those who would explore the research in AI and CALL more thoroughly or learn its programming languages on their own.

In Chapter 9, Hubbard discusses the importance of identifying, *a priori*, the philosophical and methodological approach reflected in the curriculum for which CALL materials are being considered before evaluating the courseware itself. Hubbard observes that some software may be more suitable for one type of approach than for another depending on the overall assumptions and goals of an instructional sequence. Yet most published guidelines for software evaluation focus primarily on program type and on the documentation, mechanics, content, and hardware that would be required to use it rather than on the relative correlation between the software's advertised purpose and the approach reflected in the curriculum where it may find application. Hubbard notes, moreover, that typical guidelines for software evaluation are so general that they can be used for CAI materials in many disciplines, a circumstance that belies the fact that second-language learning is fundamentally and demonstrably different from other types of learning, and therefore requires different criteria to judge (and design) its courseware. To this end, Hubbard describes a supplementary procedure (and evaluation form) specific to CALL materials that takes into consideration the characteristics of three broadly defined approaches to second-language teaching (behaviorist, explicit, acquisition) in addition to concepts related to typical and identifiable student strategies of second-language learning and other pedagogical considerations. These parameters direct the evaluation of CALL courseware for a particular application; they also provide guidance in the design of software for a specific approach. These same criteria also provide a basis for judging whether software is compatible with the orientation, content, and sequencing of syllabi that are variously structural, situational, functional-notional, or content-centered in their focus. Finally, Hubbard's criteria for software evaluation are valuable and instructive from the standpoint of courseware design, as much for the teacher who would modify existing CALL materials using an educational programming language as for the author who would endeavor to design CALL software for a particular approach. Both the above applications also hold relevance for training teachers in CALL use and CALL evaluation.

Preservice and inservice teacher education in the use of CALL, a major challenge to the profession, is the focus of Chapter 10 by Curtin and Shinall. The authors discuss the need for teachers to understand potential applications of CALL in the teaching/learning process and offer as an example a description of the syllabus for a preservice course in teacher training they have developed at the University of Illinois. The syllabus includes the following major topics: (1) background technical knowledge (CAI terminology, programming languages, hardware, networking, and databases); (2) learner needs and professional objectives as they relate to curricular goals; (3) description and exemplars of materials from five types of CAI and CALL software (tutorial, drill, simulations, problem solving, games); (4) instructional concerns related to lesson content, learning theory, and the design, execution, and evaluation of courseware; and (5) a practicum with hands-on experience in the execution of CALL-based sessions for teaching language and culture. In addition, Curtin and Shinall call attention to the kinds of basic information that should prove useful to the teacher preparing to use CALL, including models of second-language learning, learner variables (aptitude, attitude, strategies, etc.), and the role of proficiency—all topics that strengthen the basis for defining a teacher-training syllabus for CALL. The chapter closes with a brief look at what equipment the future holds in store, and alludes to what this new medium may suggest for the classroom teacher and for teacher education.

Conclusion

Computer-assisted language learning is a powerful instructional and research medium increasingly worthy of serious attention in second-language learning. The chapters in *Modern Media in Foreign Language Education* are designed to raise the consciousness of the teacher and the researcher who would study the rationale for media-aided learning of a foreign language and apply to the teaching–learning process the tenets that accrue from mediated instruction, learner variables, and the purposeful and intelligent management of the interaction between them.

References, Modern Media in Foreign Language Education: A Synopsis

1. Ahmad, Khurshid, Greville Corbett, Margaret Rogers, and Roland Sussex. *Computers, Language Learning and Language Teaching.* London: Cambridge University Press, 1985.
2. Brumfit, Christopher, M. Phillips, and P. Skehan. *Computers in English Language Teaching: A View from the Classroom.* Oxford England: Pergamon, 1985.
3. Davies, Graham D., and John Higgins. *Computers, Language and Language Learning.* London: Center for Information on Language Teaching and Research, 1982.
4. Higgins, John, and Tim Johns. *Computers in Language Learning.* Reading, MA: Addison-Wesley, 1984.
5. Hope, Geoffrey R., Heimy F. Taylor, and James P. Pusack. *Using Computers in Teaching Foreign Languages.* Language and Education: Theory and Practice, No. 57. Orlando, FL: Harcourt Brace Jovanovich, 1984.

6. Kenning, M. J., and M. M. Kenning. *An Introduction to Computer-Assisted Language Teaching.* Oxford, England: Oxford University Press, 1983.
7. Last, Rex W. *Language Teaching and the Micro.* Oxford, England: Blackwell, 1983.
8. Stevens, Vance, Roland Sussex, and Walter V. Tuman. *A Bibliography of Computer-Aided Language Learning.* New York: AMS Press, 1986.
9. Underwood, John. *Linguistics, Computers, and the Language Teacher: A Communicative Approach.* Rowley, MA: Newbury House, 1984.
10. Wyatt, David H. *Computer-Assisted Learning in ESL.* Washington, DC: Center for Applied Linguistics, 1983.
11. ———, ed. *Computer-Assisted Language Instruction.* Oxford, England: Pergamon Press, 1984.

1

Problems and Prospects in Foreign Language Computing

James P. Pusack
The University of Iowa

Introduction

High expectations and low expertise mark foreign language teaching in the matter of computing. The profession has progressed since the days when nothing was known and nothing expected, but the gap between available software and the myriad obvious ways computers can assist language learners causes concern. What conditions will lead language teachers to exploit the full potential of technology? How will interested colleagues acquire the knowledge they need to become successful authors of teaching and learning programs? Who will fund such efforts? The purpose of this chapter is to demonstrate that these questions and others like them are worth asking and answering. The problems and prospects of the field are profiled here through a survey of typical projects that language teachers might undertake. The three main sections of this chapter sketch a series of such projects—implementation, development, and research—in order of increasing complexity. A common technological basis will prove useful as the field's problems and prospects are reviewed. This introduction therefore attempts to clarify some basic concepts in instructional design, hardware, and software.

The environment for exploiting computer technology includes more than equipment and knowledge. Current attitudes play a key role. As faculty members become familiar with microcomputers through daily writing at a word processor, basic reservations give way to curiosity. This

James P. Pusack (Ph.D., Indiana University) is Associate Professor of German and Director of the Project for International Communication Studies at the University of Iowa. He is a member of ACTFL, CALICO, and AATG, and co-author of *Using Computers in Teaching Foreign Languages* (Harcourt Brace Jovanovich/Center for Applied Linguistics). DASHER, his foreign language CAI authoring system, is published by CONDUIT, where he also serves as language series editor.

is a positive shift. Administrators, who must provide equipment and released time for major projects, also recognize the potential of technology; the greatest danger on this front comes from those who would promote technology at the expense of the faculty's other priorities. Publishers of foreign language textbooks have embarked cautiously on development projects, but are inevitably guided by short-term market considerations; they view foreign language software—courseware—as an adjunct to their primary product, the textbook.

The area receiving least attention today is the systematic development of the requisite support infrastructure—the experts and facilities that will help faculty create and deliver computer-assisted language learning (CALL) to students. Short-sighted administrators think that a teacher and a machine will work miracles. Far-seeing administrators realize that undertakings like those described below cannot succeed without a staff of language laboratory and computer-center professionals who can translate faculty initiatives into well-designed, carefully implemented software.

The list of objectives sketched here is certainly not all-inclusive. Its hallmark is hard-nosed practicality. These are projects that can be accomplished with today's technology and that can benefit students in systematic rather than haphazard ways. Many other clever tasks can be imagined that put language learners and computers together. The ones chosen for inclusion here strive to improve the productivity of both teacher and learner and thus improve the quality of language learning.

Typologies and Terms

The least edifying environs of foreign language computing lie in the jungle of acronyms. CAI, CBE, CMI, CAFLI, and CALL often fail as signposts because there is little agreement about their meaning; for most listeners and readers, these acronyms differ but do not distinguish clearly among concepts. One group of terms (CAI, CMI, CBE) applies to all forms of instructional computing, not only to work in foreign languages. Computer-assisted instruction (CAI) usually refers to interactive teaching programs, while those programs whose approach derives from programmed learning concepts are sometimes called "traditional CAI." Learner control has begun to predominate in interactive software; as this and other changes take place, CAI as a generic term will probably survive by changing its connotations.

Computer-managed instruction (CMI), in contrast, is used to designate the use of computers to guide students through a course of study, much of which may be "off-line," that is, away from the computer; CMI does extensive recordkeeping to track student progress through traditional or computer-based materials. Computer-based education (CBE) encompasses nearly everything that students can do to learn via computers: study programming; practice the application of concepts; use word processors to write essays; design graphics; gather and manipulate data with spreadsheets, databases, or statistical programs. CBE (and its alias, CBI, for computer-based instruction) is therefore the most inclusive term.

Foreign language teachers engaged in CAI have long sought a compact way to label their mission. Acronyms containing the letter "I" appear to stress the machine as *instructor;* those with an "L" strive for a *learner*-centered interaction. Thus one can find both CALI (computer-assisted language instruction) and CALL (computer-assisted language learning). CAFLI (computer-assisted foreign language instruction) has also been proposed. Fashion will no doubt lead us in the near future to CALA (computer-assisted language acquisition). In the meantime, the profession's focus on the learner and the benefits of easy pronunciation suggest the use of CALL, pronounced as a word, rather than separate letters. Most of our colleagues, however, cannot be expected to recognize anything briefer than "foreign language CAI."

Workers in the area of CALL have proposed a number of typologies or classification systems that help make some basic distinctions in discussing foreign language software. Many general treatments of computers in education distinguish four fundamental categories: drills, tutorials, simulations, and management (CMI). Pusack and Otto (13) have constructed a matrix of possible applications by examining traditional areas of language teaching (grammar, listening, culture, etc.) in terms of four approaches to CALL: (1) practice and diagnosis; (2) tutorial; (3) simulation and problem-solving; and (4) utility. Each of these approaches is described briefly below.

Practice. Current practice programs usually offer discrete-item drill on a sequence of structural features of the target language. Simple drill programs that present items in a fixed sequence and undertake little processing of student input tend to fall into the oft-scorned class of software dubbed "computer flashcards" or "electronic workbooks." Reflecting the best insights into language-teaching methodology, many CALL projects today attempt to embed all practice in a meaningful context and to treat student responses as linguistically analyzable utterances. Nevertheless, most of the available CALL courseware occupies the very limited space defined by the intersection between the *grammar/structure* area and the *practice and diagnosis* approach. An appropriately constructed bank of practice materials can also be employed as a *diagnostic tool* by the teacher or by learners themselves.

Tutorial. Tutorial programs have the goal of presenting language skills and concepts in a more efficient or effective fashion than textbooks or classroom explanations. These programs exploit the computer's power to present information dynamically, adjust materials to the learner's own abilities, and keep careful records of student progress. The potential of language tutorials has not yet been fully realized and to date there are no complete, commercially available CALL tutorials that could be used, for example for home study of the basics of a foreign language.

Simulations and Problem-solving. Simulations place learners into a small model of reality in order to expose them to cultural content or foster use of the target language in a lifelike context. In most simulations, the task posed by the simulation takes precedence over correct production of the target language; the emphasis is on comprehension and meaningful expression. Adventure games fall into the category of simulation. Problem-solving programs likewise pose a task, but may not stress the student's involvement in a fictional situation as strongly as do simulations. Reading and listening comprehension programs that require the learner to extract complex information, often involving critical thinking skills, can be viewed as problem-solving software. The boundary between simulations and problem-solving depends on the level of illusion the learner is willing to accept and the degree of control the language learner has over his or her progress through the tasks offered by the computer.

Utility. Utility programs place a very high priority on the ability of students to make decisions in using the computer for language learning. Word processing (e.g., target-language composition) is the most familiar example. The emerging generation of software will bring with it many programs that give students tools for evaluating their own writing, for reading texts more efficiently, and for diagnosing their own weaknesses. Even tutorials, which are classically the most directive and prescriptive kind of software, will be designed explicitly as complex learning utilities that the learner can control fully and therefore ignore selectively.

It should be clear by now that the above four terms constitute not only categories, but also characteristics. For example, a given piece of courseware may have elements of both the tutorial and the problem-solving approach. Authors of software increasingly blend these various design characteristics into their products in order to increase their effectiveness and appeal.

Developing foreign language courseware demands expertise. Teachers in the field generally recognize that high-quality software will not spring from their own efforts to learn computer programming. In describing any development model, it has become accepted practice to refer to three discernible roles: the *subject-matter specialist* (or content expert), the *instructional designer,* and the *programmer.* In addition, graphics design expertise has become increasingly important. For CALL, this tripartite division of labor suggests that the language teacher will provide linguistic and pedagogical expertise, while the programmer will cause the computer to carry out the desired tasks. The instructional designer understands both programming and teaching and can therefore improve the working relationship between the other two. In addition, the instructional designer brings to a CAI project a storehouse of experience with instructional software; this critical knowledge forms a starting point for any project that aspires to break new ground and meet current expectations. The following sections assume no particular developmental model; rather, the roles of the instructor/author, the instructional designer, and the programmer at times coalesce. In some cases, however, distinctions are made that derive from the complexity of the task under discussion.

Hardware

Hardware intimidates everyone. No matter how much one learns about products, technologies, vendors, prices, features, and the like, it remains too much and not enough. There is too much information to evaluate in terms of pedagogy and never enough to guarantee that one is up to date. Industrial laboratories already hold technologies that will not be advertised for three years or used by the public for five. What level of information is then appropriate?

One must be guided by one's institution and one's peers in the use of *mainframes, minicomputers,* and *microcomputers.* Fortunately, each school and college supports a small set of machines. There may be a large mainframe computer or a powerful minicomputer with many terminals attached; there may be a small microcomputer cluster used by students from many departments. The national standard suggests a mixture of both, with the microcomputer sometimes acting as a timesharing terminal in order to help in the transfer of programs and information. If one's institution does not appear to be at the cutting edge, especially in technologies that apply to CALL, national conferences offer the best opportunity to see vendors' wares and the burgeoning number of colleagues' projects.

Inevitably, language instructors are concerned with various *supporting devices* used to print text, store large amounts of information, and foster communication among teachers and students. The hardware needed for these tasks becomes more economical and powerful with every passing month. For example, the first Apple® computers came equipped with 16 kilobytes (K) of memory—only a few bold purchasers bought additional memory chips; today, it costs less than $50 to add 400K to the memory of an IBM PC-compatible microcomputer. Paradoxically, the longer one waits to acquire a given device, the more likely it is that a better alternative will appear on the market. Delay can be beneficial as well as frustrating.

Printing foreign language characters no longer poses a problem for modern computers. Teachers who use a word processor will find that the publisher of good software will tout its foreign character capabilities and will therefore be able to indicate which printers can be used. Vendors, of course, should be able to demonstrate the desired capabilities. Instructional software—in contrast to software for research and teaching support—seldom requires a printer. A student workstation should be equipped with a printer only if students will be engaging in composition on the computer, in which case a version printed on paper is usually required; even in this case, fewer printers than computers will be needed.

Most microcomputer systems store programs and data on diskettes, which are useful for personal transfer of information, but have limitations. They are easily damaged, pirated, or stolen; they may not have enough capacity for some programs; and they require that someone issue and collect them. The emerging alternative to diskettes is a larger storage device, the magnetic hard disk or CD-ROM optical disk drive, which may be linked by wires to a whole group of microcomputers. A network recovers on a small scale the advantages of minicomputers and mainframes. Students may have their own data diskettes, but obtain access to programs and large information bases via the network. Networking also allows students to exchange information with each other at their individual microcomputer workstations. This option stimulates the development of software for meaningful student-to-student communication. Unfortunately, maintaining a microcomputer network requires a much higher order of expertise than that needed for a simple, self-contained machine.

Traditional keyboards, augmented by various arrows and function keys, place limits on the kinds of interaction that can be designed. Reading practice takes on an entirely different aspect if learners can express their understanding by indicating (via a pointing device) which portions of a text meet some criterion, as well as simply typing characters. Simulations and games work much more effectively if students can relate their responses directly to positions on the two-dimensional screen display, rather than indirectly via the keyboard.

The most familiar pointing device is the *mouse,* which relates motion of a tracking device on a table to motion of the cursor on the screen. An "inverted" mouse, called a *track ball,* sets up a similar analogue between hand movement and screen; *joysticks* do the same; there are even infrared devices that base their effects on head movement. Two very different technologies, the *light pen* and the *touch screen,* allow the learner to engage in fairly intuitive hand/arm motions relative to the screen. Although not yet in widespread use for CALL, pointing devices are likely to grow in popularity, especially as they become more widely used for word processing. This trend should have a positive impact by allowing graphics to convey CALL tasks in a more faithfully represented context and by enabling language learners to interact more intuitively with texts that develop comprehension skills.

Software

There is really only one issue that defines the current status of foreign language computing: the quality of software. While hardware dictates to some extent what software can do, the language-teaching profession is so far behind in realizing the capabilities of current inexpensive technology that hardware limitations must be considered moot. Of course, new applications with speech synthesis, speech recognition, or even holographic projection can be imagined, but each impulsive leap forward to a new technology will cause one to ignore valuable opportunities with the machines now on student desks. What follows is an overview of the major software options available to language teachers using basic computer equipment. (See also Chapter 4 by Wyatt in this volume for another perspective of CALL software; a second volume of *Modern Media in Foreign Language Education* will hold chapters that deal with development of courseware for audio and video devices.)

A commercially available, documented, and supported piece of software is called a *package*. It may contain one or more programs, consist of several modules, and come on more than one diskette, and it may or may not be copiable. From an instructional point of view, a package can be viewed best as the realization of someone else's language pedagogy. Since language teachers subscribe to a wide variety of methodologies and are often in disagreement about which is the most efficient or suitable approach for a given audience, it should be clear that no courseware package is likely to be judged satisfactory in all respects. Most available packages, for example, offer drill; teachers who despise drill will find them unacceptable. On the other hand, what might be called second-generation CALL software has started to come of age. The first generation was developed chiefly by individuals working alone; it found its way into the hands of publishers and eventually became available commercially. Second-generation packages may be the intellectual product of individuals, but they have been developed by larger teams working to overcome many of the weaknesses of early packages. This approach usually results in better instructional design, more effective graphics, and more sophisticated handling of student responses.

All software requires *programming,* and original forms of instruction require original programming. Since most language teachers are not programers, programming has become the bugaboo of CALL. The solution is straightforward: language teachers should author software, but they should not program it. It is tempting to let the dictum "Don't program!" stand without further comment. There will certainly be exceptions, but more projects will benefit from assuming this rule than from expecting the opposite. There is much to be said, however, in favor of language teachers gaining a basic understanding of elementary programming techniques in the context of a broader introduction to CALL. Without the demystification that a taste of programming can bring, the CALL instructor/author may develop false expectations about the nature of computer logic and intelligence. (See Chapter 10 of this volume by Curtin and Shinall for an expanded view of this issue.)

Any potential CALL instructor/author should consider developing software using an *authoring system*. An authoring system is essentially a package empty of lesson content. The instructor creates courseware by supplying certain kinds of linguistic information. In the case of CONDUIT's DASHER (12), for example, the teacher must type exercise instructions, questions, and answers; the program then handles presentation of the items and evaluation of the student response according to a predetermined algorithm. A simulation requires scenes, actions, and objects; a reading program requires texts, glossaries, and comprehension goals; structural practice must be supplied with sentence-generation tasks and solutions. Once the materials have been inserted into the authoring system, a fixed set of interactions is presented to the learner. Under these conditions, the instructor/author has complete control over the content but virtually none over the program logic and operation. More extensive criteria for high-quality foreign language authoring tools for CALL have been developed by Otto and Pusack (9).

The advantage of using an authoring system is that the author can apply his or her language-teaching expertise intensively without concern for problems of programming; this is extremely efficient and can lead to the development of large amounts of high-quality courseware in a short period of time. The disadvantage lies in the constraints imposed by the authoring system. The system must offer a valuable teaching/learning strategy; if it does not, no amount of authorial creativity will compensate for this flaw.

The term *template* (pronounced TEM-plit) is virtually synonymous with authoring system. It is usually applied to highly structured authoring mechanisms, such as vocabulary drill programs, into which one must insert lists of language data. Since some commercial packages allow the user to replace the original content with material supplied by the instructor, these packages can also be viewed as templates.

Authoring languages occupy the middle ground between programming in a general computer language like BASIC or Pascal and authoring systems. They offer a set of high-level features useful in authoring instructional courseware but require that these features be programmed by assembling a correct and logical sequence of instructions. Designers of authoring systems attempt to give an author the built-in power of preprogrammed features combined with the flexibility to design his or her own interaction with the learner. Authoring languages usually offer extremely valuable assistance with difficult programming tasks, including graphic display (including character sets), control of audio and video devices, evaluation of student responses, branching, and recordkeeping. The most advanced authoring systems also permit the author to use general programming languages when needed. This vital option means that any straitjacketlike effects of the authoring language can be overcome with the assistance of a programmer.

PILOT is the most widely known authoring language for microcomputers. Implementations of PILOT differ greatly, so care must be taken to discover which is the best version for a given computer. Many authoring languages have been designed to support traditional frame-by-frame CAI of the programmed-learning variety. These languages work well for industrial, business, and military training purposes, but may have little to offer the foreign language author. On the other hand, some authoring languages boast features designed to support foreign language instruction; *TenCORE* (15), for example, has excellent graphics for foreign-character display and a built-in answer-evaluation routine derived from the PLATO system. Because there is a business market for CAI authoring languages, teachers may discover that potentially interesting products have prohibitively high prices. Even at prices in the thousand-dollar range, however, institutions should be able to justify purchasing a carefully chosen authoring language on the basis of the time and effort it can save. For this reason, a very experienced software author or programmer will also consider using an authoring language if it meets the needs of a given project.

The basic concepts of design, hardware, and software described above will become more tangible as they are applied to specific examples of courseware useful for CALL. The following section sketches a series of introductory-level projects that can be accomplished by any dedicated language instructor.

Implementation Projects

For many faculty, the first approach to CALL should probably be the implementation of an existing, self-contained piece of courseware. A straightforward "implementation project" allows language teachers to overcome some of the basic hardware and software obstacles. First, teachers will find that it is difficult to gain consistent access to hardware without demonstrably useful courseware; on the other hand, without a minimum of several machines for faculty and student use, it is difficult to explore and integrate software at any level. Second, even if computers are available, their effective use requires that teachers develop expertise in software evaluation. Yet most institutions do not have a wide array of software for teachers to examine as a preliminary step to determining whether they should develop new materials or adopt existing packages. There is no simple solution. A sustained effort to read reviews, attend workshops, visit software booths at conferences, and travel to other institutions can have a cumulative positive effect in preparing any language teacher to decide on an approach to this technology. As a first initiative, the safest may be an implementation project, that is, one that requires no programming or authoring, but rather involves using an existing system or piece of courseware.

Implementing software takes effort and patience. The more interactive and comprehensive a good instructional package, the more likely it is to contain elements not completely congruent with a given teacher's methodology. It is safe to say that *no* computer program taken over from another source will be completely satisfactory. As a result, passions often run high in the critique of software; seldom does one hear such unequivocal—usually negative—statements about textbooks as one hears about computer software. This can be viewed as healthy skepticism, but ought not to lead teachers who would use CALL to reject all available options and plunge immediately into ambitious new projects. Furthermore, when an acceptable package has been found that is compatible with one's available hardware, the work is still not over. The correlation between one's syllabus and the package must still be worked out in detail. (Ariew discusses the ramifications of this process in Chapter 2 of this volume.)

What kinds of software could form the basis for a worthwhile first use of CALL? Given the state of the art, there is a dearth of materials that can make a significant impact on the curriculum. Catalogs of software for a given foreign language reveal very few packages that form, in themselves, a coherent contribution to students' learning. A few miscellaneous programs provide a change of pace, a motivational supplement, or a bit of work on vocabulary, but these disjointed components cannot be assembled easily into a viable strand in the syllabus.

The issue here is whether the effort that goes into acquiring expertise and marshalling a support system for CALL can be justified unless some major impact on the curriculum can be felt. While machines cannot replace teachers, teachers should be able to sense a qualitative difference over the long term in their students' learning. This means that any project—from basic implementation to full-fledged research—should be based on some larger curricular objective. Such objectives might be increased conversation in class because drill is conducted by machine, an added reading component to an otherwise conversation-oriented syllabus, or more time available for the teacher to prepare classes because homework and individualized tutorials are delivered via computer. Realistically speaking, such encompassing goals cannot be accomplished overnight, but we should keep them in focus as we decide where to invest effort in CALL.

Courseware Evaluation

Since implementation projects rely on available courseware, expertise in judging the quality of a package ranks high among the basic skills needed for teachers to inaugurate CALL. Four major concerns deserve careful consideration in package selection: *content, approach, design,* and *delivery.* Unfortunately, evaluation by a simple checklist technique often fails; many dimensions must work in concert to form an effective piece of courseware. The best way to determine the value of a package is to confront it with one's own objectives, use it with students under real learning conditions, and compare it with the alternatives. Compromises of one sort or another can seldom be avoided. In this sense, evaluation of courseware differs little from textbook evaluation. Language teachers need practice to do both tasks fairly and productively.

Content.   The content area addressed by a package is always the starting point in evaluation. Advanced reading activities will scarcely benefit first-year students. Arcade-style vocabulary games will probably alienate most graduate students striving for Ph.D. reading proficiency. The capacity of the package to complement or parallel the textbook should also be considered carefully, although this topic is difficult to treat thoroughly without actually executing every module, lesson, or exercise. An increasingly important final issue confronts every serious user of computer software—authenticity. Video, audio, and textbook materials in language courses strive for more and more authentic use of language, where possible, in a communicative context. Many software packages will be found wanting on this score.

Approach.   The approach used by the developers of a package reflects their linguistic, pedagogical, and programming knowledge. No single set of questions, however, applies to every package: utility, problem-solving, simulation, tutorial, and drill programs all approach learning with different strategies that must be fully fathomed before their effectiveness can be judged. The pace and liveliness of the courseware, the degree to which it interacts with the learner, and the clarity of instructions exemplify the kinds of questions one can put to any package.

One specific topic relevant to many CALL packages is the way the program handles natural language. Some kinds of language learning, to be sure, lend themselves to dichotomous choices (yes/no, right/wrong, true/false), or multiple-choice treatment of student input. Many simulations, for example, achieve a level of design complexity that compensates for the use of such techniques; one fine example that can be used in the ESL classroom is the package *Where in the World Is Carmen Sandiego? A Mystery Exploration Game* (2). Nevertheless, language teachers have every right to expect CALL software that attempts to analyze student responses, diagnoses or predicts typical student errors, uses linguistic rules to parse student input, and ultimately understands what the learner says to the computer. Pusack (11) analyzes the nature of answer processing and error correction in CALL, with special attention to various kinds of diagnostic feedback.

Design. The detailed design of a package may have a great influence on its effectiveness under real learning conditions. Our standards in this area rise as we gain experience from both instructional programs and general-purpose software, such as word processors. The visual appeal of the program, its ability to adapt to various learning situations, the degree to which records are kept on student performance, and the program's ease of use all deserve scrutiny once it has been determined that the content and approach of a package meet one's needs.

Delivery. The final criterion for evaluation, delivery, comprises a whole series of questions that should be asked last, but must usually be asked first. By asking which equipment a given package will run on, one funnels the pool of available software to a disappointing trickle. Other typical delivery issues relate to copy protection, educational discounts, the quality of documentation, and the need for special equipment (pointing devices, extra memory, etc.). The realities of academia dictate, unfortunately, that many teachers must launch CALL by determining just what courseware fits their machine, rather than first evaluating their precise curricular needs.

Hope, Taylor, and Pusack (5) offer a comprehensive checklist of evaluation criteria (pp. 80–85). Cornick (3) has developed a point-scoring system for foreign language software evaluation that covers five major areas in detail: content, support material, presentation, stimulation of student interest, and computer techniques. Hamerstrom, Lipton, and Suter (4) specifically address their comments to the high school teacher who is evaluating software and compress their results into a handy half-page form treating content, features, instruction/documentation, creativity, and technical quality. (See Chapter 9 in this volume, by Hubbard, for further discussion of courseware evaluation.)

Textbook Packages

The first and simplest approach to implementing CALL probably lies in using a commercial software package designed to accompany the course textbook. Over the past two or three years, large textbook publishers have become active in developing or sponsoring various kinds of CALL. Often such packages consist of multidisk sets of exercises tied closely to the text or even drawn from it. When exercises closely follow the text, instructors who want to substitute computer homework for paper-and-pencil homework will find their needs are met. Some publishers' materials are based on the textbook but offer language practice beyond what the text provides;

instructors who seek to broaden students' opportunities to use the language outside of class will be well served by such packages. This category of software often includes vocabulary practice with graphics, tutorials, cultural simulations, and conversationlike activities that allow students to apply their skills in meaningful situations.

Unfortunately, publishers are just beginning to invest in software to accompany their foreign language textbooks. Complicating the issue is the fact that, as the methodology of language teaching comes to stress communicative over manipulative practice, the development of good software becomes more expensive. Publishers offer textbooks with up-to-date methodologies, but there are few models of good software to stimulate conversation, build reading skills, or engage students in motivating cultural situations. Even when good software concepts become clear, publishers will find that the cost of worthwhile courseware beyond the level of drill may be prohibitive. Finally, commercially developed packages that employ interactive video and audio are unlikely to appear at all because the available base of hardware is too restricted to justify the expense: too few schools could afford the workstations. CALL with these interactive media will depend on noncommercial efforts by universities and government agencies.

Generic Packages

At the same time that established textbook publishers are exploring ancillary software packages, newer software companies have begun to offer "generic" packages, which represent a second option for those considering an implementation project. Such packages consist of tutorials or exercises suitable for almost any beginning or intermediate curriculum and therefore represent another kind of implementation project. These packages are usually the product of university-level efforts in foreign language CAI. Some may have their origins in early software developed on mainframe computers as far back as the 1960s. Generic tutorials are obviously attractive to software publishers because the market for generic tutorials is not limited to institutions that adopt a specific foreign language textbook. This fact usually works against generic packages being offered by textbook companies.

Generic packages are touted as "stand-alone" materials usable by any student. In practice, it is virtually impossible to create either tutorials or exercises that can be used equally well with all commercial textbooks or that mesh fully with every instructor's syllabus. The sequence of grammar and vocabulary presentation has not reached canonical status, so learners who attempt to use stand-alone packages will find themselves continually frustrated by unfamiliar words and stymied by the courseware's assumptions about known grammar. The teacher who hopes to implement a generic tutorial or exercise package must carefully review the material to establish which units of the software correspond to which units of the textbook.

The control of vocabulary in large stand-alone packages is a critical element. Even when the package author has made a concerted effort to hold vocabulary to a very small corpus, students in the early weeks and months of a first-year course will still encounter unfamiliar material. On the other hand, more sophisticated packages typically offer at least one solution to this problem by providing interactive on-screen glossaries for students to call up whenever they encounter unfamiliar words.

Grammar sequencing does not lend itself easily to on-screen help. if stand-alone tutorials and exercises are composed of relatively short, self-contained units and offer learners easy mechanisms for selecting appropriate topics, students may be able to tolerate some discrepancies between the software package and their textbook. Whenever computer work is constructed out of explanations or operations that rely on knowledge of one linguistic feature—a tense or a case—to teach another, stand-alone packages will be unacceptably frustrating for elementary students. On the other hand, intermediate students engaged primarily in review and reinforcement of previously studied concepts should not be susceptible to these incongruities between syllabus and software. This may mean that implementation of a stand-alone package is best exercised in the intermediate curriculum.

Orchestrated Miscellany

The third option for initial implementation of CALL consists of the arduous and treacherous journey through the forest of software miscellany. Careful review and screening of small packages from a variety of software houses may yield enough usable material to form a regular—if not completely coherent—computer component for an elementary or intermediate course. The advantage of this approach is that the limitations of one package may be overcome by the strengths of another. One week, students may engage in small-group work with an adventure game as the basis for conversation or composition; the following week, reading comprehension activities may inform students about peculiarities of behavior in the target culture; and the third week, a difficult grammar topic may be treated through individualized tutorial and practice at the computer. Testing and placement may be aided by use of a computer-based achievement test. Composition can be stimulated by introducing students to the use of a foreign language word processor; in this area, newer and better options come onto the market almost monthly.

An eclectic approach also permits growth from semester to semester as new packages become available and as packages acquired previously lose their appeal after students use them. Those who implement large-scale textbook or stand-alone packages seldom have this freedom to reject unacceptable segments; they may feel locked into a decision made when their expertise was low because no new software has appeared that offers the same organizational advantages as their current courseware without the pedagogical drawbacks.

The above series of implementation projects illustrates the fact that valuable and productive work in CALL need not become a language instructor's all-encompassing concern. The next step beyond imaginative use of others' courseware, however, demands a commensurate increase in resources of various types.

Development Projects

The second level of work in CALL begins with the actual development of new coursework. Although the border is not always distinct, the characteristics that distinguish the tasks of implementation from more ambitious development projects all relate to the kinds of *effort* and *expertise* required. An implementation project focuses the instructor's effort to adapt the curriculum, the syllabus, even the daily lesson plan; the expertise needed lies well within familiar pedagogical and methodological terrain. Anyone embarking on a development project, however, accepts some degree of involvement in the unfamiliar process of authoring software. This will entail various aspects of instructional design, construction of content material, use of an authoring tool or programming language, selection of hardware, and other related tasks. The exact expertise required will depend on the developmental environment at one's institution.

The following sections illustrate the full range of projects that can be considered developmental. These are described in order of increasing complexity, beginning with small-scale work involving simple changes performed on off-the-shelf software. At the high end of the developmental range come large-scale projects that border on the experimental, but involve few risks or problems. The detailed illustrations both amplify the concept of developmental projects and stimulate development efforts.

Drill and Games Using Simple Templates

A number of commercial packages offer a good first approach to developing software by allowing the instructor/author to fill in simple lexical or grammatical materials into very narrowly defined templates. Most of the teacher's decisions relate to content, rather than program operation. The actual interaction between learner and computer may well be quite complex, include communicative tasks, or depend on very complex programming and design techniques, but the instructional content is simple enough to permit the teacher to "plug in" new elements based on his or her own syllabus. The result is a tailored, course-specific program or package that closely follows the structural and lexical progression familiar to one's students. Of course, the final product will be only as good as the original template.

Customizing Modifiable Packages

Modifiable packages consist of more comprehensive tutorials or exercise collections that span the entire breadth of a course or textbook. Modifying them to suit a particular syllabus encompasses more than simply supplying lists of words and expressions. In some cases, the content of whole instructional segments may require adjustment. Grammar explanations may need to be brought into conformity with the textbook, and the sequence of units must be carefully examined and reconfigured to reflect the week-by-week progression of topics. The complexity of this task depends on the way the original package was designed and created. If modifications of this sort were foreseen by the authors of the original software, it may be possible to reconfigure significant aspects of the package by responding to various prompts or by using other parameter-setting mechanisms. If the package was created from a well-documented authoring system or language, changing textual elements in the courseware may be relatively easy and serve as an excellent introduction to how instructional programs are designed. Software written in general-purpose programming languages like BASIC, Pascal, and C may be modifiable by experienced programmers if the line-by-line operation of the computer code is extraordinarily clear and contains extensive annotation explaining its operation. This is seldom the case, however. Programmers usually regard tinkering with other people's programs as distasteful and unrewarding.

In general, software that is not expressly advertised and distributed as modifiable will probably not offer proper access for modification: license agreements may explicitly forbid changes, disks may be locked by protection schemes, or the computer code may be stored as low-level machine language that would defeat all reasonable attempts to make even small changes. Noncommercial software acquired from colleagues at other institutions may lend itself to modification if proper program documentation is available.

Creating a Test Item Bank with Existing Software

Large computer systems have long offered teachers the use of sophisticated test-generation software. Such programs support the creation of large pools of test items, the printing of tests according to very detailed item-selection criteria, and posttest recordkeeping on the effectiveness of the tests. As similar software becomes available for microcomputers, the use of item banks will become an attractive option for teachers. The tests can be administered either at the computer or with machine-readable forms and other paper-and-pencil methods. Depending on its design, a comprehensive test bank can be used for student placement, regular in-course achievement tests, and diagnostic purposes when students beyond the elementary level need advice about topics for review and remediation.

The task of creating an item bank using an existing system can be an effective first approach to CALL for several reasons: item banks are expected to grow over many semesters; computer-generated tests can be administered without a large number of machines if paper-and-pencil versions are used; and the time savings for the teacher can be felt very soon in the development process. Item banks have a number of disadvantages as well: if they are not administered on the computer ("interactively"), extra work or equipment may be needed to record student answers on a separate medium in order to analyze the items' effectiveness; most teachers have no special training in designing reliable test items; machine testing often implies the use of multiple-choice formats that allow little room for variation in testing formats, especially those that strive to measure communicative ability.

Practice or Diagnosis Using an Authoring Tool

A comprehensive set of original practice materials in reading or language structure can emerge from work with an authoring system or language. The authoring system will limit the scope of the exercises but allow the instructor/author enough freedom to focus chiefly on the approach and content of the materials. An authoring language requires much more time to master for those involved in creating the materials. Even if the language teacher serves only as subject-matter expert and can direct the services of graphics specialists, instructional designers, and programmers, the capabilities of the available authoring language must be fully understood, an appropriate language must be chosen, and prototype lessons must be written. In some instances the authoring language may not have all the capabilities demanded by the instructor/author. In this case either specialized programming will have to be commissioned, or the ambitions of the author will have to be brought back to reality. While working in a typical authoring language, teachers will frequently find it impossible or extremely difficult to engage in procedures that exploit the language-generating and language-parsing capabilities of modern computer systems. Nevertheless, powerful and useful sets of lessons can be generated with this approach. The work will doubtless be highly labor-intensive, since each lesson may consist of a set of instructional frames that must be composed one by one on the basis of very explicit designs prepared by the foreign language teacher.

Short-Answer Drill Using a Programming Language

The advantage of creating new materials using a programming language lies in the opportunity to devise entirely new types of interactions. Although work in an authoring language often permits a wide range of formats, programming in BASIC or Pascal or another general-purpose language opens up new kinds of access to the power of the machine to analyze student responses. This approach commits the project to acquiring a new level of expertise, either by having participants learn to program or by hiring a programmer. The results of such a project may be far more humble, at first, than the extensive materials that could flow from work with an authoring system over the same period of time. Original programming should be viewed therefore as a long-term investment that serves as the basis for interesting future endeavors, whether or not these have been fully spelled out.

Self-Contained Tutorial Units

CALL tutorials on aspects of structure or culture can be created in relatively efficient fashion using an authoring language. Since most tutorials contain some level of practice within their sequence of activities, projects of this sort constitute a step beyond practice programs. If the tutorials amount to nothing more than a few screens of information linked by instructions to press the RETURN key, their usefulness will be minimal. Good tutorials rank among the most challenging of projects because each topic must be molded into a stimulating, individualized, appealing, and foolproof whole. Foreign language faculty members who would not consider writing a textbook (or at least a textbook chapter) should probably steer away from tutorial projects, since interactive tutorials demand a large amount of developmental time in relation to the resulting student learning time. Informal estimates of this ratio put authoring time at anywhere from 400 to 500 hours for every hour of lesson time. The more animation and other graphics, remedial help, alternate forms of explanation, and sequenced practice activities that are included in the tutorial design, the greater must be the author's effort for a single unit. For this reason, language faculty may be advised to embark upon a tutorial project by commencing with a few topics that inevitably baffle most students (difficult tense forms, complex agreement problems, confusing prepositional usage) rather than with Week One of the syllabus. A topic like the present tense of regular verbs will seldom justify extensive authoring time and is also unlikely to serve as a sufficiently complex prototype for further developmental process.

Utility Programs to Manage Instruction

Those who want to build programming skills over the long term should consider writing a small set of programs generally useful in support of instruction. Such projects might well be tools used by the teacher to prepare materials or reduce burdensome paperwork. Examples are quiz generators that select vocabulary at random or print tables of verb forms for students to fill in as a quick check on their mastery of morphology. Although grade-book programs are commercially available, the instructor/programmer may find benefits in writing programs that help perform weighted grade calculations and print out scores and comments to students. In the area of translation or composition, programs that take several student's responses to a given task and assemble them on a single handout for class discussion can serve as simple projects that hone the programming skills useful in all foreign language programming.

Branching Tutorials Using an Authoring Language

Branching tutorials that carefully sequence subsets of linguistic information add a new level of complexity to the self-contained tutorials described above. A branching tutorial must account explicitly for the fact that students plunge into a given topic with widely different backgrounds and abilities. This kind of tutorial sets up a series of tasks that attempt to pin down the student's current competency in the topic area (e.g., reading a newspaper weather report, expressing wishes in the subjunctive) and adjust the sequence of the tutorial unit accordingly. The tutorial may even branch to remedial work from other tutorial segments. This approach can still be implemented with the help of an authoring language, although it requires a high degree of subject matter and instructional design expertise.

Generative Drill for Simple Structural Features

The term "generative CAI" refers to the use of computer logic to create morphologically and syntactically correct linguistic forms as the basis for structural practice. At the simplest level, the machine can be made to conjugate the complete paradigms of verbs (to the extent that they have regular features). A functioning verb conjugator can then serve as the basis for a sentence generator. The sentence generator becomes the engine for structural exercises that have an almost infinite number of items generated at random on a given topic.

A project of this sort is probably not appropriate for an authoring language, but rather should be seen as an intermediate-level programming task. The more complex the linguistic features and the more extensive the lexicon used, the greater the challenge to the programmer, who will have to acquire a relatively thorough understanding of the structures of the target language. The computer that generates correct paradigms and sentences can be programmed to generate incorrect forms as well, in anticipation of student errors. The power of the generative program is therefore twofold: it can pour forth practice materials almost endlessly and it can invoke powerful diagnostic strategies to help the learner understand his or her weaknesses. Programs that attempt to do all this will quickly cross the boundary from development to research.

Simple Reading Comprehension Exercises

Very few reading packages are available that go beyond simple multiple-choice or fill-in-the-blank comprehension checking. Perhaps software developers have allowed their creative insights to be throttled by fears that their efforts might be termed "page turners," a label applied indiscriminately to any software that displays chunks of text on the screen. Advances in reading research already point to a wide range of skill-building activities that lend themselves to interactive computer delivery. Like generative CAI, reading programs can begin with the simpler forms of text display and move steadily into experimental areas that offer variant versions of the text; branch to easier and harder texts; supply lexical, structural, and cultural commentary; and much more. In contrast to generative CAI, reading projects probably lend themselves to implementation via a sophisticated authoring language.

Adventure Games Using Preprogrammed Models

Adventure games can form the vehicle for highly motivated learning sessions in reading comprehension and culture. The student becomes immersed in an environment vicariously, instead of focusing only on formal practice; vicarious cultural immersion is more likely to evoke the use of the language for a communicative purpose. Kossuth (6) presents a thoughtful case for more systematic work with adventure formats, relating their use to Krashen's Input and the Affective Filter Hypotheses and describing in some detail the use of adventure authoring tools. Sanders and Sanders (14) discuss the prospects for intelligent foreign language games using the language-understanding techniques of artificial intelligence. (See also Chapter 8 in this volume, by Underwood.)

Programming adventure games and other simulations can be a demanding assignment. The simulated universe contains persons, objects, places, and actions that must be carefully tracked by the program. Communication between the learner and the computer can range from well-disguised multiple choice alternatives to machine "understanding" of hundreds or thousands of expressions. In most cases, representation of events in the simulated reality requires elaborate programming of graphics. Fortunately, adventure game packages are beginning to appear commercially that provide all of the graphics and the concealed juggling of simulation data. The instructor/author is permitted to create new scenarios, design new environments, and weave all new plots for the learner to unravel. Although there may be drawbacks to such adventure construction kits—lack of foreign characters, culturally inauthentic graphics—the advantages in terms of personalizing and contextualizing language practice probably outweigh the current disadvantages.

As the above series of typical development projects shows, the creation of original courseware can place major demands on the subject-matter specialist, i.e., the language teacher. The third level of project complexity, verging on the experimental, demands even greater time and resources and has an added element of risk, since there is seldom a guarantee of success.

Research Projects

Research projects are understood here as those large-scale or experimental projects that cannot be accomplished without a significant amount of original programming or whose success depends on the complex interaction of many modules or several media. Many of the possible projects described below will also require very careful evaluation to measure the effectiveness of the learning strategies involved.

Comprehensive Tutorials with Recordkeeping

One of the prime motivations for developing tutorial programs lies in the prospect of banning the explanatory aspects of language teaching from the classroom in favor of applying language skills in meaningful contexts.

In its extreme form, a full-scale tutorial could be used to deliver individualized instruction courses, correspondence courses and related forms of distance learning, and other nontraditional kinds of language study. The tutorial projects described above assume that computer work is conducted in parallel with a traditional course and that a human tutor consistently measures student progress. The final step in designing a full-fledged tutorial package—one that might take a learner from complete unfamiliarity with the target language to, say, the Intermediate–High level (1+) on the ACTFL/ETS scale requires careful tracking of student progress.

Recordkeeping may involve data collection via pretesting and posttesting to evaluate the learner's progress; it also requires a secure system to make a record of each step of the learner's work. The responsibilities of the instructional designer are greatly increased when the computer is asked both to instruct and to evaluate student progress. The tutorial interaction must be pedagogically correct and effective; the methods used to measure the outcome must also be reliable. Success in the tutorial must bear a fair relationship to the accomplishments demanded of students in traditional instructional settings. This implies extensive testing under controlled conditions over a long period of time. Such testing may show that specific modules of the tutorial are ineffective and should be redesigned and reprogrammed. The difficulties suggested here may explain why no completely self-contained tutorial course is currently available for any foreign language. Even when tutorials of this nature do emerge, they will doubtless raise questions about the specific proficiencies they claim to foster. In the end, a variety of tutorial software will be needed that employs different means to convey (1) structural knowledge, (2) reading proficiency, and (3) writing skills.

Drill or Tutorial with Animated Graphics

Text-based presentations seldom exploit the increasing capacity of powerful microcomputers to use color, shape, and movement to clarify relationships and illustrate content. Most authoring systems offer rudimentary tools for what can be called textual graphics—movement of letters, boxes, colors to establish links between concepts and words. Projects that go beyond text animation and static illustration require sophisticated programming techniques and are therefore extremely costly. Software for authoring seems to lag far behind the power of today's machines, but developers are well advised to keep track of illustration software (with names like "graphics magic kit," "computer paintbox," etc.) and ever more powerful authoring systems that include animation features.

Computer graphics in foreign language CAI may also engender some controversy because primitive illustrations seldom capture the cultural authenticity found in visual materials in our textbooks. Commercial publishers may be able to overcome these limitations by commissioning animation from foreign artists. Language teachers can now approach the problem by using graphics-digitizing devices to actually transfer authentic images from print or video into their computer systems for use in structural practice, tutorials, or cultural simulations.

Creating Authoring Tools for Grammar and Reading

Most large-scale projects attempted today are designed around a fixed set of activities and interactions that appear throughout a whole series of instructional modules. The computer programs and routines that support these tasks form what is known as a "driver." The driver manipulates variable lesson content provided by the language teacher/author. One approach to creating CALL software for a large segment of the curriculum is to write original driver programs with the intent that they will be used as a template or authoring system.

Designing a new authoring system assumes that small-scale pilot work has already been done to discover an effective set of interaction types for a given purpose. For example, an arsenal of reading comprehension activities—including prereading tasks, skimming and scanning activities, reading utilities such as glossaries, and postreading comprehension checks—could be carefully prototyped for a single intermediate-level text in Spanish. An authoring language can be used to expedite this preliminary process. Once a satisfactory set of learning tasks has been worked out and tested by students, it is possible to accelerate the development process radically by generalizing the software so that the original text can be replaced by *any* Spanish text. In the case of reading comprehension programs, the resulting template will probably be useful for reading programs in other European languages.

By approaching the tasks of software development with the goal of creating a specially designed authoring system, one can reduce long-term costs and improve the reliability of the ultimate products. Whether one creates a new authoring system using a high-level authoring language or resorts to programming in a language like BASIC, Pascal, or C will depend largely on the power of the authoring system being considered and on the complexity of the tasks envisioned by the teacher/author.

Large Databases for Structure and Reading Practice

Once a specialized authoring system has been developed and tested thoroughly with a small set of materials, the natural next step is to exploit its capabilities to the fullest. This step should be considered a project in itself, for it requires the involvement of other faculty, assistants with excellent linguistic and pedagogical training, native-speaker proofreaders, program testers, and a documentation editor. Work on this scale requires extra equipment and a project manager. Any authoring system with a high degree of flexibility should be considered a major resource for the campus and beyond, since using the authoring system will *always* be more cost-effective than designing new software from scratch. Granting agencies and commercial textbook publishers can be approached with strong arguments for funding to implement specific sets of material using the authoring system. The success of such proposals rests on the quality of the authoring system and on the institution's ability to carry a large project through to completion on schedule.

Complex Simulations of Target Culture Situations

Designing an authentic cultural simulation for the computer can be likened to producing a major motion picture or writing the Great American Novel. The content and language must carefully replicate the culture of a foreign country. Means must be found to present the situation to the learner via text, graphics, sound, or video. Unlike a movie or a novel, alternate scenarios must be plotted and brought to a conclusion. Fault can be found with many of the simulations attempted in the past because they ignore—knowingly or unknowingly—the imperative of authenticity in the interest of exploring the dynamics and technology of the simulation. Despite these caveats, simulations remain extremely attractive to the language teacher because even the weakest simulation attempts to give the student a controlled context for language usage. This moves CALL a large step beyond discrete-point structural practice and reflects the best insights of language-acquisition theory.

Language Understanding Projects

The projects outlined above have a fundamental limitation: they treat student input as data rather than as communication. The emergence of more powerful microcomputers with more advanced programming languages as C, Lisp, and Prolog has begun to justify research projects that attempt to analyze linguistic input in terms of its syntactic structures and ultimately its semantic content. Successful packages have already been published that accept a wide range of student expression, parse its structure, and even evaluate whether it is meaningful. In his discussion of artificial intelligence (Chapter 8 in this volume), Underwood outlines in detail the tasks and promise of linguistically based approaches to CALL.

Validated Placement and Proficiency Tests

The impetus toward developing testing instruments has become stronger with the advent of a wide consensus in the profession about the need for national standards in language proficiency. Mastery of structural features of a language and proficiency in reading skills are the two areas most likely to benefit from this trend through CALL. Listening comprehension tests will also emerge with the help of advanced audio and video technologies; speaking and writing tests, however, will feel little impact from technology.

The use of the computer in language testing, however, is still in its infancy, especially where it relates to established criteria such as the ACTFL/ETS *Guidelines.* The need for computer-based reading proficiency tests that attain the adaptive flexibility of the ACTFL Oral Proficiency Interview has been recognized, but full-fledged implementation lies in the future. Despite optimistic projections by Wyatt (16) and Pusack (10), serious questions can be raised about the reliability of adaptive tests that present different sequences of items to different students. It is clear that the programming difficulties inherent in such tests are small compared to the pedagogical concerns.

The list of potential areas for CALL research projects can be extended infinitely, especially into high-technology realms where new devices make possible ever more powerful types of student–computer interaction. The above examples, however, remain within the scope of proven hardware and software and thus deserve careful consideration by advanced users of CALL.

Conclusion

Providing CALL means engaging in a long-term process. As teacher-training programs begin to take technology into account, teachers will begin their careers with a foundation for building CALL into the curriculum. Everyone concerned, however, must explore the possibilities systematically and exploit intelligently what has been done in the past. Too many projects have simply replicated previous work. Hope, Taylor, and Pusack (5) include an extensive annotated bibliography to guide more extensive readings. Marty (7) draws a number of valuable conclusions about CALL from his extensive experience during the development of high-quality French lessons on the PLATO system. Wyatt (17) offers a perspective from the ESL curriculum that has many areas of overlap with foreign-language computing. Impetus from the wider educational context can also help in the effective design and use of instructional computing. Two highly recommended handbooks with a larger perspective are Alessi and Trollip (1) and O'Shea and Self (8).

Ultimately, progress in CALL rests with only one group: language teachers themselves. Ideas from professional design experts, algorithms from state-of-the-art programmers, and market-oriented products from commercial publishers will all miss the mark if teachers do not articulate their needs. Whether it be by critiquing packages, implementing existing CALL materials, authoring new programs, or engaging in long-term experiments, all foreign language teachers can play a decisive role by insisting that they know good software when they see it. Good CALL software has one essential property: it incorporates our best knowledge about how today's learners learn languages.

References, Problems and Prospects in Foreign Language Computing

1. Alessi, Stephen M., and Stanley R. Trollip, *Computer-Based Instruction: Methods and Development.* Englewood Cliffs, NJ: Prentice-Hall, 1985.
2. Bigham, Dane, Gene Portwood, and Lauren Elliott. *Where in the World Is Carmen Sandiego?* San Rafael, CA: Brøderbund Software, 1985.
3. Cornick, Lisa B. "Evaluating Foreign-Language CAI: A Checklist." *Die Unterrichtspraxis* 17 (1984):315–18.
4. Hamerstrom, Helen, Gladys Lipton, and Sherry Suter. "Computers in the Foreign Language Classroom: No Longer a Question." *CALICO Journal* 3, 1 (1985):19–21,48.
5. Hope, Geoffrey R., Heimy F. Taylor, and James P. Pusack. *Using Computers in Teaching Foreign Languages.* Language and Education: Theory and Practice, no. 57. Orlando, FL: Harcourt Brace Jovanovich, 1984.
6. Kossuth, Karen C. "Using the Adventure Formats for CALI." *CALICO Journal* 3, 2 (1985):13–17.
7. Marty, Fernand. "Reflections on the Use of Computers in Second-Language Acquisition." *System* 9, 2 (1981):85–98; 10, 1 (1982):1–11.
8. O'Shea, Tim, and John Self. *Learning and Teaching with Computers: Artificial Intelligence in Education.* Englewood Cliff, NJ: Prentice-Hall, 1983.
9. Otto, Sue E. K. and James P. Pusack. "Tools for Creating Foreign Language CAI," pp. 96–108 in Patricia B. Westphal, ed., *Meeting the Call for Excellence in the Foreign Language Classroom.* Proceedings of the Central States Conference on the Teaching of Foreign Languages. Lincolnwood, IL: National Textbook Company, 1985.
10. Pusack, James P. "The Interactive Computer Testing of Reading Proficiency." *Foreign Language Annals* 17, 4 (1984):415–19.
11. _____. "Answer-Processing and Error Correction in Foreign Language CAI." *System* 11, 1 (1983):53–64.
12. _____. *DASHER: An Answer Processor for Language Study.* Oakdale, IA: CONDUIT, 1983.
13. Pusack, James P., and Sue E. K. Otto. "Blueprint for a Comprehensive Foreign Language CAI Curriculum." *Computers and the Humanities* 18 (1984):195–204.
14. Sanders, Alton F., and Ruth H. Sanders. "Spion: 'Intelligent' Games for German Language Teaching," pp. 141–46 in *Foreign Language Instructional Technology Conference Proceedings, 21–24 September, 1982.* Monterey, CA: Defense Language Institute, 1983. [EDRS: ED 236 910.]
15. Tenczar, Paul et al. *TenCORE Language Authoring System.* Champaign, IL: Computer Teaching Corporation, 1984.

16. Wyatt, David H. "Computer-Assisted Teaching and Testing of Reading and Listening," *Foreign Language Annals* 17, 4 (1984):393–407.
17. _____. *Computers and ESL.* Language and Education: Theory and Practice, no. 56. New York: Harcourt Brace Jovanovich, 1984.

2

Integrating Video and CALL in the Curriculum: The Role of the ACTFL Guidelines

Robert Ariew
The Pennsylvania State University

Introduction

The first part of this chapter examines the present state of the use of media in the foreign language curriculum. The potential impact of video and CALL is analyzed, and their advantages and disadvantages are charted. In the second part, the role of the *ACTFL Proficiency Guidelines* with respect to video and CALL is discussed. In the third section, entitled "Possibilities and Feasibilities," avenues are proposed for using video and CALL appropriately in the classroom. The chapter ends with a brief look at upcoming technology.

Beginning-level foreign language materials have changed considerably in the last few years. Gone are the days when a whole curriculum could be built on a text, a workbook, and an optional set of audiotapes. First-year courses have become a formidable, complex array of supporting materials and components designed to help teachers teach and students learn. Course content has changed as well; traditional orientations have given way to more practical or pragmatic approaches. But while curricular changes could have been foreseen, the explosion in the number of ancillaries composing first-year courses has come as a surprise to many.

Robert Ariew (Ph.D., University of Illinois) is Associate Professor of French and Director of the Program in Computer Assisted Instruction for the College of Liberal Arts at Pennsylvania State University, where he teaches French language, literature, and pedagogy and computer applications to foreign language teaching. He is a member of ACTFL, AATF, CALICO, and the Association for Computing in the Humanities, is Software Review Editor for the *Newsletter* of the Northeast Conference, and is Courseware Editor for *Computers and the Humanities.* He is the author of the software for *Allons-y! Utilisons l'ordinateur* and *¡Vamos! Utilicemos la computadora,* published by Heinle and Heinle.

To illustrate the magnitude of the change, one only needs to examine the descriptions of new first-year language programs that publishers send to the profession. The following is a list of materials compiled from various brochures. It represents what publishers today consider adequate for beginning language courses.

- *The textbook.* Still the mainstay of publishers, it has evolved as well. It is now an imposing volume with a variety of activities that teach grammar, culture, reading, writing, listening, and phonetics.
- *The instructor's annotated edition.* The IAE offers variations on the text exercises, additional explanations, and cultural information.
- *The teacher's guide.* In addition to providing general pedagogical information about the approach used in the text, the teacher's guide often gives useful hints for preparing tests and lesson plans.
- *The workbook.* The modern workbook is divided into two distinct sections. One contains activities linked to the audiotape program, while a second directs writing activities.
- *The audiotape program.* The tape program has grown more elaborate and now usually includes songs. It is the principal means of providing the student additional listening comprehension activities.
- *The test bank.* Often quite elaborate, the test bank provides the teacher with several versions of quizzes and exams. Modern test banks frequently include items for oral interviews.
- *The tape script and answer key.* More and more publishers see the value in publishing a tape script for teachers to use as a reference to avoid having to listen to the tapes in preparing lesson plans. The answer key, which may be published separately, provides answers to textbook or workbook exercises, or both. Teachers routinely have given students access to it to self-check workbook assignments.
- *The reader.* Many first-year packages now include a reader. Reading selections are chosen to be timely, cultural, and interesting.
- *The CALL program.* Growing rapidly in popularity, the CALL (Computer Assisted Language Learning) program has been implemented in two distinct program types: "specific" and "generic." The "specific" coordinates activities closely with the text; the "generic" makes available CALL activities of a general nature.
- *The video program.* The latest entry into the ancillary market is one or more videotapes about culture. The content of the videotapes is generally "generic," being adapted from foreign language broadcasts.
- *The video guide.* A new publication, its purpose is to suggest activities based on the videotapes.
- *The teacher's kit.* The teacher's kit is a collection of transparencies, maps, slides, and realia designed to make the teacher's presentations more lively.

How Did We Get Here?

The beginning-level language program has become a very complex set of interrelated materials. Some say it has become unwieldy, others claim that teachers have relinquished control and that publishers are providing too many superfluous materials. There are obviously two sides to the story. Teachers are beginning to realize that there is a multiplicity of ways to present foreign language materials. They request, along with the traditional textbooks, all kinds of helpful adjuncts to enliven class time—overhead transparencies, slides, audiotapes and videotapes, and diskettes for computer-assisted instruction whose motivation is clearly to make the materials more interesting, more relevant, and more "alive" to the students. Teachers also request supplements to make teaching easier and to save time—test banks, pedagogical guides, and answer keys are now essential elements of the foreign language course.

Publishers are motivated differently. They hear teachers' requests and, after some time for market research, usually provide what is requested. While most of the supplementary materials are expensive to produce, publishers make them available because, they learn from market research, there will be a net gain in sales of books—their principal products—and profit. Some publishers have even provided some ancillary materials free as a strategy to spur sales of texts. For example, one publisher offers complimentary videocassettes if a certain number of textbooks is ordered by an institution in a given year. Another, on the same basis, provides a teacher's kit that includes transparencies, maps, realia, and helpful teaching hints.

There are therefore two divergent viewpoints: instructors want more and more materials to make teaching easier and more interesting, and publishers want to sell more books. The result is a curriculum overendowed with materials lacking an organizing principle—a sort of "bloated curriculitis." While the disease is rarely fatal, one runs the risk of complications, one of the more dangerous of which is the urge to take a first-year, two-semester course and spread it across a three- or even four-semester sequence. The rationale is generally given as follows: (a) "There is just too much material to cover in one year;" (b) "Since it would be a shame to take out any of the material, we will cover it all," but (c) "to do it justice, we will cover it thoroughly over more time." After all, the reasoning goes, it is better to do things more thoroughly than more lightly. The problem with all this is that there are perfectly good pedagogical reasons *not* to stretch out a one-year course, but to finish it in one year. For those classes meeting three times a week, a syllabus with more modest goals should be adopted. First-year and second-year courses ought to have different goals, a different organization, and perhaps even entirely different approaches.

A First Proposed Solution

The first solution to the dilemma is obvious, and has been proposed by several writers: teachers must make choices, reorder text material, and adapt and supplement the materials to fit a predetermined, well-defined curriculum. (Guntermann and Phillips, 7; Flynn, 5; Muyskens, 16; Bragger, 4; Ariew, 2; Valdman, 21). For instance, Bragger states that the lesson plan "may mean a certain reordering of the sequence of presentation in the textbook itself" (4, p. 94). Muyskens is even more specific: "Although the task of textbook adaptation and supplementation is time-consuming, prospective teachers can realize that their job is 'to provide what the textbook fails to provide.' If the text does not meet program goals entirely, teachers need to adapt it themselves" (17, p. 191). In addition, Muyskens suggests that "adapting and supplementing texts should . . . play a role in the training of preservice teachers and TAs" (p. 191).

The clamor for activist, involved teachers, while understandable, is not very realistic, given the time constraints in the average teacher's schedule. Generally speaking, the large number of classes to be taught in the secondary school environment, the research requirements in the college and university environments, and graduate courses that Teaching Assistants (TAs) must take all preclude a vigorous involvement in curricular design. There are many teachers who, by dint of dedication, willpower, or individualism, do in fact shape their own curriculum; others will relegate such onerous tasks to the textbook itself. In short, for many the word "curriculum" is synonymous with "textbook."

Time, or a lack of it, is not the only element in the equation. There is at least one group that is generally not trained to make informed curricular choices: the TAs in the college or university environment. Some are interested and capable of handling curricular design, but most do not have the necessary background, experience, or interest. For them too, the textbook represents the curriculum. And since making choices, reordering, and supplementing the syllabus are troublesome processes, they are generally not undertaken. The TA who would initiate change runs several risks in making independent curricular modifications, for if a particular grammatical or cultural point is ignored in class (or given excessive breadth or depth), that circumstance is likely to show up in departmentally administered exams or quizzes. In short, instead of helping students by focusing on what's important, the TA can hurt them by lowering their exam grades.

Curricular modifications, selection of materials, adaptation, and supplementation are useful and worthwhile tasks, but they tend to be time-consuming and difficult to carry out. They also run counter to teachers' feelings about foreign language study. Most teachers will assume that: (a) One can't get enough of a good thing. Since foreign language learning is a good thing, one should not reduce it in any way. (b) Publishers and textbook authors know best. Since they know best, there must be a good reason for the wealth of material, and therefore teachers should cover it all.

A Second Proposed Solution

Beginning language courses should be designed in a less fragmented, more integrated manner. Instead of continually *adding* ancillaries, the various media should *replace* portions of the course, based on the capabilities of the media. Some movement in this direction is becoming apparent as some publishers consider "short courses" that reduce the size or scope of the textbook while retaining most of the ancillary media. The movement is proceeding cautiously, because publishers want to provide a full measure of materials. The direction is the right one, however, because for the first time media are not considered appendices to the curriculum; they have assumed more than a minor role in the teaching environment.

The Role of the Media

What role do the media play and how can they be used to best advantage? It is foolish to assume that the mere use of videotapes in the French or Spanish class will solve all pedagogical problems. More likely, using videotapes will create new problems (in equipment selection and maintenance, for example), solve some (provide motivation and opportunities for listening to real language), and do nothing for other aspects of teaching (will not address speaking skills specifically, nor provide for individual attention, for example).

Relying on modern media to support instruction requires knowing, first, precisely what they can and cannot do in foreign language instruction. Their capabilities and potentials must be analyzed and used appropriately instead of or along with the traditional audiotapes, books, blackboard, etc. All media must be assumed to form an integral part of a curriculum and to carry a primary instructional load according to their potential to explain, illustrate, and teach. Media should not be used in a "reinforcing," "additional," "adjunct," or "remedial" way, but as mainstream teaching tools.

Holmes (10, p. 104) has addressed the need to demonstrate to teachers and students the primary rather than the supplemental role media can play, a circumstance underscored by ascribing to CALL a limited though compulsory place in the curriculum.

What of the other technologies and other media on the horizon, such as video, interactive video, CALL with artificial intelligence and the compact-disk storage medium? If CALL is to be a model for their development, they will also run the risk of being relegated to the status of ancillaries, or "frills" as Holmes calls them. If their value in teaching foreign languages is to be recognized, then classroom activities will need to be reorganized to make room for them.

What Do the New Media Bring to the Class?

A first reaction to the capabilities of well-designed CALL materials is that they can do everything: interactions are lively; there is sound, color, movement; help is available when help is needed; there is instant correction. The list goes on. Similarly, at first encounter, one might think that video can solve all teaching problems. Well-chosen video programs from abroad are interesting, realistic and natural, motivating and exciting. Both CALL and video offer certain capabilities that are otherwise either difficult or impossible to introduce into the average classroom. The second reaction is to make plans to add the materials to the curriculum. The third is to wonder to what extent the materials might someday replace the teacher. All three reactions, while understandable, are not well considered.

It is true that both CALL and video add exciting dimensions to learning languages. It is not true, however, that they can support by themselves even a significant portion of the instructional load. Both have very definite limitations in their capacity to instruct students. For instance, oral skills cannot be addressed adequately with CALL, nor can written skills be targeted with video.

To add new elements to language courses, rather than to replace existing elements, leads to inflated curricula and all attendant problems.

Finally, the issue of teacher obsolescence is ludicrous, unless mechanical clones of humans with native linguistic abilities are made available in the near future. The teacher cannot be replaced by a textbook; similarly, teaching tools with limited capabilities just cannot replace a teacher.

Teachers' fears of obsolescence do have a basis in fact. The media do provide attractive and effective capabilities that, superficially at least, raise fears in some people's minds. Which teacher would be foolish enough to compete in attractiveness of presentation and realism with any competent video material? The video would win hands down. What classroom game could compete with the best of CALL games? The adrenaline-charged CALL activity would also win easily. The facts are clearly reconcilable. Affectively, both video and CALL are very powerful, and within the bounds of their limitations they can present some materials more effectively than teachers. On the other hand, equally important to recognize is that video and CALL alone are quite limited in their abilities to teach foreign languages.

Pluses and Minuses

What, more precisely, can video and CALL accomplish? The paragraphs below tally the pluses and minuses. Unfortunately, any inventory that can be established at this time will be incomplete since the widespread use of the two media is so recent that their potential for teaching has not been clearly established nor well defined. The process of discovering the capabilities of video and CALL with respect to foreign language teaching is an ongoing one; however, there are some things that can be stated categorically.

Video Advantages

Realism	Essentially a photographic medium, video brings people and places to foreign language classrooms. Paris, Madrid, or Bonn can be shown right in the classroom. Few activities have as much visual impact or realism as video screenings.
Motion	The realism is enhanced even more because of motion; scenes, actions, and processes can be illustrated with video.
Color	Although not of the highest fidelity, video color is quite believable and motivational.
Flexibility	Video can be used in small groups or for individual work. Most viewing equipment is now relatively inexpensive and easily available.

Video Disadvantages

Linear	Unless coupled with a computer, video is mainly a linear medium. One normally starts it and lets it go on. It is difficult to repeat segments of video.
No interactivity	Video is a one-way medium. Unless the computer is brought to bear, video by itself is not interactive; students cannot have any "input."
No abstractions	Abstract subjects take a great deal of time to explain on video. The medium's strengths lie in showing things with images, not in arguing complex ideas.
Low resolution	Although studio-quality video can approach photographic clarity, most videocassette material is of much lower resolution. Small details are difficult to detect. Very little text may be used on video materials.
High production costs	Most teachers prefer to use materials prepared by others rather than videotape their own because of the high production costs. Of course, "home movie" quality is relatively inexpensive to produce, but its use in the foreign language classroom is of dubious value (Bork, 3, p. 179).

CALL Advantages

Interactivity	Students can control the path of the material, and at the same time the program can respond by providing appropriate material to students.
Answer judging	Answer judging is a corollary of interactive processing; it describes the computer's ability to judge a student's input and either mark it up or give specific diagnostics on its accuracy. The computer can judge the correctness of word input, selections (as in multiple choice items), or location (the student may be asked to point to a location on the screen).
Graphics and sounds	Although not of the highest resolution or quality, both graphics in color and sounds (sound effects and melodies) are available in present-day CALL hardware. Both add an appreciable motivational factor to materials. In addition, emphases, boxes, and different font sizes and types are available.
Timing	The computer is capable of presenting textual and graphic material as a function of time. The display rate of text may be varied on CALL and also the text may be "paused" and revealed in segments. Similarly, graphics may be revealed slowly or at the student's request. None of these features is available in texts.
Animation	Low-grade animation (a corollary of timing text and graphics) is available and can be used quite effectively in CALL presentations to show for example processes, verb paradigms, and word order.
Control of other media	The computer can control other media—at the present time videodisc, videocassette players, audiodisc, and audiocassette players—thus allowing for very complex CALL presentations.

CALL Disadvantages

No voice	Although the computer can control other media, it does not presently have an acceptable voice synthesis capability for teaching foreign languages. CALL software can only be designed with text and graphics—no voice. The computer does not understand human voices at this time either. No foreign language CALL software can include audio input.
Low realism/low resolution	Even the best of computer graphics on commonly available microcomputers cannot approach the detail of a photograph. It is also hard to display more than a paragraph or two on the screen.
No "free expression"	CALL answer judging presently can handle a word, a phrase, and perhaps a sentence. Very long or very complex sentences, especially if they are "free form," are impossible to judge given the present limitations of hardware and software.
High implementation costs	Because it is a personal medium, CALL requires that several computers be made available (or several hundred depending on the size of the institution). There are benefits however to having two or three students use a microcomputer together; they tend to teach and help each other.

High production costs	Production costs for CALL are very high. It is not unusual to encounter 400 hours of development for 1 hour of instruction. Teacher-produced CALL, like its video counterpart, is of dubious value.

Summary of Capabilities

It can be stated quite forcefully at this point that neither CALL nor video has the capability to engage students in free-form conversational exchanges. Moreover, video cannot correct a written input; for that matter, video cannot accept any input at all unless it is coupled with a computer. Computers cannot produce very understandable voices (especially in foreign languages); they cannot display images of photographic quality unless coupled with a videodisk. CALL materials can accept student input, but have a great deal of difficulty making "sense" of it when it is longer than a few words. Both media, praised highly as the panacea for all foreign language teaching and learning, are, after all, limited. They are most effective when used intelligently within the scope of a progressive and multidimensional language curriculum.

Having realized that the great advances in "modern technology" merely provide new and somewhat limited tools to the foreign language curriculum, the following very radical tenet may now be proposed: *The whole of the foreign language curriculum consists of tools.* All of the components described at the beginning of this chapter are tools—even the textbooks are tools, even chalkboards, audiotapes, and classrooms, as are chairs, overhead projectors, videodiscs, maps, realia, and so on. Moreover, it would be difficult to organize a foreign language course around the teacher alone. Tools are essential. If CALL and video offer some new capabilities to teaching, they should be welcomed as new options, but their usefulness should be known in detail, according to the tasks the tools should confront.

Special Affinities

Video.   Are there any teaching tasks that can especially benefit from the application of the new media? Are there specific skills and media that have an affinity for one another? One thing is sure: neither of the new media addresses speaking. Students could not improve their speaking skills by using video, except indirectly, by having heard foreign language material. Nor does video lend itself to improving writing skills since there is no opportunity for input. Video cannot address reading, since resolution is generally too low to display much textual material. On the other hand, video's forte is in showing action and images along with sound. Video therefore has the strongest potential in teaching listening.

Using video to teach listening skills is quite an effective combination.

To view images while listening to a soundtrack is by far more interesting to a student than listening to an audio track alone—there is a semblance of reality, an immediacy and an intimacy that can hardly be matched with any other type of presentation. Fortunately too, listening skills can be practiced in small to medium-sized groups, which is precisely the type of learning situation video affords.

Cultural information can also be presented very effectively via video. In this mode, video's images are used as the primary vehicle of information while the audio track carries the message. The foreign culture can be shown with considerable impact, since it can be portrayed through actions, events, sites, vistas, locales, peoples, and sounds. It is hard to imagine providing a more focused or more realistic presentation than through authentic foreign video.

CALL.   CALL, on the other hand, without additional hardware to generate speech, does little for listening skills. Similarly, CALL does not directly affect speaking; there are no opportunities for voice input. While CALL can be very useful to teach writing skills, there is an upper limit to its capabilities: the machine (the software) has trouble dealing with more than a few words of student input at a time (Wyatt, 22, p. 395). However, CALL does provide an opportunity to make a valuable contribution in teaching reading.

Pairing CALL with reading skills has been the subject of a series of articles (Aoki, 1; Holmes, 11; Pederson, 17; Phillips, 18). In another, Pusack (19, p. 416) argues that computer-assisted testing of reading proficiency, compared to other language skills, is promising because computers are very good at the display of text—much better than they are at understanding language—and since reading skills involve discriminations that lend themselves to algorithmic analysis, the harrowing problems of language analysis can be avoided. Therefore, the tremendous memory and analytical powers of the machine are harnessed to the task of determining individual students' reading ability. For reading skills, the power of the computer can be used (1) to display textual and graphic materials, (2) to monitor student progress through the material by keeping track of strengths and weaknesses, (3) to present interactive material at an appropriate level of difficulty.

An Intermediate Conclusion

At this point, it is possible to make some statements about the two media under scrutiny. When video and CALL are evaluated on the basis of their capabilities, it becomes clear that both media are of limited value in teaching foreign languages; that is, neither can, by itself, carry the burden of teaching all four (or five) skills. It is therefore impossible to conceive of a complete language program based exclusively on either medium. Just as it is difficult to conceive of a complete foreign language curriculum based on audiotapes alone, videotapes will not be sufficient to teach a language. One could conceive of a single-track program, such as a language program for listening comprehension based on videotapes, but a complete language course is probably out of the question. Similarly, CALL, because of its inherent limitations, cannot carry the burden of the whole teaching program no matter the skill sought.

The same statement can be made about foreign language textbooks. Because of the text's inherent limitations (no audio, no action, low realism, no interaction, etc.), it is equally difficult to conceive of a complete foreign language program based on a textbook alone. Taking one step further, by itself a textbook is not a particularly good medium with which to teach foreign languages. The textbook benefits from centuries of development and use and, of course, it does have many excellent characteristics: (1) much information can be presented quickly, (2) graphics, including line art, sketches, and drawings, can be used and combined with text, (3) photographs in black and white or color can be used in presentations, (4) emphases with color, type styles, type sizes, and boxes can be used to point out important language features. All these capabilities, while useful, cannot guarantee the successful transmission of all foreign language skills. Much more is needed.

	Video	Call	Textbook
Listening	+	−	−
Speaking	−	−	−
Reading	−(?)	+	+
Writing	−	+(?)	+

Figure 1. Strengths and Weaknesses of Three Media in Relation to the Four Skills

Since none of the media, including the text, can provide all the components required to learn a second language (See Figure 1), the foreign language course should be structured around various media, taking into account their strengths in presenting or testing specific skills. One should conceive of a curriculum as made up of a large number of ancillaries (including the text), each of which is selected and used according to its capabilities vis à vis the skills being taught. Video should figure prominently when listening skills are targeted, while the text, the workbook, and perhaps a CALL unit should be brought to bear when writing skills are addressed. When reading skills or culture are discussed, the text, video, and CALL could be used as appropriate teaching media. No medium can be identified specifically for speaking skills. At this time, speaking can only be addressed by teachers making use of their experience and the examples, hints, and suggestions pedagogical guides and teachers' editions of textbooks typically provide.

In short, new media cloud the curricular issues. None can be shown to aid or encompass all teaching skills. Teachers are faced therefore with having to pick and choose from among media with various capabilities and limitations. Publishers, to whom teachers generally turn for curricular help, have not made the task easier; they provide more and more material without addressing the problem of how to integrate it into one coherent and workable course. Are we back to square one?

Not quite—there have been advances and there is some cause for optimism.

Causes for Optimism

Higgs wrote:

> I believe almost any target language data—even something as mundane as learning colors or how to count—can capture and hold students' interest, provided that it is presented in a way that directly involves the students and encourages their active participation in the presentation itself. (9, p. 200)

A first cause for optimism: the new media are likely to make an impact on foreign language teaching because they involve students and ask for their participation in the foreign language material.

A second cause for optimism: new teaching materials will have to address the issue of integration. It is inconceivable to keep adding ancillaries to the curriculum without absorbing media into the domain of textbook presentations. To that end, CALL materials are a logical substitute for some or all of the traditional workbook. Similarly, video presentations will be used to illustrate textbook dialogues and will substitute for some or all of the audiotape program. Readers will soon be published simultaneously in book and in CALL form.

A third cause for optimism, the *ACTFL Proficiency Guidelines* will certainly play a role in shaping the curriculum in the immediate future. The role of the *Guidelines* and how they may help integrate media into the curriculum is the subject of the next section.

The ACTFL Proficiency Guidelines

It is not within the scope of this chapter to provide a thorough historical narrative on the *Guidelines.* Liskin-Gasparro (13), for one, has accomplished the task admirably. Suffice it to state that the *Guidelines* are a series of descriptions of levels of proficiency for the four skills commonly taught in foreign language courses. According to Liskin-Gasparro, the *Guidelines* "can be used to structure a foreign language program" (p. 11). They describe four main proficiency levels from a "novice" (a person with no functional knowledge of the language), to a "superior" (a person who demonstrates a great deal of functionality in the language). In addition, there are also low, mid, and high sublevel descriptions for some levels.

All who have commented on the *Guidelines* have made the following statements at one time or another: (1) They are *not* goal statements. Although goal statements for specific curricula or courses may be defined on the basis of the ACTFL descriptions, the descriptions themselves are not goals. (2) They are *not* tests. They are not proficiency tests, or achievement tests, or any other kind of test. They may be the starting point for formulating a test, however; one test derived from them that has received a certain amount of attention recently is the Oral Proficiency Interview, which, when given by a certified tester, provides an accurate gauge of oral linguistic ability. (3) They are *not* a methodology. Although the descriptions suggest a focal point around which a curriculum may be structured, they do not provide any clue to how a curriculum is to be guided toward its goals (which, as stated above, are not defined by the *Guidelines*).

There is *no* methodological description to go with them, and no hint of how to achieve the levels of proficiency described therein. It has been maintained that no methodology is necessary, since none would ultimately be effective. Some have also maintained that a new method is implied by the *Guidelines,* a method termed "eclectic"—an apparent contradiction in terms (Higgs, 8, p. 4).

The purpose of this foray into the subtleties of the *Guidelines* is to determine to what extent they are helpful in integrating media in the foreign language curriculum. Of the four traditional skills, only three are addressed by the new media. Since none of the new media is able to engender oral production directly, the ACTFL description for speaking will not be considered. However, the remaining descriptions (listening, reading, and writing) will be examined to see what skill areas are addressed specifically by the media and at what skill level the media are likely to make an impact.

Listening

Video in all its forms (satellite reception, videodisc, videocassette) is the medium most likely to make an impact on students' listening skills. The capabilities of the medium (immediacy, realism, color) make it ideal for such use. CALL, on the other hand, is ill-suited for work in listening since, without additional expensive hardware, the medium cannot provide any audio. The problem addressed herein, however, is not to discern affinities between media and skills (a topic treated above), but to consider the "fit" of media with the *Guidelines.* The descriptors for listening are summarized below for quick reference.

Novice—Low	No practical understanding of the spoken language.
Novice—Mid	Understands some memorized words within predictable areas of need. Rarely understands more than two or three words at a time, requests repetitions often, confuses words that sound similar.
Novice—High	Understands memorized utterances and some longer utterances referring to daily needs. Comprehends simple questions/statements about family members, age, address, weather, time, daily activities. Requires repetitions.
Intermediate—Low	Understands utterances about basic survival needs, minimum courtesy and travel requirements. Misunderstandings arise frequently from lack of vocabulary or from faulty processing of syntactic information.
Intermediate—Mid	Understands topics beyond basic survival needs such as personal history and leisure-time activities. Some inflection and basic constructions are understood.
Intermediate—High	Increasingly able to understand topics beyond immediate survival needs. Shows some spontaneity in understanding, but speed and consistency of understanding are uneven. Asks for many repetitions.
Advanced	Sufficient comprehension to understand conversations about routine social conventions and limited school or work requirements. Understands face-to-face speech delivered at a normal rate with some repetition and rewording. Discusses current events, can handle descriptions, can deal with past, present, and future time.
Advanced Plus	Often shows remarkable ability and ease of understanding, but comprehension may break down under tension or pressure. Some weaknesses are evident because of lack of vocabulary or grammar. Makes inferences.
Superior	Understands the essentials of all speech in standard dialects, including technical discussions. Rarely asks for rephrasing or explanations. Follows the essentials of conversations between educated native speakers. May not understand native speakers if they speak very fast or use slang or unfamiliar dialects.
Distinguished	Able to understand all forms and styles of speech pertinent to personal, social, and professional needs tailored to different audiences.

Level of Use. It is conceivable to provide materials on video that could address each and every level of those described above. Students at the lower functional levels can be provided with specially selected or edited materials, while in the upper range of proficiency, unedited material can be used.

Only one major problem remains in using video materials. How does one determine what video materials are adequate for a given level? The materials must be chosen carefully, since they need to be at or slightly above the students' expected level of listening ability (Krashen's input hypothesis—see Krashen and Terrell, 12; Higgs, 9). Materials that are too advanced cannot be used, since they will frustrate students (Ur, 20, p. 27). If students only comprehend 5 percent of what is said, there is a certain possibility that they will "tune out," and, consequently, the video experience will be a waste of time—even more so if the images do not carry enough interest to maintain attention by themselves. On the other hand, materials that are too easy, too childish, or too obviously fashioned for the American student will tend to short-circuit the motivational energies generated by the medium. Students will tune them out too, just as they often do when watching "educational" programs.

Unfortunately, the *Guidelines* do not address the adequacy of materials for a particular level of listening proficiency. There is no "comprehensibility index" that could be used to gauge the level of video materials (or other listening skill materials). Unless they are able to measure the difficulty of video materials, teachers are forced to guess about the usefulness of video, or worse are guided only by publishers' representatives anxious to make a sale.

Reading

Video can have little impact on reading skills. Resolution is not high enough, nor is interactivity possible without adding costly equipment. CALL, on the other hand, offers resolution that is somewhat more acceptable; it also offers interaction capabilities that are vital in exercises to develop reading skills. The following is a summarized form of the *Guidelines* for reading proficiency.

Novice—Low	No functional reading ability in the language.
Novice—Mid	Interprets highly contextualized words or cognates within predictable areas. Vocabulary is limited to simple elementary needs such as names, addresses, dates, street signs, building names.
Novice—High	Interprets set expressions in areas of immediate need. Can read standardized messages, phrases, or expressions. Details are overlooked or misunderstood.
Intermediate—Low	Reads the simplest connected material dealing with basic survival and social needs. Can read messages, greetings, statements of social amenities using the highest-frequency grammatical patterns.
Intermediate—Mid	Understands simple written discourse for informative or social purposes. Can read announcements, popular advertising, notes containing biographical information or narrations of events. Rereads material several times before understanding.

Intermediate—High	Understands a simple paragraph for personal communication, information, or recreational purposes. Can locate and derive main ideas of the introductory/summary paragraphs.
Advanced	Reads simple authentic printed material on familiar subjects containing narration and description. There are some misunderstandings in reading; able to read facts but cannot draw inferences.
Advanced Plus	Understands most factual information in nontechnical prose. Follows sequence of events and reacts to the information. Locates and interprets main ideas. Guesses sensibly at new words. Reacts personally to material but does not detect subjective attitudes, values, or judgments in the writings.
Superior	Reads standard newspaper items and recreational literature addressed to the general reader at a normal rate of speed. Rarely misreads; almost always produces correct interpretation; able to read between the lines, but may be unable to appreciate nuance or stylistics.
Distinguished	Able to read fluently and accurately most styles and forms of the language pertinent to academic and professional needs. Able to relate inferences in the text to real-world knowledge and understand almost all sociolinguistic and cultural references.

Level of Use. As with video, it is conceivable that CALL provide materials for all levels of the reading skill. The medium itself does not present any limitations in delivering reading selections. Simple to very complex readings may be presented via CALL; however, the *Guidelines* do not address specifically how to judge the "readability level" of reading passages. The choice of material, its length and apparent readability are left completely to the instructor (or to the textbook authors).

Several types of presentations are possible, however, and benefit from the capabilities of CALL to improve on textbook or reader presentations. For instance, reading passages may be scrolled at varying rates or they may be held on the screen for a predetermined time. Passages may be illustrated with color graphics. Students may be given access to various levels of help—lexical, morphological, syntactic, or cultural information—and periodic comprehension checks. Such checks can take the form of cloze passages, reordering exercises, word-family activities, etc. Based on their results, students may be presented with more information about the passage, or they may be given the same information in a less complex form.

Since both listening and reading are receptive skills, it is not very difficult to believe that video and CALL can deliver material for all levels of proficiency described by the *Guidelines.* The media are the transmission vehicle for the material. Having selected a medium whose capabilities are congruous with the information to be presented, success is assured. In the case of CALL, however, the medium is not limited to presenting material (as with video); it is also possible to check on students' progress and to tailor further presentations dynamically on the basis of the results of evaluations. This is a new problem, one that warrants further comments.

CALL as an input medium has certain peculiar characteristics. When used to check on student progress and to evaluate results, its limitations become evident: input longer than a few words is difficult to evaluate, especially if the input is "free form." Activities such as true–false and multiple-choice exercises are easy to judge. For example, Grellet (6, pp. 39–40) suggests the use of partially complete material in which students decide which of three vocabulary possibilities complete the passage best. An activity of this type is implemented relatively easily on CALL, as are other activities, such as cloze passages, vocabulary drills, and reordering sentences and ideas. However, some activities are nearly impossible to transfer to the medium. For example, Meyer and Tetrault (16) propose the following predicting task:

> Based on the title and the first and final paragraphs, what kinds of information do you expect to find in the rest of the article? Answer in as much detail as possible. Then scan the attached text to check your predictions. [A text follows.]

Since the activity is based on a "free form" answer of sentence length, that is, an answer in the student's own words and without a predictable linguistic structure, implementing this activity on CALL is almost impossible, unless, of course, the computer is used simply to present the problem—something that could be done on paper just as well—instead of to check the student's answer.

When used as a medium of presentation, CALL is viable for all reading proficiency levels. When used as an input medium to check student answers, its efficacy falls dramatically. Nevertheless, it is not possible to specify a particular level at which CALL is no longer useful for checking reading skills. The capabilities drop off according to whether the answer to be judged is free form or not, meaning that CALL is somewhat useful for checking answers at all levels, but that not all types of answers can be judged easily.

Writing

CALL offers some capabilities to teach writing. As with reading, however, the capabilities of CALL drop off rapidly whenever free form student input is required. The following abbreviated descriptors from the *Guidelines* will be used to demonstrate to what extent the medium is able to carry some of the teaching load for writing.

Novice—Low	No functional ability in writing in the foreign language.
Novice—Mid	No practical communicative writing skills. Able to transcribe or copy.

Novice—High	Able to write simple fixed expressions and memorized material. Can write names, numbers, dates, addresses, and other simple biographic information with frequent misspellings and inaccuracies.
Intermediate—Low	Meets limited practical needs: can write short messages such as questions, notes, postcards, phone messages. Can take simple notes and can create statements within the scope of a limited language experience. Writing tends to be a loosely organized collection of sentence fragments.
Intermediate—Mid	Meets some survival needs and limited social demands. Composes short paragraphs or takes simple notes on very familiar topics. Discusses likes and dislikes, daily routines, everyday events, and the like. Makes frequent errors.
Intermediate—High	Meets most survival needs and limited social demands. Can create sentences and short paragraphs relating to most survival needs (food, lodging, transportation, immediate surroundings). Can produce present and future time and some past verb forms. Shows good control of elementary vocabulary and some control of basic syntax. Writing is comprehensible to native speakers used to dealing with foreigners.
Advanced	Able to write routine correspondence on everyday topics using both description and narration. Makes common errors in spelling and punctuation, but shows some control of the morphology of the language and of the most often used syntactic structures. Has difficulty producing complex sentences accurately.
Advanced Plus	Shows ability to write about most common topics with some precision and some detail. Can describe or narrate experiences and explain points of view simply. Often shows remarkable fluency and ease of expression. Some misuse of vocabulary is evident. Shows a limited ability to use circumlocution. Writing is understandable to native speakers not used to reading material written by nonnatives.
Superior	Able to use the written language effectively in most formal and informal practical, social, and professional topics. Can write most correspondence, short research papers, statements of position. Can express hypotheses, conjectures, and present arguments. Uses complex and compound sentences to express ideas clearly and coherently. Errors, though sometimes made, rarely disturb the native speaker.

It is undoubtedly in the area of writing that CALL appeared to have attracted the most attention, generated the most activity, and initially had the most adherents. There are uncounted software packages that "teach" some aspect of writing. Most is limited to a rather mechanical drill and practice mode that "teaches" relatively little, but provides ample practice on grammatical points. The majority of this type of material may be termed "prelinguistic"—focusing on prewriting stages. There is, however, some software that goes beyond mechanical drills and provides activities aimed at developing writing fluency. For instance, materials are available that include sentence combining, sentence unscrambling, ordering of sentences into paragraphs, and cloze passages. All of these activities can be helpful in acquiring writing skills.

Level of Use. As an input medium, however, it is clear that CALL has limitations. For example, are there proficiency levels at which CALL would be beneficial, and are there others at which it would be ineffective? It is possible to make such an assessment referring to the abridged *Guidelines* above. Magnan (14, pp. 125–127) provides a list of tasks for the first three levels. The novice-level tasks are broken down into seven categories:

1. Identifying	Given a picture of a room, students identify the typical items it contains.
2. Listing	Students prepare a list of items **not** contained in a photograph: items needed.
3. Using memorized material	Using vocabulary that was studied and reviewed in previous activities, students complete a paragraph based on a picture provided.
4. Beginning to create with language	Students write a telegram telling a friend what another student has, what the student doesn't have, what should be brought as a gift.
5. Creating with language, under teacher's directions	Students write a paragraph describing a photograph by answering a series of questions. The answers, when given in the same order as the questions, will form a complete paragraph.
6. Describing in present time	Students write a paragraph from a specific assignment. The assignment gives hints and suggestions on the structure of the finished product.
7. Accuracy check	Students answer a set of questions on their work: Is there a progression in the sentences? Is there a topic sentence? Does the final sentence summarize the paragraph? Are connectives logical? Are spelling and punctuation accurate?

Which of these tasks can be implemented on CALL?

1. *Identifying.* Identifying items in a photograph poses no problems. A graphic may be substituted for the photograph and students may be asked to identify and list as many items as possible. Answer judging can very easily check spelling and article agreement.

2. *Listing.* A listing of items *not* on a photograph or in a graphic does present programming problems. A very large number of possible or acceptable answers must be provided to implement the exercise. It can be argued that, since novice-level students do not have a very large vocabulary, most likely less than 500 nouns, all of the words could be entered as input. But even 500 nouns would tax the *memory capacity* of presently available machines. The list may more than double when one

also considers adding permutations (plurals and gender agreements, etc.). In addition, if students enter nouns that they know but that do not appear in the list, they will be frustrated. Still, this activity can be implemented with a judicious choice of high-use vocabulary and a sophisticated program. It is clear, however, that even a relatively simple novice-level activity is sometimes difficult to carry out.

3. *Using memorized material.* Since this activity does not rely on the recognition of an unlimited or open-ended amount of vocabulary and, since a paragraph is typically given as context to further limit students' choices, it is ideal for CALL implementation.

4. *Beginning to create with language; writing a telegram.* The use of an open-ended format makes this activity difficult (if not impossible) to carry out.

5. *Creating with language under teacher direction.* The activity involves free-form answers to free-form questions; thus, there are the predictable difficulties in implementation. Nevertheless, if the questions are selected judiciously and if one can assume a limited number of sentence types in the answer, the activity presents fewer problems and can be implemented, although with difficulty.

6. *Describing in the present time.* This unstructured activity is difficult if not impossible to implement on CALL.

7. *Accuracy check.* Although this activity is somewhat structured and therefore implementable, it is a continuation of the previous activity and makes most sense when done on paper, without the aid of the computer.

The activities described above are not definitive; they can be taken, however, as representative of the type of activities needed for novice-level writers. CALL's capabilities, while very useful for reading, only provide mixed results for writing. Some activities can be carried out easily, others require complex programs and even more complex linguistic data (which would tax the capabilities of present-day microcomputers), and other activities are too open-ended and are therefore not implementable, even on very large machines.

Magnan suggests the following activities for later novice- to intermediate-level tasks:

1. Working with memorized material   Students make sentences by choosing one item from each column. For example,

I	study	watch TV
you	work	listen to the radio
she	play	visit friends
he	shop	do homework

2. Working with memorized material to add cohesion to language	Students create paragraph-length discourse using the technique above. The items given in columns include such words and phrases as "in the morning," "later," "then," "while," "my friend," etc.
3. Creating a cohesive description	Students describe their typical daily activities and those of their best friends. The directions provided give hints about a well-structured paragraph.
4. Accuracy check	Students self-check the paragraph produced above using the same techniques as in the novice level (p. 126).

Here again, some activities may be carried out on CALL while others may not. The first two, because they are fairly well-structured and do not require free-form answers, may be transformed easily into CALL activities and may benefit from the capabilities of the medium. Features that may be included in these activities are answer judging, providing helpful hints, and graphics. The third and fourth activities, by virtue of being open-ended, are not easily implementable and should be done on paper.

Some later novice- and intermediate-level tasks may also be carried out on CALL. Magnan suggests the following:

1. Listing	Students list things they did yesterday, using partial sentences.
2. Creating series of statements	Students write statements describing what they did yesterday. The goal is to create simple narrations in the past.
3. Building a paragraph	Students add clauses or amplify the statements written above. The goal is to describe and narrate in the past.
4. Describing and narrating in the past	Students write a letter to a friend describing what they did last summer, giving some detail.
5. Accuracy check	Same activity as in the novice level (p. 126-27).

Activities become more free-form as one goes up on the proficiency scale; hence the number of activities that can be implemented on CALL becomes smaller. However, there is one activity that can possibly still be accomplished at the intermediate level, the first one suggested by Magnan, listing. Given a large enough linguistic corpus and checking of key words, one can imagine an activity designed to help students formulate a list of past events. The computer could check the items for accuracy as they are entered and make suggestions for new items when the student indicates that help is needed. The other three activities, however, cannot presently be done via CALL, except, of course, by using the computer as a word processor.

Implementing CALL for writing skills yields mixed results. Some activities seem transferable immediately, while others, especially at the higher ranges of the proficiency levels, require either more processing power than available now or very sophisticated programs. Neither is available at this time without enormous expense in hardware and software. Whether or not improved CALL facilities with capabilities that can solve these problems will come about in the near future is addressed in the following section.

Possibilities and Feasibilities

What can we look forward to with the new media? Several facts emerge from the preceding discussion:

1. Modern media, including video and CALL, will make an impact on the foreign language curriculum. They offer many useful capabilities that should and will be exploited in the classroom. Both media are here to stay; they will evolve and may eventually metamorphose into one medium, but they will survive as a pedagogical tool.
2. Neither medium is without problems. It can probably be argued that they add many problems relative to acquisition, maintenance, implementation, and integration of second-language skills, just to name a few; it is clear, however, that most of the problems are solvable.
3. Neither medium can, by itself, shoulder the responsibility for teaching even one specific skill. Each medium offers capabilities that are ideal for some types of presentations or activities, but there are severe limitations in the use of both CALL and video.
4. The use of the media brings about complications in the structure of the curriculum—new and complex machines introduced in the classrooms and laboratories. As a result, teachers are required to assume a greater involvement in curricular design and implementation. They are required to choose from among several possible modes of presentation, several media, and several teaching options.

In asking for more help in the classroom, teachers are getting more than they bargained for—a surplus of material and very little unifying structure. Where will the needed help come from? The *Guidelines* are likely to bring an organizing principle to the curriculum. More and more texts are being written with them in mind and, as a result, incorporate primary material that includes more communicative, better-defined, and more useful tasks. However, since the *Guidelines* do not address curriculum design specifically, much time may pass before those issues are resolved. A more immediate and more pragmatic means to solve curricular problems is needed.

One place where curricular matters can be addressed is in the Instructor's Annotated Edition (IAE) of the textbook. A few years ago, the IAE provided only marginal annotations about optional sections of the grammar. More recently, the IAE has assumed a role in guiding the curriculum as well. More and more the IAE holds additional suggested or variant activities in addition to answers to selected exercises. New are suggestions on the use of materials and hints about appropriate methodologies, as well as references to other ancillaries and to the tape program. Carrying the trend a bit further, it is not unreasonable to assume that, as video and CALL make more of an impact on the curriculum, the future IAE will become the central document to orchestrate these media. For example, a marginal notation may refer the teacher to a videotape presentation of a dialogue, or to an overhead transparency for presentation of a grammar point, or even to a set of reading activities on CALL.

Looking Ahead

To predict what new technologies will be available to the foreign language teacher in the distant future is the job of a science fiction writer. To predict what will be available in the near future (or five years from now), is not such a mystery. One has simply to look about and find out what technologies are being worked on *at this time.* Some will become commonly accepted; some will fail because they are either too costly, too difficult to handle, do not provide enough tangible benefits, or simply fail to interest enough people. The following two technological advances show some promise.

The 3M Machine

The 3M machine is a logical enhancement of the microcomputers presently in use. Several groups (universities, large and small companies) are developing simultaneously what has been touted as the all-purpose academic workstation. The new machine is dubbed 3M because it will have 1 megabyte of random-access memory, display 1 million pixels on its screen, and run at 1 million instructions per second—thus, 3 millions, or 3M. The machine will have capabilities much greater than the ones presently in use that, in turn, will make possible greater complexity in programming, greater storage capacity, and much better display characteristics. If the price is kept within reason, it is likely to be used widely by faculty and students across a broad spectrum of disciplines. The availability of a large number of 3M machines should encourage software designers to produce a large number of materials and perhaps even make possible a modicum of standardization without stifling the creativity in design the 3M machine will make possible.

CD ROM

Coupled with advances in microcomputer hardware, an equivalent advance in storage technology is in the making. The CD ROM (compact disc, read-only memory) presently under development is likely to affect strongly the way one looks at information. The CD ROM, a laser-based storage device similar to the high-fidelity compact audiodisc player, will erase the distinctions made about type of information and, at the same time, allow for much greater storage capacities. Presently one talks, as in this chapter, about computer data storage, video information storage, music storage, and graphics storage as separate kinds of information requiring separate kinds of storage devices. CD ROM technology will eliminate these distinctions and allow storage of any and all types of digitized information on the same plastic medium. For instance, a CD ROM has been used to hold on a single five-inch disk an encyclopedia (including text and graphics), music, and video information. When the user inquires about Beethoven, for example, the medium provides a display text, a graphic, and even a few bars of Beethoven's most famous symphonies.

The storage capacity of a typical CD ROM disk is phenomenal. A library of a million volumes, if it is transferred to CD ROM, could be compressed into the space occupied by one end of a teacher's desk! With such high densities for storage and with such flexibility for types of storage, CD ROM, provided it becomes accepted commonly, is bound to make its mark on foreign language teaching.

A Short Conclusion

The advent of new technologies always provokes mixed reactions. On the one hand, they are exciting to work with; they add new dimensions to the class and spark students to higher levels of motivation and achievement. On the other, they are expensive to purchase and maintain, difficult to implement in real situations, and often the cause of much frustration. When problems created by an incomplete or unintegrated curriculum are added, the situation may become untenable. The advantages brought about by the new media are more than offset by the curricular problems they create. Teachers will perceive a loss in effectiveness when they must take time to select media, materials, and methodologies carefully, for they will spend more time planning than they will gain from the capabilities that the media bring. However, there are several positive trends that counteract this caveat: (1) The *ACTFL Proficiency Guidelines* will tend to unify the curriculum, as will the customary adjustments that are brought about when a new element is introduced. (2) The media will eventually take up their respective niches in the curriculum and teachers will rely on them for specific tasks as a matter of course. (3) Publishers will continue to provide methodological information in the Instructor's Annotated Edition, but will expand it to include curricular information. (4) Finally, new technologies will add even more functionality in video and to CALL, eventually merging the two into a powerful teaching tool.

References, Integrating Video and CALL in the Curriculum

1. Aoki, Paul K. "Limitations of Current Microcomputers for Foreign Language Training," *Foreign Language Annals* 17, 4 (1984):409–12.
2. Ariew, Robert. "The Textbook as Curriculum," pp. 11–33 in Theodore V. Higgs, ed., *Curriculum, Competence, and the Foreign Language Teacher.* The ACTFL Foreign Language Education Series. Lincolnwood, IL: National Textbook Company, 1982.
3. Bork, Alfred. "Computer Futures for Education," *Creative Computing* 10, 11 (1984):178–80.
4. Bragger, Jeannette D. "Materials Development for the Proficiency-Oriented Classroom," pp. 79–115 in Charles J. James, ed., *Foreign Language Proficiency in the Classroom and Beyond.* The ACTFL Foreign Language Education Series. Lincolnwood, IL: National Textbook Company, 1985.
5. Flynn, Mary B. "Breaking the Book Barrier," pp. 35–56 in Theodore V. Higgs, ed., *Curriculum, Competence, and the Foreign Language Teacher.* The ACTFL Foreign Language Education Series. Lincolnwood, IL: National Textbook Company, 1982.
6. Grellet, Françoise. *Developing Reading Skills. A Practical Guide to Reading Comprehension Exercises.* New York: Cambridge University Press, 1981.
7. Guntermann, Gail, and June K. Phillips. *Functional-Notional Concepts: Adapting the Foreign Language Textbook.* Language in Education: Theory and Practice, no. 44. Washington, DC: Center for Applied Linguistics, 1982.
8. Higgs, Theodore V. "Language Teaching and the Quest for the Holy Grail," pp. 1–9 in Theodore V. Higgs, ed., *Teaching for Proficiency, the Organizing Principle.* The ACTFL Foreign Language Education Series. Lincolnwood, IL: National Textbook Company, 1984.
9. _____. "The Input Hypothesis: An Inside Look," *Foreign Language Annals* 18, 3 (1985):197–203.
10. Holmes, Glyn. "Of Computers and Other Technologies," pp. 93–106 in Gilbert A. Jarvis, ed., *The Challenge for Excellence in Foreign Language Education.* Report of the Northeast Conference on the Teaching of Foreign Languages. Middlebury, VT: The Northeast Conference, 1984.
11. _____. "The Computer and Limitations," *Foreign Language Annals* 17, 4 (1984):413–14.
12. Krashen, Stephen D., and Tracy D. Terrell, *The Natural Approach: Language Acquisition in the Classroom.* San Francisco: Alemany Press, 1983.
13. Liskin-Gasparro, Judith. "The ACTFL Proficiency Guidelines: A Historical Perspective," pp. 11–42 in Theodore V. Higgs, ed., *Teaching for Proficiency, the Organizing Principle.* The ACTFL Foreign Language Education Series. Lincolnwood, IL: National Textbook Company, 1984.
14. Magnan, Sally Sieloff. "Teaching and Testing Proficiency in Writing: Skills to Transcend the Second Language Classroom," pp. 109–36 in Alice C. Omaggio, ed., *Proficiency, Curriculum, Articulation: The Ties That Bind.* Report of the Northeast Conference on the Teaching of Foreign Languages. Middlebury, VT: The Northeast Conference, 1985.
15. Meyer, R., and E. Tetrault. "Real Life, Real Discourse, Real Comprehension:

An Analytic Approach to Reading and Listening." Workshop given at the annual meeting of ACTFL, San Francisco, 1983.

16. Muyskens, Judith A. "Preservice and Inservice Teacher Training: Focus on Proficiency," pp. 179–200 in Theodore V. Higgs, ed., *Teaching for Proficiency, the Organizing Principle.* The ACTFL Foreign Language Education Series. Lincolnwood, IL: National Textbook Company, 1984.

17. Pederson, Kathleen M. "An Experiment in Computer-Assisted Second-Language Reading." *The Modern Language Journal* 70, 1 (1986):36–41.

18. Phillips, June K. "Reading Is Communication, Too!" *Foreign Language Annals* 11, 3 (1978):281–87,

19. Pusack, James P. "The Interactive Computer Testing of Reading Proficiency," *Foreign Language Annals* 17, 4 (1984):415–19.

20. Ur, Penny. *Teaching, Listening Comprehension.* New York: Cambridge University Press, 1984.

21. Valdman, Albert. "Communicative Use of Language and Syllabus Design." *Foreign Language Annals* 11, 5 (1978):567–78.

22. Wyatt, David H. "Computer-Assisted Teaching and Testing of Reading and Listening." *Foreign Language Annals* 17, 4 (1984):393–407.

3

Towards a Media-Specific Methodology for CALL

David M. Weible
University of Illinois at Chicago

Introduction

The focus of this chapter is the determination of what strategies and methods are appropriate for the computer on the basis of its media characteristics. If one stops to think about it, the growth and development of the use of computers since their invention is simply astounding. Were all the computers now in use to disappear overnight, most of the services taken for granted—telecommunications, banking, etc.—would break down completely, and society would experience total disruption. One of the areas where the effect would not be so noticeable, however, is the field of education.

The use of computers in education remains unimpressive, both in terms of the quality of the software and its impact on efforts to improve learning. This is particularly so in the area of foreign languages (Baker, 2). As to why it is so, a major reason must be the general failure of software writers to exploit the computer's qualities fully. They have failed because they have persisted in treating the computer as a substitute vehicle for existing instructional techniques and methodologies. That they should do this is quite in keeping with the observations of one of the first students of the characteristics of media, Marshall McLuhan.

David M. Weible (Ph.D., University of Kansas) is Associate Professor of German at the University of Illinois at Chicago where he is also Director of the Audio Information Service/Language Lab. Recipient of an Exxon Education Foundation grant in 1975–76 to develop courseware in German for the PLATO system, he is currently Editor of *Die Unterrichtspraxis* and has served as a consultant in technology and multimedia instructional packages for the Goethe-Institute, the U.S. Department of Education, and others. He is a member of ACTFL, AATG, CALICO, and the International Association of Learning Laboratory Directors (IALLD).

McLuhan's dictum, *the medium is the message,* has been a commonplace for twenty years (McLuhan, 13). The truth of this notion seems to be supported by the various phenomena attending the shift in orientation from printed to pictorial media that has taken place throughout the modern industrialized world. The rise in popularity first of the cinema and then of video has had a profound impact on our culture, particularly upon the educational process. The relative decline in significance of the word (written or spoken), the decreasing ability to perform abstract analysis, and the corresponding increasing emphasis placed on visually oriented conceptualization are regarded by many as signs of cultural impoverishment. This helps to explain why education, particularly at the college and university level, has generally been slow to embrace computers (Olsen, 15). Some educators, perceiving computers to be more for the visually than the verbally oriented, fear that their widespread introduction in education may, instead of aiding in the learning process, lead to its further degradation.

To a certain extent, this battle has been joined once before. McLuhan saw the rise in interest in teaching machines in the early sixties to be a side effect of the impact of television on society.

> One of the major pressures of TV has been to encourage the "teaching machine." In fact, the devices are adaptations of the book in the direction of dialogue. These teaching machines are really private tutors, and their being misnamed on the principle that produced the names "wireless" and "horseless carriage" is another instance in that long list that illustrates how every innovation must pass through a primary phase in which the new effect is secured by the old method, amplified or modified by some new feature (p. 292).

There are a number of points of interest in this quotation that one can relate as well to the computer and its milieu. The description of the teaching machines of twenty years ago as an "adaptation of the book"—thus primarily a text-oriented medium—"in the direction of dialogue"— through a limited sort of interactivity, with student responses generally of a true–false or multiple-choice nature—seems to fit much of what is seen in present-day computer-assisted instruction materials. Moreover, the misnomer "teaching machine" was for McLuhan a further instance of a process that occurs with any major innovation, that is, the unavoidable tendency to explain, name, and view the innovation as simply a modification of an already familiar device or method—a tendency that delays the full perception of the innovation's true characteristics and potential.

In their turn, computers as an educational medium also have to go through an initial phase of discovery. One aspect of this phase has been the association of the hardware with the earlier "teaching machines" and computer-assisted instruction with the instructional methodology associated with them: programmed instruction and the emphasis of rote drill and practice over cognitive interaction. Over twenty years ago, Nordberg (14) indicated the use of teaching machines under these six dangers:

1. Whatever lacks abstract intelligence is not able to initiate, transmit or receive ideas. . . . The most that a machine can do is take concentrated symbols built into it by an intelligent being and rearrange them according to a schema also built into it by somebody. Thus governed, the machine can tell a pupil that he has or has not the "right answer," but it cannot deal with interpretive problems that might arise beyond what has been programmed into it.

2. Whatever cannot deal with paraphrasing is somewhat handicapped for meaningful teaching. Educational psychologists generally agree that the two best proofs of meaningful, solid learning are paraphrasing and application. Machines can deal with applications only in an isolated, superficial way, and they have yet to do much with paraphrasing. . . . A teaching machine will penalize a student who has the right idea but the "wrong" words, and reward one who has memorized the "right" words but has the wrong idea. Therefore, they are somewhat handicapped for meaningful teaching.

3. Whatever cannot deal with organization and expression of knowledge is handicapped for meaningful teaching. Most educators agree that, beyond such arbitrary meanings as the alphabet and numbering system, to arrange and articulate one's knowledge in a holistic way is of the essence in learning. But machines cannot deal with organization and expression of knowledge. That is because they must be "objective" in the same sense as an "objective test," that is, a test that anyone with the key can grade with the same results as anyone else. All programs for automated learning that the writer has seen deal with rather trivial bits and fragments of knowledge, and it is hard to see how it could be otherwise. The creed of the machine, as of those who find machines fascinating, is that everything is the sum of its parts.

4. Whatever encourages preoccupation with details poses dangers for meaningful teaching. Facts, parts, data, are necessary but acquire meaning only in relation to ideas, patterns, the whole. . . . But machines encourage preoccupation with details, for reasons already argued. Therefore, they pose dangers for meaningful teaching.

5. Whatever leads towards a nationalized curriculum discourages creativity and thought in some fields. Experience suggests that nationalized educational systems are invariably mediocre. Standardization is never the royal road to genius! But teaching

machines lead towards a nationalized (and almost certainly secu-
larized) curriculum.
6. Whatever minimizes the importance of the sheer metaphysical
presence of the teacher jeopardizes good teaching. For, teaching is
essentially the confrontation of two intelligences, and tends to be
more effective when that confrontation is flexible and direct.
When a teacher is smiling at *me,* looking at *me* (not an *image* of a
teacher on a TV screen or her alter ego in the gears and pulleys of a
machine) this is something irreplaceable. Naturally, mechanists
do not understand how this could be, and regard those of us who
have any criticisms of teaching machines as incompetents who
fear to lose our jobs (pp. 1–4).

Against all of this Nordberg could find only one positive attribute of the
teaching machines of his day. He noted that anything that facilitated individualized drill can aid in teaching *arbitrary meanings,* "those facts and
concepts which from the standpoint of the learner at the time he learns
them, have no rationale. The cannot be anticipated or deduced; they must
simply be experienced and committed more or less blindly to memory"
(14, p. 5).

What perhaps surprises one most while reading these six dangers (and
the one advantage, as well) is how easily they could be applied to the CAI
(computer-assisted instruction) programs of today. This is surprising
because computers are far more sophisticated and powerful than the
teaching machines of twenty years ago. Unfortunately, that additional
power and sophistication will remain largely unavailable to language
teachers until a substantial body of CALL (computer-assisted language
learning) software is created that makes full use of the computer's potential as an instructional medium. This will not be so easily done. As
McLuhan observed, people are slow to perceive the true nature of innovations precisely because they go beyond everything with which they are
familiar. In order to get some idea of the sort of mistaken assumptions and
wrongheaded uses likely to be made of the computer, consider the development of another modern communications medium that has been
around for most of this century: the cinema.

The Development of Cinema

In the years preceding the advent of sound in motion pictures, it was taken
for granted that the visual element should dominate in the telling of the
story. The use of words was restricted to the occasional appearance of
"titles." When sound was added in the late 1920s, it exercised a great novelty appeal, even though the use to which it was put was hardly original.

For example, music in the sound track often simply replaced, albeit on a grander scale, the performance on the movie house's organ or piano.

Another change brought by the addition of sound to the cinema was the opening of the realm of "sound effects." It should be noted that truly creative and original uses of sound effects were slow in coming to the movies. On the whole, directors and their audiences were extremely pleased if the sound track succeeded simply in reproducing the most basic effects (bells, whistles, gunshots, etc.) with acceptably close synchronization to the image. The rise in popularity at this time of the detective/police/gangster genre may be in part attributed to the popularity of the rather obvious sound effects that accompanied them—a further illustration of the medium being the message (Geduld, 6, p. 266).

Nevertheless, many wholly unnatural and inappropriate uses of sound remained common practice for a decade or more into the sound era. To some extent, that was due to the primitive technology of those early days. For example, whenever someone entering a room closed the door behind him, absolute silence ensued—all noise from outside was totally shut off. Now, given the presence of a moderately lively party going on beyond that closed door, one would normally expect to hear at least a faint murmur of conversation, even with the door shut. However, this expectation went beyond the capabilities of the early sound systems. They were not up to producing clearly audible faint murmurs due to the high level of ambient hiss and splutter generated in the primitive recording process.

The most vivid and dramatic advantage of sound movies over silent ones was the ability it gave the actors to speak their lines instead of miming them. This opportunity was seized with a vengeance, and the "talkies," as they were called, became very talky indeed. Mystery/detective melodramas benefited from this development as well.

> They offered superabundant opportunities for talk and noise, for stretches of dialogue in which police and detectives [or] gangsters and other villains sometimes strained the patience of audiences with long-winded explanations or self-revelations; for interminable courtroom scenes (Geduld, 6, p. 266).

On a loftier artistic plane, many leading stage actors were now attracted to the cinema for the first time. Witty dialogue, snappy repartee, and just plain chattiness became leading characteristics of the films of the thirties and forties. Many of these films, too, have a rather theatrical quality, as though this new medium were to be regarded as an electronic and more modern version of the stage—a further instance of an innovation's nature being masked by a seemingly near relation (Geduld, 6, p. 253; Robinson, 17, p. 167). In that sense, the motion picture medium can be said to have suffered from an identity crisis at this point in its history, a point where, in the opinion of some, it was just beginning to find itself as an art form

(Geduld, 6, p. 222). The visual element continued to be of importance, but in very many cases it served primarily as illustration for the spoken word. One aspect of the medium by virtue of its novelty had assumed an exaggerated importance.

In the last two decades, there has been a significant shift away from this position so that now, more often than not, image (together with music and sound effects) generally dominates the verbal element. The nature of that image has itself undergone a number of transformations due to technological changes. The traditional square visual field gave way in the fifties to new wide-screen formats. These encouraged the use of sweeping panoramic photography. More recently, there has been a move back to more intimate, close-up photography with little of significance taking place on the edges of the visual field, a trend that has resulted from the increasing impact of television in the marketing and distribution of motion pictures.

The Development of the Computer

As McLuhan observed, any new medium must undergo this process of definition. The process is a rather slow one for two reasons. The more radically new the medium, the more unknown it is and, consequently, the longer it takes to explore its possibilities. Also, ongoing technological advancements expand the range of possibilities continually necessitating additional experimentation and exploration, just as sound did with the cinema. Can it then be any wonder that considerable uncertainty remains with regard to the computer's potential for instructional applications in language learning? The computer is quite possibly the most radically new information medium mankind has ever invented. Moreover, improvements in computer hardware and systems design follow one another with tremendous rapidity, forcing constant redefinition of the computer's capabilities. It started off as a data processor, pure and simple. The addition of a cathode ray tube display device (CRT) and full screen, text-based direct input and output (I/O) produced something of an identity crisis in this medium as well, focusing more on the computer as a booklike purveyor of textual information and drawing attention away from its data-processing powers. More recently, the computer has drawn even more popular attention to itself as a game-playing device, both in the home and in so-called video arcades. Given these very different perceptions of its character, how can one get a clearer notion of this new medium?

Perhaps a sensible course would be to ask not what the computer can do, but rather what do we want it to do—operating on the hopeful assumption that, with time, it may be able to do virtually anything. That, however, is not very practical in the short run, in terms of the design and execution of programs we wish to see implemented as soon as possible. Moreover, one would then also have to assume as a corollary that the computer has no intrinsic media qualities, that it is infinitely adaptable, while we know this is, at least at present, far from being true. As Schank (19) points out:

> The operations that a computer can execute are embodied in the programming languages it can understand. Any time you wish to break new ground in computer understanding you have to figure out how to explain everything to the computer in terms it already can understand, namely, a programming language at a lower level (p. 77).

Schank then goes on to observe that while a programmer "is someone who is familiar with the levels of understanding which computers so far have been given" and a computer scientist is "someone who attempts to find new ways to get computers to execute programs more efficiently or new ways to enable people to communicate with computers more effectively," researchers in artificial intelligence are attempting to "raise the level of understanding that computers have" (p. 77). Once they succeed in this, quite a lot may be expected from CALL.

Even at present, however, a good deal more can be expected from computers than from the teaching machines of yore. "The choice is not simply between mechanical drill at one extreme and human-like simulated intelligence at the other" (Underwood, 21, p. 47). There are, in fact, "many in-between levels of partial understanding, what we might call 'semi-intelligent systems,' that can be extremely useful as interactive instructional aids" (Underwood, 21, p. 47). Unfortunately, to judge by most of the material produced for CALL to date, one must conclude that these "in-between levels" have been consistently set too low.

This low-level focus can be explained in part by the reasonable excuse that a good deal of time must elapse between the formulation of a concept and its practical implementation. The CALL software currently available in the marketplace represents the conceptual level of one or two years ago. The danger posed by the existence of these programs, many of them being marketed by reputable publishers in the field of foreign language education, is that they may be regarded mistakenly as models to be emulated when, in fact, they should be subjected to the severest scrutiny.

That is so because users of CAI allow the present capabilities of the medium to define their expectations. Actually, it is worse than that; in reality, the *perception* of present capabilities of the medium is allowed to define expectations, and this perception is too often based on a limited view of the computer as a data processor and, perhaps, an electronic book, when in reality it is much more than that, and essentially different. Even a realistic assessment of the medium's present capabilities is insufficient because, as was noted earlier, these capabilities are being expanded at such a dizzying rate that it is unwise to permit current capabilities to limit current expectations. Whoever will attempt to write useful instructional software must strive constantly to achieve the maximal appropriate utilization of present-day technology, guided by an apprehension of immediately foreseeable developments.

Admittedly, just what constitutes *appropriate* utilization is a debatable issue and relates to the still larger questions of second-language acquisition theories and their significance for the design and implementation of CALL materials. There may well be, as Higgins and Johns (9) suggest and Underwood (21) maintains, major arguments against using traditional programmed instruction modes. These may indeed, in Krashen's (12) terms, contribute to *learning* more than to *acquisition.* Just how important that really is, in terms of facilitating (or retarding) the acquisition of second-language competence, while an issue of great importance, is peripheral to the topic of this chapter, whose focus is on what constitutes appropriate utilization exclusively with reference to the qualities of the computer as an instructional medium.

Three Unique Qualities

To be specific, there are three particularly important qualities that no other instructional medium possesses and that developers of CALL materials have as yet largely ignored: First, computers are able to structure the student's interaction with the subject matter in a precise manner; that is, they not only present the subject matter but are also capable of presenting and teaching learning strategies. Second, unlike print, which is an essentially static, fixed medium, computers are process-oriented, a quality that could be very helpful in avoiding the need for reliance on grammatical terminology in teaching various features of the target language. Finally, when programmed properly, the computer is able to modify the presentation of instructional material to meet an individual learner's needs and/or abilities. At the same time, programs which utilize this ability could also become valuable sources of new data on how second languages are learned, given appropriate data collection and evaluation procedures (a topic developed by Pederson in Chapter 5 of this volume). The sections that follow discuss each of these qualities in some detail and offer recommendations for authors and teachers who would use CALL software in their classes.

Structured Interaction

Perhaps the most striking difference between computers and other instructional media is the fact that the computer's operation is governed by a program. Its presentation of instructional material embodies a programmatic approach to that material; that is, *it defines precisely the nature of the student's approach to and interaction with the subject matter.* As Steinberg (20) notes:

> The CAI author must make instructional and managerial decisions that are not an issue in other media. A textbook author may insert questions or problems in the book but does not have to decide how many questions the student should answer. The student or the instructor decides. The CAI author does have control and must decide not only how many questions to ask, but whether to force the student to answer them and whether to require a given level of mastery before allowing the student to proceed. Clearly, the author has many more decisions to make than how to present the lesson content (p. 5).

Admittedly, the degree to which the program affects the student's interactions with the subject matter varies greatly and depends on the design goals of its author. A "page-turning" lesson, one that simply presents successive pages of information for the user to read, is the lowest degree of interaction and, in fact, hardly provides it at all, but one might also argue that—in terms of its media-specific impact—such a program is not really a computer program, for it does not utilize the capabilities of the medium to any significant degree.

But even programs of the flash-card drill variety that are only slightly more ambitious than the "page-turners" suggest things to the student about the nature of second-language learning that the program's author most likely never intended. The author may have wished simply to provide an aid to vocabulary memorization and, to do so, transported the familiar flash card format to the computer. This seemingly innocent translation of a given methodology from one medium (print) to another (the computer) is, in fact, cause for serious concern. Any student using traditional printed flash cards is free to use them as he or she sees fit. The number of flash cards to be done, whether or not to randomize their appearance, whether or not to review missed items, whether or not to cheat, all this is left entirely to the student's discretion. And perhaps most importantly, no undue significance is placed on the role of flash-card drilling in language learning. Students who feel that such aids help them can use them, others do not.

However, when this drill approach is "computerized," a number of things happen. Students seem, at least at the beginning, to find working with them more interesting than working with printed flash cards. As Hope, Taylor, and Pusack (10) put it, "by having each item pop up as though from nowhere, and by responding in some way to the student's answer, the program transforms otherwise inert exercises into active material" (p. 3).

At first glance, this may seem to be a justification for producing such programs. After a bit of thought, however, one can see that the student's reaction is actually rather worrisome. Computerized flash cards possess no intrinsic advantage over printed ones. Indeed, their lack of portability is a disadvantage. Why then do students respond to them more enthusiastically? Clearly, they are being seduced by the medium itself. Increased familiarity with computers will doubtless lessen this effect eventually, but at present there can be no doubt that many, probably most students find working with computers on instructional tasks fascinatingly novel. Computers occupy a special position in their imagination, and they interact far more intensely with them than they do with print media.

Again, this "attraction" seems to speak strongly for the use of computers in instruction. But it must also serve as a warning to authors (and teachers) to be careful of methodological design. The casual, occasional use of printed flash cards may indeed be helpful to some students in their study of a foreign language. But the programmatic use of a flash-card mode in an intense drilling situation is likely to reinforce in the learner certain common and counterproductive assumptions about the nature of second-language acquisition.

The programmatic determination of word meanings through the memorization of paired associate items devoid of contextual reference strengthens the naive learner's tendency to view reading comprehension, for example, as a decoding exercise with each lexical item to be decoded in turn until the entire sentence is revealed. This approach may work fairly well for students at the outset of their foreign language studies, but with time it becomes a significant barrier to progress, not only in reading but in speaking and writing as well. One has to doubt the value of any instructional program that pumps the user full of information in such a way as to render its integration into a broader overview of the subject matter more difficult (Nordberg, 14, p. 3).

In short, when students use a CALL program, they tend to learn its methodological approach as well as the subject-matter elements it contains. What is more, the prolonged use of a program tends to program the user. Evidence of this phenomenon is perhaps found most easily in the improvement in performance of video game players. A video game is really an interactive structure, and the players do increasingly better in the game as their knowledge of the game's structure and its hidden rules improves. Both the speed and the accuracy of their responses benefit by continued exposure. Similarly, it is possible for a CALL lesson to present, along with the obvious subject matter, a "hidden agenda" consisting of useful approaches to facilitate the student's learning and/or acquisition of new features of the target language. Thus, the use of CALL materials could have an effect that would carry over into the student's work with the textbook, in the classroom, and even in an unstructured target language environment. Insofar as teaching students to learn rivals in importance teaching them subject matter, every effort must be made to see that CALL lessons incorporate and inculcate appropriate learning strategies so that the students who use them will be, so to speak, programmed for successful language study. Just as important, care must be taken that inappropriate or even counterproductive learner behaviors not be incorporated inadvertently into CALL materials.

What is the best way to do this? First of all, the author in testing out his or her material must observe carefully the behavior it produces in its users and make sure that this behavior is desirable from the point of view of learning psychology. Weible (22) gives an example of the importance of this. A principal instructional goal of a German reading program was to teach the students to infer the meaning of unknown lexical items from contextual indications. The students were presented with a series of reading passages. They were to read the text through, inferring the probable meanings of the German items from their (known) context, and then test their inferences on an item-by-item basis.

The program's initial design suffered, however, from a critical flaw. Following the classic tenets of programmed instruction, the student who failed to infer the word's meaning correctly was immediately given the correct answer as a form of positive feedback. Observation of actual student behavior showed, however, that while some of the students were using the material as intended, others had discovered they could get through the material without having to try to infer the meaning of any of the items. All that was necessary was to ignore the reading passage entirely, enter any sort of nonsense in the item-checking section, copy down the correct answers as corroborated for each item, then run through the item-checking section once again, plugging those same answers as needed into the appropriate items. While students had not altered the program's apparent purpose of teaching certain new vocabulary items, they had subverted completely the more important pedagogical aim of the program—teaching the contextual dependence of word meanings.

A CAI program must reflect its author's pedagogical intent faithfully. In this case, the program was subsequently altered so that the student had either to achieve a correct response rate of at least 33 percent or to have already passed twice through the item-checking section unsuccessfully before help would be given in the form of correct answers. This, plus a few other minor changes, ensured that the pedagogical goal of the material would be achieved by its users (Weible, 22, p. 490).

The ability to do this, to structure the student's interaction with the material in a precise and detailed manner, is surely a major aid in achieving and implementing a coherent instructional design. Does doing this make the computer, to use Higgin's (8) term, a *magister*?

The *magister* wears a gown to show that he is qualified. He is paid a salary every month. He carries a stick, real or metaphorical, with which to beat the children who give wrong answers. He makes assessments: right or wrong, good worker or lazy student. Most important of all, he chooses the order in which things happen, what is to be learned, and what kind of activity the learners will carry out. . . . For years people have been trying to turn the computer into a *magister*. They do this by making it carry the learning system known as Programmed Learning (PL). Underlying PL is the belief that a body of knowledge can be reduced to a set of very small steps, each of which is easily learnable. Each step is turned into a frame which contains a line or two of exposition and a comprehension question. PL in fact does not need a computer or any other machinery; it can be used just as effectively in paper form, and computers which are used exclusively for PL are sometimes known disparagingly as page-turners (p. 4).

Note that Higgins echoes one of Nordberg's dangers, the concern regarding the underlying belief of programmed learning (or programmed instruction) that a body of knowledge can be reduced to a set of very small steps, that the whole is nothing more than the sum of its parts. Higgins seems to equate the determination of the instructional goal and methodology (principal characteristic of the *magister*) with the utilization of one specific methodology, programmed instruction. This may simply be his reaction to that body of CALL lessons that, in fact, do imitate in a most unimaginative way the approach of the programmed instruction texts and machines of decades ago. At any rate, Higgins sees another role for the computer as preferable: the role of the pedagogue, or less ambiguously, the *paidagogos*—the Greek slave who escorted the young master to school.

When the young master snaps his fingers, [the slave] comes forward to give information, answer questions, or perhaps, if that is what the young master wants, to conduct an argument or give a test. He may be expert, but his expertise only emerges on demand (p. 4).

The chief reason Higgins gives for his preference that the computer play the role of *paidagogos* rather than *magister* is as follows:

At many stages of learning we need and expect a magisterial approach. But an exclusively magisterial method, particularly one undertaken with a large class, entails that the teacher does nearly all the initiating and the learners get practice only in responding. Such one-sidedness can have practical and motivational drawbacks (p. 4).

This objection does not really cover the various qualities he ascribes to his *magister*. In particular, the computer as *magister* does not typically deal with a large class but rather with the individual learner. One has to wonder whether the real concern here is not that the computer may become too magisterial in a broader sense, even dictatorial, evoking the idea of "big brother."

Steinberg (20), too, admits to an objection to computer control of instruction, but hers is the pragmatic concern that "computer control is more costly than learner control" (p. 97). While she notes that many CAI authors believe that giving the student control of the learning process will improve student achievement, she doubts this to be the case.

> For the most part, only adults who are high performers in the subject will be skillful managers of the sequence of instruction and will perform equally well (not better) under learner than under computer control. Other students usually perform worse under learner than under computer control. Experience and research are in agreement with common sense. If a student knows little or nothing about a subject, how can you expect her to choose a reasonable sequence of topics (p. 98)?

Unfortunately, Steinberg does not give a specific reference to the research studies that support this claim. Still, it seems a reasonable one, granting the assumption that the pedagogical and methodological aspects of the program are well taken care of. The computer can indeed function as a *magister,* but it need not do so in the limited and limiting way described by Higgins. To see why this need not be so, those other qualities the computer does not share with the print media must be addressed. Moreover, as shall be seen below, it is possible to give the student indirect control of the program, i.e., control of variables such as sequencing, level of difficulty, length of study, etc., which the student controls through interaction with the lesson.

The Process Orientation of the Computer

A second quality often overlooked is the fact that computers, unlike books, are process-oriented. The heart of a computer is its "central processing unit" (CPU). The primary use of the computer is as a data processor or, in the case of verbal "data," a word processor. A computer "spreadsheet" does not merely display columns of figures; it calculates them according to the relationships and formulas specified by the user. If an entry is altered for any reason, all of the totals resulting from that entry can be reprocessed speedily and automatically.

The ability of computers to process data rapidly also permits them to simulate processes. There are, for example, computer programs that offer realistic simulations of piloting a plane, performing chemical titrations, and breeding generations of fruit flies. This ability could be put to good use in CALL materials as well.

The most obvious analogy are programs that would simulate actual target language usage and permit the learner to apply it more or less communicatively. Programs such as *Spion* (Sanders, 18), *Familia* (Underwood, 21, pp. 75–79) and *Die Programmiersprache SuperPILOT* (Harroff, 7) are all very promising beginnings in this direction. However, they are extremely complicated programs and, with the possible exception of *Familia,* may seem to most classroom teachers to deal with instructional points of only marginal interest. Perhaps of more interest to many teachers would be the use of the computer as a tutorial instructor.

The ability of computers to simulate processes also means that those aspects of language learning that relate to linguistic processes or processlike linguistic features, such as the derivation of a new and unfamiliar form, either lexical or morphological, from a known one, can be presented directly, as a process. Where the medium of print limits the user to the description of processes, quite often utilizing a highly specialized terminology that itself, until it is mastered, represents a barrier to understanding, the computer permits the author quite often to display the process as a process, without extraneous commentary.

Most regrettably, not much use of this ability has been made to date in foreign language instructional programs. One example, however, is provided by some CALL materials Ariew (1) has authored. To explain the formation of the imperfect tense, first a first-person plural form is shown, then the stem is derived by blanking out the personal ending, finally the various imperfect endings are appended sequentially to the stem in conjunction with the appropriate personal pronouns. Where this differs significantly from a textbook presentation is in the total avoidance of grammatical terminology or indeed of an explanation of any kind. The learner observes the process, analyzes it, and then imitates it. The attempt to acquire a new concept through the use of a grammatical metalanguage that may itself be largely meaningless to the user is here replaced by a dynamic representation of the process, forcing learners to discover how it works on their own.

Of course, the objection can be made that grammatical terminology should be taught, that the learning of abstract grammatical concepts is in itself an important part of foreign language instruction—a view that may have fallen somewhat out of favor, but is doubtless still widely held (see Chapter 7 by Garret in this volume). The students can, however, always be taught the formal description of a linguistic feature *after* they have already acquired practical mastery of it. Most important, surely, is the likelihood that this use of the computer may greatly facilitate the acquisition of new language concepts, particularly those that find no parallel in the learner's native language. If we have indeed become a more visually oriented culture, then clearly computers with their ability to use animation along with color and sound are at a great advantage over textbooks in the presentation of some features of a foreign language, for example the teaching of morphology, accidence, concordance and other formal aspects of language learning whose textbook exposition seems, at least in the United States, to meet increasingly with blank incomprehension.

Automated Individualized Instruction

A third quality of computers as an instructional medium that should be observed by authors who wish to ensure that users of their lessons become better language learners is the ability to provide for maximally efficient use of the material by different kinds and levels of students. In the best instance, the author will provide the program with the ability to "learn" about the individual user's needs and to act on this "knowledge" by modifying the presentation of the subject matter. This modification may be no more than having the program "interrupt" itself to provide advice (Chambers and Sprecher, 4, p. 124). A more extreme variation of this would have the program modify the order and/or manner of the presentation of its content in response to indications it has been programmed to pick up from the student's performance. This effect can carry across between programs on different diskettes if they have been designed to have a common student database and if there is some means of collecting individual student data independently of the lesson disk, whether through the use of a second "floppy" data disk or the incorporation of a centralized hard disk storage unit. In this manner, the student will contribute to the ultimate form of the program as he or she encounters it—that is, the student, while being "programmed" by the program, will also exercise a sort of programming power over it and be able to alter it to his or her greatest educational advantage, so that the end result will be a synthesis of the author's intent and the student's needs (Barrutia, 3, p. 37).

Far more than the first two abilities of the computer described above, this particular ability of the medium has been acknowledged widely for some time. Despite that circumstance, practically all of the CALL materials currently available force each and every student to go through them in the same, identical manner. Clearly, here too there is much to achieve before it can be said that adequate and appropriate use of the computer's potential as an instructional medium has been made.

Conclusion

Doubtless, too, there are other important qualities of the computer that have been passed over here—some of them perhaps as yet wholly unnoticed. For this reason, it is important to try occasionally to step back and get a fresh perspective on what computers really are and what their potential is for any and all aspects of second-language acquisition. That may seem not so difficult, but it is not as easy as all that to assess such things accurately, as these words from Thomas A. Edison (5) testify.

I believe that the motion picture is destined to revolutionize our educational system, and that in a few years it will supplant largely, if not entirely, the use of text-books in our schools. Books are clumsy methods of instruction at best, and often even the words of explanation in them have to be explained.

I should say that on the average we get only about two percent efficiency out of school books as they are written today. The education of the future, as I see it, will be conducted through the medium of the motion picture, a visualized education, where it should be possible to obtain a one-hundred-per-cent-efficiency" (pp. 78–79).

If the "Wizard of Menlo Park" could be so wrong in his rosy assessment of the instructional potential of cinema, surely our own beliefs and pronouncements about CALL must be regarded with some skepticism.

Just as innovations and modifications in the cinema forced a reevaluation of that mediums' significance in our culture, so too our perception of the computer's potential will be altered by developments related to its own increasing power and declining costs, the development of higher-level computer languages, the use of interactive audio and video, improved speech recognition capabilities, and, most important, advances in the field of artificial intelligence. Exciting studies, such as MIT's Athena Project (Kramsch, Morgenstern, and Murray, 11) are underway to explore and help realize more of the computer's enormous potential for foreign language learning. But again, the process will be a slow one and will require active involvement on a broad scale.

The emergence of motion pictures as a new art form went hand in hand with the emergence of a new subculture, a new set of professions made up of people whose skills, sensitivities, and philosophies of life were unlike anything that had existed before. The story of the evolution of the world of movies is inseparable from the story of the evolution of the communities of people. Similarly, a new world of personal computing is about to come into being, and its history will be inseparable from the story of the people who will make it (Papert, 16, p. 189).

What makes the development of CALL so exciting is the fact that, in this case, the people in the story are foreign language teachers. This is their own new world that is coming into being, and it will be up to them to make its history.

References, Toward a Media-Specific Methodology

1. Ariew, Robert. *Tête à Tête*. Boston: Heinle & Heinle, 1986.
2. Baker, Robert L. "Foreign-Language Software: The State of the Art, or Pick a Card, Any (Flash) Card." *CALICO Journal* 2, 1 (1984):6–10, 27.
3. Barrutia, Richard. "Communicative CALL with Artificial Intelligence: Some Desiderata." *CALICO Journal* 3, 1 (1985):37–42.
4. Chambers, Jack A., and Jerry W. Sprecher. *Computer-Assisted Instruction: Its Use in the Classroom*. Englewood Cliffs, NJ: Prentice-Hall, 1983.
5. Edison, Thomas A. *The Diary and Sundry Observations of T. A. Edison*. Edited by Dagobert D. Runes, New York: Philosophical Library, 1948.
6. Geduld, Harry M. *The Birth of the Talkies*. Bloomington: Indiana University Press, 1975.
7. Harroff, Stephen. "A Microworld for Second-Language Acquisition." *CALICO Journal* 3, 3 (1986):31–33.
8. Higgins, John. "Can Computers Teach?" *CALICO Journal* 1, 2 (1983):4–6.
9. _____, and Tim Johns. *Computers in Language Learning*. Reading, MA: Addison-Wesley, 1984.
10. Hope, Geoffrey R., Heimy F. Taylor, and James P. Pusack. *Using Computers in Teaching Foreign Languages*. Language and Education: Theory and Practice, no. 57. Orlando, FL: Harcourt Brace Jovanovich, 1984.
11. Kramsch, Claire, Douglas Morgenstern, and Janet H. Murray. "An Overview of the MIT Athena Language Learning Project." *CALICO Journal* 2, 4 (1985):31–34.
12. Krashen, Stephen D. *Principles and Practice in Second Language Acquisition*. Oxford, England: Pergamon Press, 1982.
13. McLuhan, Marshall. *Understanding Media: The Extensions of Man*. New York: McGraw-Hill, 1964.
14. Nordberg, Robert B. "Teaching Machines—Six Dangers and One Advantage," pp. 1–8 in J. S. Roucek, ed., *Programmed Teaching: A Symposium on Automation in Education*. New York: Philosophical Library, 1965.
15. Olsen, Solveig. "Foreign Language Departments and Computer-Assisted Instruction: A Survey." *The Modern Language Journal* 64 (1980):341–49.
16. Papert, Seymour. *Mindstorms: Children, Computers, and Powerful Ideas*. New York: Basic Books, 1980.
17. Robinson, David. *The History of World Cinema*. 2nd ed. New York: Stein and Day, 1981.
18. Sanders, Ruth. "PILOT-Spion: A Computer Game for German Students." *Die Unterrichtspraxis* 17, 1 (1984):123–29.
19. Schank, Roger C. *The Cognitive Computer: On Language, Learning, and Artificial Intelligence*. Reading, MA: Addison-Wesley, 1984.
20. Steinberg, Esther R. *Teaching Computers to Teach*. Hillsdale, NJ: Lawrence Erlbaum, 1984.
21. Underwood, John H. *Linguistics, Computers, and the Language Teacher: A Communicative Approach*. Rowley, MA: Newbury House, 1984.
22. Weible, David M. "Teaching Reading Skills through Linguistic Redundancy." *Foreign Language Annals* 13, 4 (1980):487–93.

4

Applying Pedagogical Principles to CALL Courseware Development

David H. Wyatt
Specialized Curriculum Design
Consultants and Trinity College

Introduction

In order to gain an accurate picture of the field of computer-assisted language learning (CALL), it is essential to make a crucial distinction between the medium itself and approach and methodology. It will be argued here that the computer medium is not tied to a particular type of pedagogy, but can potentially be used as a component of a very wide range of different approaches and methodologies. In recent years, increasing attention has been focused on second-language acquisition and natural approaches to second-language learning. As a medium for language learning, the computer may have as much potential for fostering acquisition and communication as more traditional tools.

Before examining the prospects for developing different types of CALL courseware, the relationships between the capabilities of the computer (and computer-controlled technology) and the main approaches to second-language learning will be clarified. Common types of CALL programs will be reviewed briefly under the familiar classification scheme (tutorial, drill-and-practice, etc.). A "relational" classification will then be proposed (based on the relationship between and roles assumed by learner

David H. Wyatt (M.A., Cambridge University) is the Director of Specialized Curriculum Design Consultants and a Lecturer in the Trinity College (Washington, D.C.) Masters Program for Computers in Education and Training. He has been instrumental in the installation of more than 1500 microcomputer systems for CALL. He is also Computer Editor for *System,* the author of *Computers and ESL* (Harcourt Brace Jovanovich/Center for Applied Linguistics), a member of ACTFL, TESOL, and CALICO, and past President of the Society for Microcomputer Applications in Language and Literature.

and computer) to define (1) instructional, (2) collaborative, and (3) facilitative types of programs. It will be shown how this newer classification scheme lends insight into a wide range of issues in the use of computer software and hardware in language courses. This tripartite classification will also be used as a basis for explaining why published reviews of CALL software are so often unintentionally misleading, and why the possibilities for valid computer applications in some newer approaches to language learning have been almost completely overlooked. Finally, the new classification will be used as a basis for discussing important aspects of CALL design and development. Teacher involvement in the development and intelligent use of CALL is essential to its success; thus, this chapter will also indicate how the three major approaches to producing CALL programs allow for different types and levels of teacher participation.

CALL and Pedagogy

One of the most fundamental issues in the field of CALL is the "fit" between the computer's capabilities and the demands of language pedagogy. Neither is static; both have undergone very significant developments in the last decade, and continued change is to be expected. Nevertheless, it is illuminating to examine the question of "fit" in terms of currently accepted pedagogical principles and widely available microcomputer technology. Over the last ten years, microcomputers have become the first type of computer technology available to the language-teaching profession on a significant scale. Microcomputers at first appeared to have certain well-defined pedagogical capabilities (such as the presentation of mechanical language drills) and limitations (for example, an inability to handle open-ended student responses). As a result, much of the early CALL software was of the drill-and-practice variety, and microcomputers rapidly became identified with just one approach to language pedagogy—the audiolingual method. The introduction of an earlier technology—the tape recorder—should have alerted teachers to the danger of leaping to this type of conclusion. In the case of the language laboratory, the obvious "fit" between the technology and language learning appeared to lie in the provision of speaking practice. It was only later that the value of this kind of speaking practice was questioned and more valid possibilities for the development of listening comprehension were recognized for the medium.

Unfortunately, much of the debate over the use of computers in language learning has been based on their unilateral identification with mechanical audiolingual techniques. Drill-and-practice CALL materials of this type have been welcomed by some writers (Davies, 1; Wyatt, 13) but strongly criticized (Sanders and Kenner, 11; Underwood, 12) or rejected (Krashen, 7) by others. Whatever the merits of this type of software, it is important to realize that CALL is not limited to and should not be identified with any single approach and methodology. In short, computer applications in second-language learning are potentially at least as relevant to the natural approach as they are in an audiolingual or cognitive code setting.

Types of CALL Programs

The discussion of computers and language learning that follows is limited to the largest class of computer applications—programs intended for *direct use* by students. Other applications are outside the focus of this discussion, as is the use of the computer and computer-controlled technology by the teacher as a demonstration medium in the classroom. A basic computer system can be used as a powerful "electronic blackboard," particularly in the teaching of reading and writing skills, provided that a large enough display device is available. With the addition of a computer-controlled videodisc or videotape player, a new spectrum of video-assisted language teaching (VALT) techniques become possible (Wyatt, 17). Two other significant areas beyond the scope of this chapter are computer-assisted language testing (Wyatt, 15) and teacher support (Higgins and Johns, 4).

Software for direct student use includes a bewildering variety of forms. Figure 1 shows some of the most common "types," but does not attempt to provide a complete listing. Related accounts of software types may be found in Davies (1) and Higgins and Johns (4).

Program Type	Examples of Functions and Contents
1. Tutorial	introducing new material—e.g., the Cyrillic alphabet in beginning Russian
2. Drill and practice	allowing mastery of material already presented—e.g., grammatical forms, culturally appropriate behavior
3. Game	adding elements of peer competition, scoring, and timing to a wide variety of practice activities
4. Holistic practice	providing higher-level, contextualized practice activities—e.g., cloze passages
5. Modeling	demonstrating how to perform a language task—e.g., how a good reader handles difficult sections of a reading passage
6. Discovery	providing situations in which linguistic generalizations can be made—e.g., inferring rules for generating comparative forms
7. Simulation	allowing students to experiment with language use—e.g., levels of formality in a conversational simulator

8. Adventure reading (interactive fiction)	offering "participatory" reading materials—e.g., student as detective explores murder location, gathers clues
9. Annotation	providing a wide range of language "notes" (vocabulary, syntax, plot, etc.) available on demand during reading or listening activities
10. Idea processor	planning and editing outlines—e.g., before writing activities, after listening to lectures
11. Word processor	creating and editing written assignments
12. On-line thesaurus	expanding vocabulary, improving writing style
13. Spelling checker	guarding against errors during or after writing activities
14. Textual analysis	revealing structural and stylistic aspects of written work—e.g., complexity and variety of sentence types, subject/verb agreement errors

Figure 1. Some Types of Programs Used in CALL

Much discussion of CALL software has been conducted on the basis of categories such as those in Figure 1. Unfortunately, these categories can be very misleading. Software in a "game" format, for example, often consists of disguised drill-and-practice materials. "Tutorials" are frequently taken to imply mechanical approaches to language learning, whereas tutorial CALL formats can equally be used to implement functional and communicative language learning.

More insight into CALL approaches can be provided by examining the interactional relationship between student and computer. On this basis, three fundamental categories of language-learning programs can be distinguished: instructional, collaborative, and facilitative (Wyatt, 16).

In *instructional* CALL programs, the computer presents language-learning materials in a highly structured, predetermined manner. In essence, the student plays the relatively passive role of responder and the computer functions as an authoritative instructor. The language-learning objectives of instructional CALL programs can be very precisely specified, as can the learning path or paths to be followed by students in attaining the goals. Tutorial, drill and practice, holistic practice, and many types of game software (items 1 through 4 in Figure 1) are examples of instructional programs.

Despite their high degree of structuring, instructional programs need not appear rigid or mechanical. Students may be given considerable freedom to select program formats, move on to new programs, and the like. Based on their needs as demonstrated in their responses at the computer, students may be routed in very different ways through an instructional program and may receive individualized learning materials not presented to other students. Nevertheless, instructional programs are generally characterized by highly predetermined sets of learning goals and paths, regardless of whether this is apparent to the learner.

Collaborative software casts students in a much more active role and depends on them to take responsibility for their own learning. The computer may function in a large range of roles—as an interactive world in which the student plays the part of detective or adventurer, as an environment for linguistic discovery, or as a conversational partner, etc. In all cases, however, the student must make decisions and take the initiative in working with the program.

In some types of collaborative programs (for example, adventure reading), learning objectives can be expressed only in very general, holistic terms, while in other cases (such as annotation and discovery courseware) they may be specified in as much detail as in instructional programs. One key feature of collaborative programs, however, is that there is no attempt to create predetermined learning paths. Students will interact with these programs and draw on their pedagogical resources in a wide variety of ways. Items 5 through 9 in Figure 1 are examples of collaborative program formats.

Facilitative software differs from the above two categories in that it is essentially empty of direct pedagogical content. With purely facilitative materials, the program itself embodies no language-learning paths or objectives. Rather, the software serves as a tool in language-learning activities. In Figure 1, items 10 through 14 are examples of programs that can be used facilitatively in second-language learning. Of these, word processing programs are the most familiar, already finding considerable use in writing activities where the ability to edit and rework materials quickly and easily is important to the learning process. This use of word processing illustrates the main function of facilitative software—to minimize the "inauthentic labor" (Kemmis et al., 6) involved in the learning process.

The three-way relational classification of program types, summarized in Figure 2, clarifies a number of aspects of CALL.

Approach	Characteristics
A. INSTRUCTIONAL e.g., tutorial, drill and practice, holistic practice, many "games"	• Students are responders, not initiators, despite their high level of activity
	• Detailed set of high- and low-level learning objectives
	• Predetermined learning path(s)
	• The computer instructs the student; students learn *from* the computer

B. COLLABORATIVE
e.g., modeling, discovery, simulation, adventure reading,
annotation, some "games"

- Students are initiators, take more responsibility for their learning

- May only be possible to specify learning objectives in high-level terms

- No predetermined learning paths

- Elements of discovery learning; students learn *with* the computer

C. FACILITATIVE
e.g., word and idea processing,
spell check, on-line thesaurus,
text analysis

- Students are initiators, entirely responsible for their learning

- Learning objectives and paths not specified or embodied in computer program

- Students use computer as *tool* to reduce "inauthentic labor"

Figure 2. Relational Classification of CALL Approaches

Instructional approaches in CALL represent the older traditions of computer-assisted learning. At their best, they are extremely sophisticated elaborations of the proven techniques of programmed instruction. The more precisely the learning objectives can be specified and the learning paths predicted, the more effective this type of software is likely to be. Researchers have generally reported significant reductions in average student learning times in language arts areas with instructional courseware (Edwards et al., 2; Ragosta et al., 8). A recent study (Robinson, 10) suggests that the computer program's ability to assess individual student's problem areas and provide practice in them is effective in second-language learning. However, much research remains to be done to assess whether the results in language arts can be replicated in appropriate areas of second-language learning, and this type of research is fraught with problems (Hope et al., 5; Pederson, Chapter 5 in this volume).

The strengths of instructional CALL software include a high degree of student involvement and activity, student self-pacing, practice materials appropriate in quantity and challenge to each student's level, and other aspects of individualization. In general, these benefits can only be realized if each student works at a separate computer. As a result, a relatively large number of computers is usually a *sine qua non* for the appropriate use of instructional software.

To achieve and maintain computer-mediated individualization, detailed recordkeeping on each student's work is often a feature of instructional programs. For greatest convenience and maximum ease of use, this requires an additional layer of computer technology to network the individual computers and provide centralized information storage. In general, instructional CALL therefore implies more expensive and sophisticated computer systems than other approaches.

It should be apparent that much of the debate concerning the use of computers in language learning has been conducted as though CALL were synonymous with instructional software. Historically, this was perhaps an understandable error—much of the earlier CALL software was instructional, with particularly strong ties to the audiolingual and cognitive code approaches. In the mid-eighties, however, it seems high time to set instructional software in its proper context as just one of three distinct approaches to CALL.

It is also important to recognize that instructional software can serve as part of many communicative approaches to second-language learning. Newer instructional programs employing communicative approaches are already appearing. Moreover, some proponents of the natural approach advocate the provision of grammar-oriented materials for out-of-class study (Krashen, 7); in these circumstances, well-designed instructional software offers all the advantages previously outlined.

On the other hand, there may be little or no "fit" between some communicative approaches and instructional CALL, and this should be acknowledged openly. It serves little purpose for a reviewer opposed to the use of drill techniques to attack the use of computers in language learning based on a detailed critique of drill and practice and other instructional programs. Presumably the same reviewer would also reject a majority of the textbooks currently used in language learning because of the prevalence of drill activities; it is the methodology, not the medium, that generally lies at the heart of such debates. (See Chapter 9 in this volume, by Hubbard, for further discussion of software review and evaluation.)

Collaborative CALL provides a sharp contrast to the instructional approach. In all collaborative activities, the prime linguistic focus is on process, function, and communication. It is the students who decide how the pedagogical resources of the program are to be used.

Some important types of collaborative software are designed for use by groups of students. Group-oriented collaborative programs are fundamentally different from the single-student approach typical of instructional programs. In many CALL simulations, games, and discovery activities, for example, the student group discussions that precede each new "move" at the computer are one of the most valuable aspects of the program.

Certain types of collaborative software are primarily intended for single-student use. Reading skill modelers and annotated listening programs are examples of single-student collaborative software that takes advantage of the computer's ability to individualize the learning process. However, there are two crucial differences from the way the individualizing capabilities are used in instructional CALL. In these collaborative programs, the reading or listening activity proceeds transparently—without apparent computer intervention—until students decide to ask for assistance or check their understanding. Secondly, when help is requested, it is the student who selects from and decides how to use the range of learning aids provided.

Since many collaborative program formats are group-oriented, this approach to CALL can be implemented even when relatively few microcomputers are available. Because many group-oriented approaches derive their value from student interactions rather than from explicitly programmed learning sequences, a careful selection of existing games and simulations for native speakers may be directly usable in the language classroom. Basic microcomputer systems are adequate for most applications, as recordkeeping features are generally absent from this type of software. Thus, group-oriented collaborative CALL may be the most practical starting point for a majority of teachers and institutions.

In their purest form, programs used in facilitative CALL embody no assumptions about language teaching and learning. As examples, consider the use of word processing and spelling-checker programs in language courses. It is now widely accepted that writing should generally be treated as a process, not a product (Raimes, 9), and so students' written assignments should go through at least one cycle of editing and rewriting. Similarly, research indicates that teacher responses to students' written work should emphasize more global problems such as planning, rhetorical structure, and content (Griffin, 3) rather than focus only on form. With handwritten or typed student assignments, rewriting can be laborious at each stage. When assignments are word-processed, however, even global changes can be incorporated quickly into successive drafts. Spelling checkers, now becoming standard components of many word processor programs, can both remove a burden and focus attention on problem items.

There are many existing microcomputer programs in foreign language as well as English versions that can serve effectively in CALL for purely facilitative applications in the teaching of writing. Such programs have no built-in pedagogical bias, so they are adaptable to any approach to second-language learning. Usable programs are often available for even the least sophisticated microcomputer systems. The only drawback is the need for a great deal of available computer time. Obviously, straightforward work on writing assignments in the classroom requires one computer per student. Even if the word processing is done out of class in a campus computer laboratory, students must still have ready access to computers for relatively lengthy periods. As institutions and students continue to acquire microcomputers at a rapid pace, however, this constraint on facilitative applications is likely to diminish.

A trend that tends to mask the identity of facilitative approaches is the combining of instructional and collaborative elements with a basically facilitative program. For example, software (such as Quill) is beginning to appear that attempts to integrate instructional programs on planning a writing assignment with word processing. In debating the merits of such combined programs, the reviewer must be careful to specify which elements of the software are being discussed vis à vis their purpose and overall objective.

In summary, the three-way classification of CALL applications may provide a new perspective in the debate over computer applications in second-language learning. The appropriateness of the computer in a given approach may vary widely according to the category of CALL. In particular, there may be little or no "fit" between instructional CALL and some communicative approaches; on the other hand, there may be considerable scope in theory and practice for agreement between communicative approaches and collaborative and facilitative CALL.

Illustration of CALL Approaches to Pedagogy _____

The three main roles for computers and computer-controlled technology can be illustrated by considering a few of the possibilities for teaching listening comprehension via CALL. In this regard, one extremely promising strategy involves the use of a videodisc player under the control of a simple microcomputer system (Wyatt, 17).

For an instructional approach, the video materials generally need to be custom scripted and filmed so as to be fully integrated with the computer-based activities. The computer programs might present a careful sequence of listening exercises designed to develop various aspects of listening comprehension skills. Videodisc operation is under computer control throughout and presents the listening segments on which each student activity and items are based. Clearly, in an instructional approach of this type, the development of computer–video materials is expensive and time-consuming.

In some types of collaborative approaches, such as annotated listening, learning materials are based on existing video materials such as news broadcasts, documentaries, and movies. Computer programs are developed to provide a wide variety of assistance to students, ranging from minimal listening comprehension hints and vocabulary glosses to the provision of complete scripts. After beginning an activity, students listen uninterruptedly to the video materials until help is needed. At any point, students can touch a computer key to halt the video presentation and select the kind of collaborative assistance they want. Computer help is keyed directly to the current position in the video material, since the computer keeps track of the videodisc's progress. Such collaborative materials are relatively quick and inexpensive to develop for those abreast of the technology.

Existing or custom-filmed video materials can be used in a facilitative approach. Here, the computer simply functions as an intelligent video controller. The program knows where each scene or topic starts and ends, providing students with rapid, convenient control over the video materials. Such a system also provides an ideal classroom aid for the teacher. A "template" computer program, once developed, would serve both teacher and student applications with minimal time required for adaptation to each new videodisc.

CALL Program Design and Development

The following paragraphs focus on two related considerations: how computer software is developed, and which developmental methods are appropriate for the different approaches to CALL. The discussion is based on the types of computer hardware and software generally available now and in the immediate future. Much more sophisticated technology is already in existence; unfortunately, its cost will keep it beyond the reach of virtually all educational institutions for a number of years.

The three main methods of producing CALL programs are through the use of (1) educational authoring systems, (2) educational programming languages, and (3) general-purpose programming languages (Wyatt, 14). In terms of current technology, each method has different implications for the role of the language teacher in the development process and the types of CALL programs that can readily be designed and produced.

Educational Authoring Systems

Educational authoring systems offer the greatest opportunity for teachers to develop their own CALL materials. The main purpose of these software systems is to permit the creation of relatively sophisticated student programs while requiring a minimum of learning and production time for the developer. With an authoring system, materials developers are not required to learn how to program a computer or deal with an operating system. Instead, they need only master the rules of the system, which are designed specifically for rapid learning and educational applications. In principle, teachers with no previous computer programming experience should quickly be able to begin developing their own CALL materials. In practice, however, the performance of many authoring systems is far from the ideal. Of the large number the writer has reviewed personally, well over half suffer from very poor user design. In many cases, assistance from someone with computer programming expertise would be necessary to operate even very "simple" systems. Other systems are riddled with programming "bugs" or contain surprising built-in limitations to their stated capabilities.

Many authoring systems are designed solely for the production of instructional types of CALL materials. Some are placed onto a single-screen format, as with many cloze exercise generators. Others employ a question-and-answer structure that, used imaginatively, can produce a large number of superficially different screen formats and activities, all of which are fundamentally drill-and-practice in nature. If the instructional approach is acceptable for some purposes, however, these very limited systems may well be worthy of consideration. Some of the simpler systems are indeed easy to learn and will operate without flaws.

There are still other authoring systems that transcend these limitations. For example, both teachers and students can readily develop creative reading activities with certain authoring systems. A different type of collaborative CALL material can be produced with adventure authoring systems, although these are generally more difficult to master. A small number of very powerful authoring systems will permit much greater flexibility, as described below, but involve greater expense, complexity, learning periods, and development time.

Educational Programming Languages

Educational programming languages such as PILOT constitute the second developmental route. This method generally offers significantly greater flexibility in the type of CALL materials that can be produced. Potentially, both collaborative and instructional materials can be developed, although facilitative programs are beyond the capabilities of most educational programming languages.

As the term implies, the use of educational programming languages requires a knowledge of programming. In the original version of PILOT, for example, the programming language was designed to be extremely simple, so that learning to program basic (instructional) student exercises would take only a few hours. Thus, educational programming languages such as PILOT were intended to provide teachers with a quick entry point into developing computer-assisted learning materials. Unfortunately, the original simplified programming languages quickly earned the reputation of being unsuitable for producing worthwhile courseware. The emphasis is now on power and sophistication, not simplicity, and recent versions of PILOT reflect the trend toward full-featured educational programming languages with certain authoring-system capabilities. Languages such as EnBASIC and SuperPILOT are not intended to provide quick access for nonprogramming teachers. They are powerful, time-saving programming tools meant for relatively expert programmers.

In most cases, developing collaborative or instructional CALL materials using educational programming languages therefore implies a team approach involving at least one language teacher and one programmer. If possible, however, there should be at least two language teachers on the team. One should have familiarity with CALL applications and some programming experience, while the other should have as few preconceived ideas about CALL as possible and little or no computer experience.

As noted previously, however, there is considerable application for existing programs (originally written to entertain or educate native speakers) in collaborative CALL. Carefully chosen programs such as simulations, adventures, and games may be usable directly, without any need for reprogramming. Teacher-prepared handouts for use before, during, or after the work on the computer can enhance the value of the software for second-language learning. In this manner, nonprogramming teachers may be able to develop excellent collaborative activities on their own.

General-Purpose Programming Languages

The remaining method of producing CALL materials is through the use of general-purpose programming languages (BASIC, Pascal, Assembler, and the like). In essence, these languages offer unrestricted access to the computer's full capabilities. Virtually any type of CALL application— instructional, collaborative, or facilitative—can be produced. Except for those willing to undertake considerable study of programming, however, language teachers will need to form teams with programmers to produce materials using this method.

General-purpose programming languages are the only realistic option for the development of original facilitative programs. Where possible, however, it is important to consider the alternative—adapting carefully selected existing programs, through teacher planning and handouts, for facilitative CALL. Word processors are a case in point. "Educational" word processing programs have been appearing, designed specifically for the classroom and, in a few cases, even for foreign language courses. Such programs aim at ease of learning and may have special capabilities designed for the classroom environment. However, they may sacrifice so much power and speed as to represent a poor bargain, especially when compared with a full-featured professional program carefully selected for user-friendliness. Because of the complexity of facilitative software development, the language teacher's energy and expertise can generally be best spent in choosing the most suitable of the extant programs and developing imaginative ways of using them.

Conclusion _____

This chapter has provided arguments for challenging two prevalent views of CALL. One is the misconception that computers fit into only one pedagogical style and approach to language learning, a misconception based on the characteristics of instructional CALL. As computers become more available to students and teachers, their value as language-learning aids in collaborative and facilitative activities will be more widely recognized.

The second has challenged the assumption that language teachers wishing to become involved in CALL materials production must turn themselves into programmers when, in fact, nonprogramming teachers have a particular value as members of software development teams. Nonprogrammers can also produce effective CALL programs with carefully chosen authoring systems. Finally, there is considerable room for imaginative adaptations of existing non-CALL programs for the second-language classroom.

References. Applying Pedagogical Principles to CALL Courseware Development

1. Davies, Graham. *Computers, Language and Language Learning.* London: Centre for Information on Language Teaching and Research, 1982.
2. Edwards, Judith, Shirley Norton, Sandra Taylor, Martha Weiss, and Ralph Dusseldorp. "How Effective Is CAI? A Review of the Research." *Educational Leadership* 33, 2 (1975):147–53.
3. Griffin, C. "Theory of Responding to Student Writing: The State of the Art." *College Composition and Communication* 33, 3 (1982):296–301.
4. Higgins, John, and Tim Johns. *Computers in Language Learning.* Reading, MA: Addison-Wesley, 1984.
5. Hope, Geoffrey R., Heimy F. Taylor, and James P. Pusack. *Using Computers in Teaching Foreign Languages.* Language and Education: Theory and Practice, no. 57. Orlando, FL: Harcourt Brace Jovanovich/CAL, 1984.
6. Kemmis, Stephen, Roderick Atkin, and Eleanor Wright. *How Do Students Learn? Working Papers on Computer-Assisted Learning: UNCAL Evaluation Studies.* Norwich, England: Centre for Applied Research in Education, 1977.
7. Krashen, Stephen. "The Power of Reading." Plenary presentation at the annual TESOL Conference, New York, 1985.
8. Ragosta, Marjorie, Paul Holland, and Dean Jamieson. *Computer-Assisted Instruction and Compensatory Education: The ETS/LAUSD Study.* Washington, DC: U.S. Department of Education, 1982.
9. Raimes, Ann. "What Unskilled ESL Students Do as They Write: A Classroom Study of Composing." *TESOL Quarterly* 19, 2 (1985):229–58.
10. Robinson, Gail, John Underwood, Wilga Rivers, José Hernández, Carollyn Rudesill, and Clare Malnik Enseñat. "Computer-Assisted Instruction in Foreign Language Education: A Comparison of the Effectiveness of Different Methodologies and Different Forms of Error Correction." San Francisco: Center for Language & Crosscultural Skills, 1985. [EDRS: ED 262 626.]
11. Sanders, David, and Roger Kenner. "Whither CAI? The Need for Communicative Courseware." *System* 11, 1 (1983):33–39.
12. Underwood, John. *Linguistics, Computers, and the Language Teacher: A Communicative Approach.* Rowley, MA: Newbury House, 1984.
13. Wyatt, David. "Computer-Assisted Language Instruction: Present State and Future Prospects." *System* 11, 1 (1983):3–11.

5

Research on CALL

Kathleen Marshall Pederson
Buffalo Grove High School, Buffalo Grove, Illinois

Introduction

The question most commonly asked about computer-assisted language learning (CALL) by language teachers is no longer "Are you using CALL?" but "What kind of CALL do you use?" Assumptions about the value and the potential of the computer as a teaching tool abound. In fact, both Ragsdale (62) and Hurly and Hlynka (34) have argued that blind faith in the power of the computer has strongly shaped current American educational practices. The momentum toward the electronic classroom is so swift and so powerful that many second-language educators echo Teichert's (87) assertion that becoming computer literate and incorporating CALL into the curriculum is a matter of professional survival.

Although it could be argued that Teichert's dilemma is perhaps too extreme to characterize the profession at large, his sense of urgency about incorporating CALL into the curriculum portrays accurately the thinking of a growing number of language teachers who, in general, reflect a new enthusiasm for technology-aided language learning. Seemingly innumerable testimonials to the observed learning benefits and the yet untapped potentials of CALL are commonplace. Alatis (3) reminds the profession that if it wishes to take the humanistic value of second-language study seriously, then it must not shy from technological learning aids, but should explore all possibilities. In all fairness, this penchant for embracing innovation is one of the profession's most admirable qualities. When,

Kathleen Marshall Pederson (Ph.D., The Ohio State University), former Assistant Professor of French and Chair of Languages and Literature at Northwestern College (Orange City, IA), is currently a teacher of French and Spanish at Buffalo Grove High School in Buffalo Grove, IL. The 1986 recipient of the Emma Marie Birkmaier Award for Doctoral Dissertation Research in Foreign Language Education, she is a member of ACTFL, AATF, and CALICO.

however, testimonials are permitted to sway important curricular decisions without corresponding research evidence, enthusiasm becomes a serious flaw.

Consider, for example, a typical and seemingly simple endeavor such as designing a CALL program for practicing the differences between the Spanish preterite and the imperfect. The instructional designer is faced with an array of ways the computer can deliver instruction and must decide, among other possibilities, how and when to use graphics, sound, feedback, branching from one learning task to the next based on learner response or request for new material, and how to display all these coding options accurately and efficiently. Simply stated, the CALL instructional designer is too often forced to make decisions that affect courseware design and content without the benefit of adequate research results that generalize to language learning contexts when the various coding options available in computer-assisted instruction are utilized in specific ways.

Stern (84) observes that "the teaching of language is often regarded more as a matter of practical intuition, inventiveness, and sensitivity than as a suitable subject for research" (p. 53). He and others, however, are quick to remind the profession of the seriousness of its last technological blunder, the blind trust given the language laboratory's projected impact on learning in the early 60s. Nevertheless, the careful instructional designer searches controlled research in vain for guidance on CALL. Simply stated, there is little information about how to use the computer's capabilities to enhance CALL lesson delivery (Hope, Taylor, and Pusack, 29; Meredith, 49; Underwood, 89).

Not only has little research been conducted on how to use the computer's coding options to improve learning, the numerous studies that have questioned whether computers do make a difference in achievement have shown, generally, that "there are no learning benefits to be gained from employing any specific medium to deliver instruction" (Clark, 12, p. 445). In short, findings showing no significant differences have prevailed in spite of utopian projections to the contrary (Schramm, 74; Salomon, 68). Recent CALL research, however, suggests that the *design* of computer software to cause adjustments in cognitive processing, not the *medium* used to deliver instruction, stands the best chance of affecting learning outcomes. Only recently a few CALL studies have been conducted that illustrate that certain learning tasks for certain learners can be facilitated by the use of CALL (Pederson, 59; Robinson et al., 64). In other words, compelling evidence is beginning to emerge that CALL is highly context-bound and must, therefore, take such variables as learner differences, learning task, and the computer's coding options into account.

While no success has resulted from attempts to demonstrate that computer-assisted instruction is more effective than some other mode of instruction, these results should not be surprising. In the past two decades, foreign language educators have become increasingly aware of the fruitless nature of what have been coined "broad methodologies comparisons" (Smith and Berger, 78; Scherer and Wertheimer, 73). Comparative research that endeavors to identify a superior medium or a superior method is doomed to provide murky and usually uninterpretable results because the essential variables that might make a difference in a given language-learning context cannot be isolated, manipulated, and examined adequately.

Generally speaking, appropriate and feasible research in computer-assisted instruction (CAI) has lagged far behind vigorous materials development, especially in the area of CALL (Meredith, 49; Putnam, 61; Wyatt, 91). Although this situation is understandable (foreign language educators cannot wait until every research question is answered about how CALL can best be designed before beginning to use the medium), the profession needs to give serious consideration to the likely effects of such a lopsided approach.

There are many ways to ensure the best possible use of CALL. Surely careful programming, thoughtful instructional design, good sense, intuition, and sensitivity to students' needs all are necessary; but they are not sufficient. The profession must undertake research that provides an empirical base for assumptions, strategies, and applications of the computer in language teaching, lest another powerful tool for language learning not realize its potential. Starting form a historical perspective of research on the language laboratory, the purpose of this chapter is (1) to analyze and evaluate comparative and applied research on CALL, (2) to provide a theoretical base that illustrates the need for more basic research on CALL that considers computer capabilities, learner differences, and the learning task in concert, and (3) to evaluate basic research in CALL.

Media in Perspective: The Language Laboratory ⸺⸺⸺⸺

The language laboratory of the late 1950s and the 1960s is viewed by many in retrospect as an unfortunate venture that resulted in a loss of credibility for language education and a growing suspicion among teachers about the value of mediated language teaching in general. The major flaw of the language lab movement was the introduction of the medium with virtually no systematic research except on its engineering aspects (Stern, 84).

A perusal of the literature from 1959 to 1962 reveals that the language lab was viewed as a miracle worker too often foisted upon the unwary (Smith, 79). Most language teachers, however, welcomed the pseudo-credibility that the new technology afforded the profession and touted its potential as a "taskmaster" (Siciliano, 76, p. 224), a "private tutor" (Young, 92, p. 221), a milieu for a "fully automated language workout"

(Mathieu, 44, p. 352), a means by which the teacher could "enter into a much closer individual relationship with each of his students" (McGraw, 47, p. 218), a resource that would "multiply the good teacher" (Hocking, 25), "the most important technological aid to language teaching" (Huebner, 33, p. 109), and "the most important advance in language teaching efficiency" (Stack, 82, p. x).

These plaudits were rebuffed by others, however, who were skeptical about the lab's value. For example, Koekkoek (39) and Mustard and Tudisco (54) indicated that in spite of optimistic projections, many teachers had basic questions concerning the language lab, which adherents failed to answer. In words that would ring equally true today, Dostert (18) warned teachers to be less enamored of sophisticated hardware and to work instead at creating flexible and appropriate materials.

From its earliest use to its widespread dismantling in the late 1960s and early 1970s, the failure of the language lab concept has been blamed on a lack of appropriate audio and visual materials (Davies, 16), oversell (Holmes and Kidd, 27; McCoy and Weible, 46), inflexibility (Underwood, 89), and negative reactions from students (Rivers, 63). All these explanations are partially accurate in describing the decline of the lab, but they fail to identify the major source of the problem: No research was conducted on how best to utilize the technology to enhance language learning. The limited comparative studies (e.g., Keating, 38; Lorge, 42; Smith, 80) added little to knowledge about the technology and provided almost no direction on how best to manipulate specific potentials of the medium. Without adequate research to enable appropriate software to be designed, the language laboratory was doomed to fail.

CALL: Have We Learned Our Lesson?

One parallel between the profession's anticipation of miraculous results from the language laboratories of the 1960s and the impact expected of CALL in the 1980s is particularly noteworthy: There is still little research on effective pedagogical manipulations of the medium to guide the instructional designer, author, or practitioner.

For example, in discussing principles to follow when designing CALL, Curtin and Shinall (14) assert that students "should be challenged but in control of the material" (p. 12), without providing evidence why. But recent research in first-language computer-assisted reading indicates that program rather than user control of the display rate of a text typically results in higher reading speed and increased reading comprehension (Belland et al., 6). And at least one CALL study has indicated that program control over the display of a reading passage during comprehension checks via questioning results in more retention (Pederson, 58; 59).

Other testimonials similarly fail to cite research results largely owing to the inadequate investigatory procedures used to tout the computer's potential for effective CALL. What are cited are informal observations and attitude questionnaires (Taylor, 86), personal experience and student responses (Scanlan, 70), and surmised superior efficiency (Post, 60). In an article describing the positive reactions of students using CALL in first-year French, Hope (28) counsels that the need for research into CALL is exaggerated since "all devices are effective to the extent to which they are used efficiently and enthusiastically" (p. 350).

Second-language education is not alone in its failure to investigate theoretical issues and societal assumptions in the application of technology to education. Diamond (17) has observed that instructional design throughout much of its history has based most of its success on hunches and personal experience across disciplines. In the same vein, Eisele (20) observes that "scarcely anyone is now opposing the use of computers for learning; but, neither is anyone able to pronounce the *real* value of their use with any degree of confidence based on research" (p. 34).

Is it inevitable that "the bandwagon-to-pratfall history" of the language lab will be repeated (Arthurs, 4, p. 38)? Will CALL software ever begin to reach the level of pedagogical sophistication that many have claimed for it? What can be done to provide the complex information that instructional designers need to make informed decisions about how best to manipulate the many coding elements inherent in CALL? In short, what kind of empirical findings can best add to the highly limited theoretical base that exists in CALL and direct its applications?

Research in CALL: Analysis and Prognosis ——————

Whether foreign language educators decide to commit themselves to dispassionate, controlled research on CALL and its potential will determine to a large extent its ultimate credibility, longevity, and efficacy. The financial and human resources available for conducting this research are, unfortunately, quite limited. Holmes (26) warns, with respect to the use of computers to teach languages, that the profession must ask, "Do the benefits justify the time, energy, and money?" (p. 414); so too, must the profession consider carefully which CALL research efforts to fund. Studies should be undertaken that have the greatest probability of (1) providing language teachers and instructional designers with the greatest amount of and the most useful information possible, and (2) achieving longevity (i.e., not being obsolete before they are even printed) in spite of the rate which technology is expanding.

The following sections consider several different types of research and the likely resource (cost-time-energy) benefits that each stands to provide. An analysis of the purposes and limitations of several types of research (comparative, evaluative, basic) along with representative CALL studies that have been conducted to date should provide direction for future CALL research efforts.

Comparative Research Studies

Sample CALL Projects. Comparative research (medium A versus medium B) predominated prior to the mid-1970s. Morrison and Adams (52) conducted an exploratory investigation on the difference in achievement between first-year college students of German who studied using CALL and students who were taught using ALM language lab materials. Results after one year showed no difference between the CALL group and the lab group in overall achievement nor, similarly, in the four skills.

Other studies that compared CALL with traditional classroom learning (Adams and Rosenbaum, 2; Barrutia, 5) found no significant differences in learning that could be attributed to the CALL treatment. Williams (90) conducted an investigation to determine whether students enrolled in second-semester college French could learn five grammar points effectively through computer-assisted instruction as could others enrolled in conventionally taught language classes. The overall findings were that CALL students learned as well as but not significantly better than traditionally taught learners. Mellgren (48) attempted to determine the effect of computers on achievement in junior high school students of Spanish, but found no difference between the treatment group that completed written tasks with paper and pencil and the one that performed all assignments on the computer. These studies, however interesting, provide little usable information outside of their specific setting; for all, in one way or another, fall into the trap of attempting to attribute learning gains to the medium itself rather than to the way the medium was manipulated to affect achievement.

In recent years, researchers have shown marked improvement in the design of CALL studies though, unfortunately, many still overgeneralize the results and apply experimental outcomes to contexts not investigated. For example, Schrupp et al. (75) undertook to justify the cost of interactive video (IAV) equipment (video instruction driven by a CALL program) for language teaching at the U.S. Air Force Academy by demonstrating evidence of learning gains from use of the medium through study of a construct defined as "interactivity." On first consideration, the investigation appears appropriate and the results applicable to other institutions, until one stops to consider the fact that "interactivity" encompasses a wide range of IAV variables, including multiple trials, feedback (in the form of hints and provision of correct answers), remedial video replay, and unlimited time on task. Schrupp et al. write that the study endeavored "to measure any quantifiable advantage in learning outcome attributable to computer-assisted instruction [IAV treatment]"

(p. 17). Since the same comprehension questions that had been used as a strategy for practice in diverse treatments were reused as the dependent variable, the experiment was skewed seriously at the outset in favor of the IAV treatment whose students, not surprisingly, performed best. Clearly, any outcome of this experiment cannot be attributed with confidence to any one of these or any other unknown variable; in short, the results are of limited generalizable value beyond the specific experimental milieu.

Teichert (87) described an experiment to test the usefulness of the computer in aiding first-year college students of German to learn vocabulary and grammar, limiting one of the independent variables to "the materials." The CALL materials, however, were not described and delimited adequately for the reader; therefore, to ascribe to "the computer" itself the ability to bring about learning gains is entirely misleading, for the results were actually a function of the unknown characteristics of the CALL software used. As a result, any statistically significant differences cannot be ascribed to a replicable variable. Teichert identified 21 grammatical structures from the syllabus studied in class; the control group studied them via conventional workbook exercises and the experimental treatment completed CALL modules. As compared to the control treatment, the CALL modules held these features: immediate feedback, suggestions for review, repetition to 80 percent mastery, and "help." The results indicated that the CALL treatment group scored 10 percent better on the departmental posttest; however, in addition to an incomplete description of lesson content, the problems involved in interpreting these results are many. First, Teichert reported that it is "possible" that the CALL group practiced the material more than the control class, an uncontrolled difference that illustrates one of the built-in limitations of comparative research. Perhaps more important, even if the legitimacy of the 10 percent differential between groups were unquestioned, results attributed to CALL treatment overall can be neither interpreted nor ascribed ecological validity—the likelihood of being replicated elsewhere (Bracht and Glass, 8). In short, there is no way of knowing exactly what variable(s) in the CALL materials in question caused the reported results.

Dursky (19) compared the effectiveness of a CALL instructional format versus programmed learning for teaching Latin and Greek derivatives to first-year college students. Dursky hypothesized that because one medium is interactive (computer) and the other is somewhat passive by nature (programmed instruction), learning via the two would interact with personality types and learning styles. The research design, which moves a step beyond those that attempt to show that computers can teach any student as well as or better than some other medium, still holds a major flaw: the independent variables are not conceptualized theoretically and then described adequately. Dursky found that no differences emerged from the two treatments as measured by end-of-term tests and that none of the learning styles or personality-type variables interacted with the mode of instruction to affect achievement.

Even as recently as 1985 a major comparative project was conducted by Lozano et al. (43) at the University of Colorado to determine whether adding a weekly 45-minute CALL lab in place of one 45-minute language lab period for first-year college students would result in more effective teaching in listening, speaking, reading, writing, or grammar for beginning Spanish. After careful piloting, pretesting, validation, and revision of the criterion instruments, the experiment was conducted for an entire semester. The results indicate that the CALL group performed better than the lab group in the writing skill alone. Unlike much CALL comparative research that preceeded this experiment, considerable care was taken to ensure that (1) the intact classes were comparable, (2) other aspects of the teaching that occurred in both treatments were the same for both groups (including assignment of teachers to treatment groups, time of day classes were taught, and learning tasks) and (3) specific skills, as opposed to simple overall achievement, were tested.

The results indicated that some combination of the ways this particular CALL instruction was coded combined with the fact that the CALL group received 45 minutes less lab practice than the lab group resulted in better writing skills. But, because the independent variable (herein, mode of practice) is not delimited clearly for the reader, similar results could not be expected in the same practice format but with different software even in the same setting. In fact, the authors caution that all CALL software is not created (coded) equal. That the researchers were forced to write software to fit the students' needs illustrates the "situation-specific" nature of the experiment and, hence, the ungeneralizability of the outcome.

Theoretical Limitations.   Comparative research on computer-assisted versus noncomputer-assisted language instruction is incapable of providing generalizable results for many reasons. First, there is no way to replicate the conditions of the experiment exactly; therefore, the results lack consistency (reliability) from place to place. If the independent variable, for example, is "use of the computer versus use of a traditional method," how can the classroom teacher in another setting be assured that his or her use of the computer will be identical to that of the primary study? Second, there is no valid way to ascribe with confidence the causes for differences in the dependent variables to the independent variables. Without adequate controls, all of the possible causes for learning differences between one medium and another cannot be explained adequately, and the researcher is left with the dilemma of concluding that apples (CALL), for example, are superior to oranges (the language lab). Third, such studies usually fail to hold hypotheses based on language-learning theory, and, as a result, it is impossible (1) to integrate their results into the constantly expanding language-learning theoretical research base, and (2) to utilize the outcomes for adjustments in classroom teaching that will result in improved second-language learning.

Consider a typical, though fictitious, comparative study designed to show that CALL drill and practice is superior to paper-and-pencil workbook drill and practice. Suppose that the findings indicate that the CALL group of students perform better on the posttest than does the traditional workbook drill-and-practice group. Can it be asserted that CALL drill and practice, in general, is more effective than traditional drill and practice? What if the expected proficiency level of the students is changed; will the same results emerge? And what if students at a different age level are studied or the language of study is different? How can the researcher know which of the following variables might have affected learner outcomes:

novelty	learner expectations
feedback	place of practice
content	display mode and form
practice	cognitive response
answer-processing	motivation
response mode	audio
lesson format	. . .etc.

The point, however obvious, needs to be restated: *CALL, in and of itself, does not result in more and better learning; rather, it is the specific way instruction is coded in CALL software that has the potential of affecting learning positively, for specific learners in specific contexts.* All one can learn from the large comparative research efforts in mediated instruction is simply that if learning differences emerge in favor of one set of learners who used an unreplicable set of learning materials in an undefined context on a one-time basis, more learning occurred for one group than another, but one cannot ascribe the differences with confidence to any one variable.

In summary, researchers in instructional technologies have been discouraged countless times in the last decade from engaging in comparative investigations that attempt to show that one medium delivers instruction better than another. Hurly and Hlynka (34) have chided educators for placing emphasis upon a machine independent of its users; Ragsdale (62) reminds us that "one of the consequences of searching for ways to use computers has been a tendency to build from computer strengths rather than to build toward student weaknesses" (p. 3); Clark (12) notes that metanalysis after metanalysis of comparative studies from "five decades of research suggest that there are no learning benefits to be gained from employing different media in instruction, regardless of their obviously attractive features or advertised superiority" (p. 450); in fact, Clark warns that "studies comparing the relative achievement advantages of one medium over another will inevitably confound medium with method of instruction" (p. 451); Schramm (74) reminds us that "a common report among experimenters is that they find more variance *within* than *between* media—meaning that learning seems to be affected more by what is delivered than by the delivery system" (p. 273); and finally Salomon (68) explains "the cumulative finding is that media per se have no consistent differential effects on learning" (p. 144). Unquestionably, the temptation is great to conduct a research effort that will demonstrate, once and for all, that CALL compared to other modes of language learning (however defined) results in more learning. Given all the pitfalls of such broad comparative research, however, the profession simply cannot again indulge in such naive solutions to complex problems. The question must be, "How do computers make a difference?" Appropriate CALL research is needed to provide *theoretical, explanatory,* and *practical* information about the specific ways the computer can deliver instruction that is particularly well-suited to specific language learners who, in turn, perform clearly defined learning tasks.

Evaluative Research

Purpose and Potential.   Evaluative research is the most common form taken by applied research in CALL. Applied research is usually defined in relation to basic research. Basic research attempts to develop a theory of language learning and to provide explanatory principles for learning differences that emerge from ethnographic observations or controlled experiments; the purpose of applied research is to achieve practical objectives (solve problems, for example) in a specific learning situation or with a specific set of learning materials. To that end, the appropriateness of engaging in evaluative research is unquestionable.

One obvious practical problem in CALL is to provide evidence that a given software package is designed and programmed effectively. McCoy and Weible (46) note that reviewers must evaluate software packages intelligently, "reacting neither out of fear nor witless enthusiasm, but judging them truly on their merits" (p. 140). Haas (24) argues that sufficient guidelines for the testing and evaluation of CALL must be developed. Although intuition may play an important role in making the final match between software and student, evaluative research provides useful information on learning gains that may be achieved by specific users of a CALL package before the software reaches countless language learners. First, more precise documentation from software publishers is needed. In general too much leniency in this regard has been accorded software publishers. Courseware documentation rarely identifies the target learners, in fact the documentation from some CALL software claims that a given lesson can be "adapted" to fit a learner of nearly any age, at nearly any proficiency level, in nearly any context (Kyle, Pons and

Barnett, 40). Clearly, language teachers would never tolerate such vague marketing in the case of textbooks. Furthermore, the software reviews provided in nearly all professional journals (as useful as they are) can be no substitute for rigorous formative and summative evaluations during the process of creating the materials and readying them for market.

Steffin (83) offers useful guidelines for establishing the validity of software packages. They call for quantifiable data that (1) relate to specific educational objectives, (2) differentiate between the likely variances in potential users, (3) take the likely variations in instructional settings into account, (4) document opinions of a variety of users (not just software publishers or computer enthusiasts) concerning the software's quality. In short, language teachers should beware of evaluative research that claims more generalizability of uses and users than it can logically garner. The wise language teacher should examine evaluative research reports carefully for clear educational objectives, a specific target audience, and an adequate evaluative consensus from classroom teachers, students, and CALL experts. Only in this way can a good estimate be made of the quality of the match between the software and the potential student-user.

Finally, because evaluative research is software-specific, its results should not be published as research articles in professional journals. This recommendation does not diminish the importance of formative and summative evaluative research; it simply acknowledges the fact that most software evaluations become rapidly obsolete. Publishers make adjustments in CALL software on a continual basis. Thus CALL research that should be reported are those basic projects that offer new theoretical information about the psycholinguistic nature of language learning and the way in which a specific computer capability of delivering instruction—its coding elements—has been shown to affect or interact with the learning process. Such studies will stand the test of time.

Example Evaluative Projects.   An additional form that evaluative research may take is the informal survey conducted, for example, by a language department that may wish to determine the degree to which students are satisfied with the CALL software being utilized. Several such surveys have been reported in the literature (Hope, 28; Scanlan, 70; Simonsen, 77; Taylor, 86), but unfortunately too often they are used as a vehicle to substantiate claims of medium superiority. Surveys are generally regarded as accurate indicators of student attitude and perception of learning gains (Moore, 51), but the results cannot be applied to a larger population than the one from which the sample is drawn (as is the case of comparative research). In addition, the learners' experiences are software-specific, and the research results should not be generalized beyond the software in question.

Other CALL evaluative research is designed to provide formative and summative data during and after the development of new materials. These studies attempt to evaluate a variety of factors. For example, May

(45) engaged in a rigorous series of pilot investigations that generated data to develop and refine a computer-based program to teach basic writing skills to ESL students. Terry (88) developed a useful model for determining cost per user-hour in his evaluation of MONIQUE, a French drill-and-practice driver program. O'Brien (55) ran a prototype feasibility/pilot study to examine if it would be possible logistically to implement CALL for drill and practice in his German department. Brebner, Johnson, and Mydlarski (9) utilized a comparative research design to evaluate nine drill-and-practice lessons in French. No differences in learning resulted between traditionally taught students and the experimental group.

Finally, a rather encouraging development in the area of evaluative research on CALL has emerged recently. Language programs are beginning to turn to a consultant or a group of consultants to provide an analysis of CALL software needs, and of how best to meet them. Fought et al. (21) have recently completed an extensive project on behalf of the Defense Intelligence Agency. After in-depth interviews with potential users, a review of CALL software and of possible short-term and long-range solutions, several workable suggestions for the implementation of CALL have been provided to the DIA, all of which respect Steffin's (83) counsel that learner differences, the context, and the purpose for language study, as well as previous evaluations of the software, need be considered in evaluative research.

Basic CALL Research

Purpose and Potentials.   Recently, CAI theorists have become aware of the need for a greater percentage of future research to move beyond evaluative models toward more theoretical (basic) designs. Spitzer and Kielt (81) have observed that "through the standard procedures of evaluative research we are rarely able to understand the complex nature of the effects of the educational technology with which we are dealing" (p. 20). Another major benefit of engaging in basic CALL research in second-language education is that the researcher is constrained to adopt a dispassionate attitude toward the medium. Unlike comparative research (which has as its purpose providing evidence that CALL is effective) and unlike evaluative research (which attempts to document the quality of a given software package), the purpose of basic research is to discover something about the way students best learn a second language. Meredith (49) calls for more studies such as those conducted by Omaggio (57) and Mueller (53), which were designed to determine how variations in the use of a specific medium affect language learning. If a difference can be shown in favor of the way a specific coding capability of the computer can deliver instruction in a given circumstance for a given set of learners for a given learning task, then basic researchers should attempt to integrate what is already known about language learning into their discussion of how this new knowledge supports, refutes, or elaborates the theoretical base that already exists (Jarvis, 36). Likewise, such research results should provide CALL instructional designers with needed information that cannot be gathered solely through hunches, extrapolation, and intuition.

A Theoretical Base: Gavriel Salomon.   Gagné (22) asserts that it is time for a new approach to the study of media and points to Salomon (66, 68) for a theory that abandons the atheoretical bent of the past and provides a much-needed, convincing, and workable model for designing media research. Salomon's model takes into account the three most important variables in mediated instruction: the learner, the learning task, and the coding elements.

There are five basic tenets of Salomon's theory that are of particular importance to the design of CALL basic research:

1. *The ways a medium stores and delivers instruction (its coding elements) rather than the medium itself stands the best chance of affecting cognition.*

   The way CALL materials are designed and not the simple use of CALL versus some other medium is what will probably affect learning outcomes.

2. *These coding elements often mirror or activate a cognitive subskill in human learners (focusing, organizing, highlighting). These subskills are often those most affected in students as a result of the use of the coding element.*

   Word order accuracy, for example, will probably be affected by use of the computer's ability to remove cues from the screen during written answering, because this coding element activates that subskill in the learner.

3. *Different learners are affected in different ways by the use of any given coding element.*

   The removal of cues for early beginners performing written pattern practice, for example, may prove to activate and enrich the skill in high-verbal-ability learners, while it may serve to frustrate low-verbal-ability learners.

4. *Different learners are affected in different ways by their perceptions of the task expectations related to their use of instruction that is transmitted via a given coding element.*

   If a learner perceives, for example, that the instructor is not particularly concerned about accuracy in the placement of diacriticals, then the use of the computer's display coding element of highlighting errors and requiring correct insertion of accent marks before moving on will probably result in less retention of correct use of diacriticals than if the learner is aware that learning how to place accent marks is very important to success in his or her language class.

5. *A medium's coding elements often will interact with related learner differences and related learning tasks.*

For example, students whose learning style lends itself to accuracy will respond differently to the above example than ones who tend to fail to pay as much attention to detail. As a result, it is likely that degree of retention of diacritical placement will probably reflect the following declining order:

a). Accurate learners who believe the instructor requires accuracy

b). Inaccurate learners who believe the instructor requires accuracy

and

Accurate learners who believe the instructor does not require accuracy

c). Inaccurate learners who believe the instructor does not require accuracy

Salomon relies heavily upon Cronbach's Aptitude-Treatment Interaction (ATI) model (Cronbach and Snow, 13), which predicts that most students' individual differences will interact with the way they are taught and result in differential learning outcomes (see number 5 in the box above). Thus Salomon adds to aptitude and treatment a third variable, coding elements of a medium. In media research, the coding element rather than the medium itself stands to make the greater difference in instruction. Salomon encourages researchers to conduct studies that investigate relations among aptitude, learning tasks, and coding elements, because this type of investigation allows the most essential attributes of a medium and their related psychological functions to be studied together toward identifying how specific learners can be taught most efficiently and effectively. The three important elements of Salomon's design are detailed below.

Symbol systems and their coding elements.   Salomon (68) defines media as "our cultural apparatus for selecting, gathering, storing, and conveying knowledge in representational form" (p. 3). Any medium, such as CAI, is made up of many symbol systems, among other components. For example, in CAI, one important symbol system is *display.* The subcategories of a symbol system are its coding elements, those potentials of the symbol system to deliver instruction in particular ways. The symbol system display consists of many coding elements, including color, graphics, rate, timing, format, clarity, and print size. Symbol systems are of crucial importance to the instructional designer and researcher because they isolate particular ways in which a medium "relates cognition to learning" (p. 1). Rather than assuming, for example, that a medium as complex as CAI can be shown to make a difference, Salomon emphasizes the need to isolate an essential attribute of a medium that may affect learning and to examine it in relation to what is known about language learning.

Furthermore, Salomon asserts that, in spite of misconceptions, the subcategories of a medium's symbol systems—its coding elements—are not invariant (65). For example, a coding element such as "random access" can be utilized in such disparate media applications as a videodisc slide presentation (in which, for example, a computer can randomly access visuals to assist a student of French in reviewing various architectural aspects of major monuments in Paris) and flash cards (in which, for example, a beginning student of Russian can shuffle the cards to practice identifying letters in the Cyrillic alphabet).

In short, Salomon insists that no coding element can be attributed solely to one medium. Each medium, however, does "translate" coding elements in ways that will result in some differences from other media's utilization of them (e.g., the videodisc is capable of performing random access tasks much more efficiently than a person shuffling a deck of flash cards).

Task requirements.   Research on use versus nonuse of coding elements alone cannot be expected to yield satisfactory results. The learner's task orientation (perception of what is supposed to be learned) will determine the effect of a given coding element. Salomon describes this interaction in terms of selective attention. In short, students tend to assume that certain ways in which CALL is presented deserve special attention, depending upon their perception of the task they are expected to perform. In essence, students extract the information from CALL materials in a way that leads to optimal success in completing the learning task while at the same time internalizing (as noted by Weible in Chapter 3 of this volume) strategies of understanding and application that are reflected in future, related learning tasks. The wise instructional designer uses coding elements that learners perceive will help them to perform well.

It stands to reason, then, that a learner who believes the task of reading French is a matter of comprehending strings of words will respond differently to the use of the coding element "delayed display" (i.e., the timed, sequenced display of a reading text that adds one word at a time) than the learner who views reading French as a higher-level processing task in which frequent forward and backward eye regressions are needed. Hosenfeld (30, 31) illustrated how language learners are extremely conscious of task orientation. She found that language students tend to be very efficient problem-solvers and know how to take shortcuts. For Salomon, the essential research question in choosing the combination of coding element and task variables to investigate is whether the mental activities that the coding element activates are task-relevant. For example, because the use of the coding element "color display" (as opposed to monochromatic display) probably would have little bearing upon the retention of a reading text, it is unlikely that a study investigating the effects of color enhancements upon retention in reading will yield much useful information to CALL instructional designers. Much more useful would be investigations concerning display rate, display size, length of reading passages, frequency of interspersed comprehension questions, and other, more task-relevant coding elements.

Finally, Salomon has shown in research on film (67, 68) and television for children (68) that "increased experience with coded messages improves one's skill in extracting information from such messages" (68, p. 113). Put simply, the interaction of the coding element with the task can "short-circuit" a skill (perform extra processing that noncoding would normally require of the learner instead, such as "shuffling" the deck of Cyrillic alphabet cards); it can also code elements so that they can "activate" and "supplant" existent cognitive skills. Salomon has found that children who lack cognitive skills (such as focusing on the major point) can be taught to activate them by practicing these skills through their interaction with video presentations that use related coding elements effectively. Investigations should be conducted on the ways in which well-designed CALL software that uses coding elements efficiently may be able to activate and cultivate dormant but needed metacognitive strategies (developing strategic competence, acquiring vocabulary through listening comprehension, imitating phrases that are "turned" in a novel manner in the target language, raising the level of processing from a syntactic to a semantic level) in nonnative speakers. Such research has the potential of providing information to instructional designers toward delivering instruction that teaches languages while teaching students how to learn them.

Learner variables.   Salomon relies heavily on Cronbach and Snow's (13) analysis of the importance of individual learner differences but rejects the notion that any medium's coding element can serve all learners equally well. Goodman (23) concurs that in CAI research student variables are among the least likely factors to be given consideration by researchers in spite of their crucial nature.

Learner differences are complex and perplexing. The researcher needs to take into account such disparate contributing factors as cognitive development, preference for learning style, aptitude, and experience (available schemata). Because learners vary in their ability and willingness to adapt to task and coding demands, one can expect that (1) a specific use of any coding element will not be best for all language learners, and (2) that some interactions among aptitude, task, and coding element will emerge in CALL experiments. Therefore, in research design, Salomon urges the choice of the coding element that seems to be in best "correspondence to—or in contiguity with—the mode of internal representation that an individual with a given cognitive make-up and task can best utilize" (68, p. 73). Lesgold and Reif (41) cite convincing evidence for basing coding choices on known human information processing rather than on computer potentials, a necessary approach because discerning the match between the cognitive demands of a learning task and the processing demands of a coded message offers the best choice of providing experimental results that can be used as a model to enhance learning.

Research that fails to take learner differences into account falls into a trap similar to that of comparative research that seeks to demonstrate that one medium communicates better than another. Tasks that are coded by one medium cannot be expected to require the same amount of translation (cognitive drive needed to integrate the new material into an individual's cognitive structure) or elaboration (higher-level processing needed to make sense of new information) by all learners. Goodman (23) and Montague (50) note the key role that mental representations such as cognitive mapping play in cognition and call the inadequate consideration of these constructs in research the most untapped theoretical base; similarly they counsel that this area may be the most potentially fruitful for advancement in CAI research design.

In short, because language is processed internally by individuals with many different aptitudes, learning styles, and learning preferences, the key learner variable(s) that are called into play must be considered in research design along with task(s) and coding element(s). Without consideration for individual differences, the design of media research assumes that specific language-learning tasks are always best coded in specific ways. Although this type of research moves a needed step beyond that which compares, for example, learning in a traditional context versus learning via CALL, it still falls short of accounting accurately for the likely causes of variance in learning outcomes.

Salomon's model for media research in education can be applied easily to CALL. Such studies should be based on a foundation that takes into account the psycholinguistic factors that are known to play a crucial role in language acquisition. Furthermore, research on educational media should be holistic in the sense that it examine three crucial variables: coding element, task, and learner differences (Salomon and Clark, 69).

Types and Examples of Basic CALL Research _____

Experimental Research

The most obvious type of basic CALL research is experimental in nature. Such studies attempt to investigate the effect of the existence or manipulation of independent variables (learning styles, aptitude, learning task, the coding elements of the computer) upon dependent variables (achievement or attitude). Experimental studies are controlled and disciplined. Variables are chosen on the basis of language-learning theory, and the researcher develops one or more hypotheses that the independent variables under study may result in differences in the dependent variable (usually achievement) or interact with them.

One of the earliest basic CALL experiments was conducted by Schaeffer (71, 72) who studied how students are able to understand the content of materials presented in a drill or exercise format, that is, their levels of processing. The results of Schaeffer's research reaffirmed that value of higher-level processing (meaningful language practice) and extended our understanding of the value of contextualizing even language drills, while providing a needed first indication that meaningful practice is possible on the computer. Schaeffer hypothesized that the beginning language learner will usually exert the smallest amount of effort possible to accomplish a learning task. He therefore predicted that, in their interaction with CALL materials, learners would attend to semantic features of the language in drill-and-practice sentences only if such additional processing beyond the syntactic level were necessary for completing the learning task.

In a highly controlled experiment, undergraduate first-semester students of German were placed in one of two treatments after having received instruction on the present perfect tense. The first group practiced sentence-length exercises that focused on structure and required attention to the predicate only. The second group practiced semantic exercises that required focus first on the meaning of the sentence and secondarily on form. After one hour of study, the semantic group scored significantly higher on the semantic items in a criterion-referenced posttest composed of both syntactic and semantic problems. Although the difference between the two treatments in the syntactic items' postscores was not significant, the semantic group scored somewhat higher on that measure as well. Schaeffer attributed the differences between the two measures to the task variable (syntactic or semantic practice) and concluded that "while knowledge of the grammatical structure was the only requirement [for success] on the structural subtest, the key to successful accomplishment of the semantic task [demonstrated] a deeper level of [cognitive] processing" (71, p. 70). Schaeffer's seminal study demonstrated that even in the much-maligned drill-and-practice format, students can be oriented to process language meaningfully as a result of the careful preparation of learning materials.

Johansen and Tennyson (37) investigated the degree to which learner control of instruction (and learning gains) can be facilitated by using the computer to instruct the student on how to make instructional choices. Students were expected to learn punctuation rules for English via one of three treatments: advisement and full and partial learner control. The advisement learner-control group received guidance on how to proceed through the program (what branching choices to make) based on success in mastering the material, but after a short preliminary lesson was permitted to make its own decisions. The full learner-control group was able to choose its own practice units and could review at will with no guidance from the program based on learner success. The partial learner-control group was provided with a program-controlled preliminary CAI practice lesson on punctuation-rule learning and then was told to make its own choices (about what to practice or review) without advisement thereafter.

A comparison of results indicated that the advisement learner-control group performed best on a criterion-referenced posttest, providing evidence that instructional designers may code CALL software in such a way as to use the computer to teach strategies of instructional management. This study thus provides support for Salomon's assertion (66) that optimally coded CAI can activate dormant or underdeveloped metacognitive strategies. Perhaps even more important, it offers instructional designers needed preliminary information concerning how best to code CALL learning materials. Additional research is needed, however, to determine if advisement learner control interacts with related learner variables (field independence, locus of control, and aptitude).

In a related study in second-language education, Pederson (58, 59) examined three hypothesized independent variables related to levels of cognitive processing during CALL reading practice in French: verbal ability, type of comprehension question, and passage availability. The investigation was based on previous second-language research that indicated clearly that task orientation and level of processing (meaningful reading) are crucial variables in language practice. The coding element, passage availability, was defined as the computer's capability to keep a reading passage displayed on screen or remove it from the monitor during comprehension questioning. It was hypothesized that removing the passage would induce a higher level of processing in second-language readers, and thus, like the Schaeffer experiment, result in higher retention of the material presented in a reading text. The 2 x 2 x 2 factorial design (indicating three independent variables, each with two different treatments) was based on passage availability versus passage unavailability; low-level comprehension questions versus high-level comprehension questions; and low verbal ability versus high verbal ability. Students participated in the experiment for a single 50-minute period. All students read the same selection but, depending on their random assignment to treatments, answered either high-level (integrative) or low-level (vocabulary) questions, with or without the passage available for reinspection during questioning. After practice, learners wrote down as much as they could remember about the selection they had read. These data (protocols), in turn, were scored using a weighted propositional count (a listing of all idea units in the text, which were assigned values according to their relative importance to its overall meaning) to determine the dependent variable, recall. In addition, several simultaneous, unobtrusive measures (trials, correct responses, response latencies, and time on task) were collected by the computer for the purposes of hypothesis generation.

Experimental results indicated that passage unavailability during the answering of comprehension questions led to more retention. Furthermore, low-verbal-ability subjects showed less capacity to derive learning benefits from passage unavailability than did high-verbal-ability subjects. Finally, as expected, those subjects who answered high-level questions recalled much more from the reading than those who practiced low-level questions. This study reaffirmed that unneeded adjunct comprehension aids (e.g., low-level questions) may have distracted high-verbal-ability readers from attending to the meaning of a text, causing them to recall less than had they not been questioned.

The results from Pederson's investigation, while extending the research base that indicates that meaningful (contextualized) practice is better than mechanical (isolated) practice, illustrates that the particular use of a specific computer coding option (such as passage availability) can result in learning gains that are statistically significant for both high- and low-verbal-ability learners. Furthermore, these results lead to many other questions that are deserving of investigation: Can second-language learners be taught to reconstruct a reading text mentally and systematically while avoiding consultation of the text during comprehension questioning in order to enhance retention? Will long-term interaction with maximally coded CALL reading materials lead to purposeful reading strategies that help the learner even when the student is reading from the printed page? Are there any learner variables (such as locus of control or field independence) that will interact in CALL with the facilitative effects that have been shown for passage unavailability?

Two studies have provided useful information on the interaction of some of these learner differences and CALL. In the first, Chapelle and Jamieson (11) conducted a carefully controlled experiment to discern if ESL learners' choice to engage in CALL practice would serve as a predictor of success in language acquisition. Students in an intensive English program were invited by letter to participate in the research project that incorporated ESL CALL lessons in grammar, listening, and reading delivered on PLATO software. Unlike much previous comparative research, Chapelle and Jamieson provide a detailed description of the CALL programs used and the acknowledgment that "CALL effectiveness cannot be looked at as though CALL represented one form of instruction and all students were in need of that kind of instruction" (p. 42).

The variables examined were field independence/dependence (where field independence was defined as the ability to discern multiple meanings for ambiguous speech acts), ambiguity tolerance, motivational intensity, English-class anxiety, attitude toward CALL, voluntary time spent using CALL, and proficiency in English. The first research question—whether cognitive/affective variables would be related to attitudes and time spent using CALL—revealed a significant negative correlation between field independence and time spent using CALL. Likewise, a negative correlation emerged between field independence and attitude toward CALL. A positive correlation was found between CALL use and students who had high motivational intensity. Neither English-class anxiety nor ambiguity tolerance revealed a significant correlation with CALL. The data were analyzed to determine if both high motivational intensity and field independence were necessary to account for the variance in CALL use. The results of multiple regression analyses indicated that field independence was the exclusive predictor for time spent using CALL. Field-independent students did not like and failed to use the CALL lessons voluntarily in comparison with their field-dependent counterparts. Chapelle and Jamieson attribute these results to the coding of PLATO's ESL lessons, rather than to CALL in general, stating, "it is likely that the field independent students, who are capable of and accustomed to using their own internal referents, found the structured approach of the lessons in the ESL PLATO series to be inconsistent with their learning styles. They may have found it irritating to have information and exercises structured in a way different from how they would have done it themselves" (p. 38).

The second research question Chapelle and Jamieson examined was whether CALL would serve as a predictor of achievement in English beyond what can be estimated by entry-level achievement or affective/cognitive characteristics (field independence, ambiguity tolerance, motivational intensity, English-class anxiety). The researchers found that time spent in CALL was not a significant predictor of end-of-semester English proficiency.

This study provides useful preliminary indications of the necessity of giving adequate consideration to learning styles and attitudes in the design and use of CALL, and the need to include learner variables in the design of CALL experiments. Clearly, learner characteristics are capable of accounting for both learning differences and of interacting with other variables. Without attention to such constructs, research into CALL risks arriving at results that cannot be generalized with confidence to equal populations of students.

In a related study, Jamieson (35) used the computer as the medium of instruction for several purposes: (1) to investigate the effects of cognitive style (field independence and reflection/impulsivity—*studied* versus *quick* decision-making) upon achievement and (2) to identify work styles—deliberate approaches toward task completion—exhibited by learners interacting with CALL and their relationship with cognitive styles and achievement.

Advanced ESL students utilized CALL materials to practice spelling and dictation. The computer's accurate and untiring ability to count student errors and to record response latencies was the sole means used to determine work styles related to accuracy and speed. Various components of the TOEFL test were used as dependent measures. Results indicated that field independence was related to all measures of language achievement, while reflection was related to improvement on the TOEFL structure test. It was found that interaction rate (a combined measure of time and accuracy in responding) and monitoring of linguistic input (number of times students requested to hear cues from audiotapes) related negatively to achievement. Monitoring linguistic output (as measured by the number of edit/erases of the learner) was not related to any of the achievement measures. Work styles and cognitive styles exhibited some relationships. For example, field independence and impulsivity both related to response time (subscore of interaction rate). Reflective subjects both were slow while working on the CALL lessons and also requested to listen to the audio cues more often than impulsive students.

These findings show that computer software design needs to take both cognitive style and likely work style into account in the provision of options, timing, and the way scored exercises are tallied in order to enhance student motivation and student control. However, much more research on specific issues will need to be conducted before implications for specific instructional design decisions can be drawn with confidence.

Studies that use the computer as a research tool for data collection provide information that has long been unavailable to language education researchers (Abraham, 1; British Council, 10; Dalgish, 15; Simonsen, 77). Simultaneous practice measures (response latencies, trials, time on task) that have the potential to provide evidence about learning strategies during CALL practice and to generate data for statistical analyses concerning strategy/learner style interactions should continue to be collected in future CALL research efforts.

Perhaps the most ambitious CALL experimental endeavor to date has been conducted by Robinson et al. (64) at the Center for Language and Crosscultural Skills (CLCCS) in San Francisco. The authors posited several hypotheses (each based firmly in second-language education and psycholinguistic research) concerning the ways in which the computer's coding variables may stand the best chance of interacting with second-language learning. The purpose of the research was not to prove the effectiveness of CALL in general, but to provide evidence of how the manipulation of certain CALL coding elements may be particularly well suited to encouraging meaningful, communicative, and maximally facilitative CALL. In short, the CLCCS research design illustrates a pedagogical rather than a technological rationale for generating research questions and selecting variables.

Six pedagogical and four answer-judging hypotheses were posited. The pedagogical hypotheses predicted improved achievement as a result of the following types of materials presentation:

1. Integrated context for discrete structural items
2. Meaningful practice of structural items
3. Reference to people that students knew
4. Use of humor or emotion in order to involve the learner personally
5. Student choice of general context
6. Higher-level cognitive tasks (drawing inferences or problem solving)

The four answer-judging hypotheses predicted greater learning gains for

students who, when they answered incorrectly, were
1. Given feedback that caused them to discover their error
2. Provided assistance with a degree of personal control whether or not to use it
3. Provided with implicit rather than explicit correction
4. Given the same items to practice again at spaced intervals

Students were given two tests prior to the study: the Pimsleur Language Aptitude Battery (PLAB) and a specially constructed test of prior knowledge of Spanish, based on the language material to be covered during CALL practice, also used as a posttest. For nine days, junior-high students practiced Spanish with CALL materials designed especially for this experiment. Each hypothesis was tested using identical materials except for the single variable under inspection. Each day, after approximately 20 minutes of CALL practice, the learners were given a short test to determine any progressive learning gains. Several posttests of achievement, attitude, and aptitude were administered after the entire series of subexperiments was conducted. The results showed that the experimental group (students who practiced with CALL vis à vis the ten hypotheses above) significantly outperformed the control group (students who practiced under the opposite conditions) in cumulative achievement and when scores were mediated by prior knowledge. That is, the results suggested that meaningful and discovery-oriented CALL leads to more learning than CALL that is less communicative and more directive. Although the study clearly identified and isolated variables in the experimental treatment, these larger findings may have limited value for future CALL development owing to the problem of ascribing gains in *cumulative* achievement to any one particular variable. It should be noted however, that the CLCCS study did emphasize variables that have a strong pedagogical base in the research that shows meaningful practice and discovery learning both result in higher achievement in language learning than does mechanical practice.

On the other hand, the results from the individual subexperiments on various types of answer judging defined in the CLCCS study provide the most specific and therefore immediately useful information for CALL instructional designers. In three cases, all of them answer-judging experiments, the experimental group outperformed the control group significantly—student discovery of errors, combination of student control over and program feedback for help, and implicit correction. These particular results provide compelling evidence for the future coding of answer processing in CALL materials in ways that will cause the learner to be engaged actively in discovering his or her errors.

The statistically significant results in favor of the control group are less instructive, for example, where the CALL lessons named persons known to the students and provided meaningful rather than simple manipulative practice, the control groups outperformed the experimental groups. The researchers suggested many reasons that a discrepancy would emerge between daily subtest scores for the pedagogical hypotheses and cumulative achievement scores, the most plausible being that immediate recall (which was accessed in the day-to-day subtests) is an unreliable and even inappropriate measure of learning. The entire investigation probably would have benefited from delayed retesting to allow more accurate measures of differential learning to occur, but that was not feasible in this experimental setting.

The CLCCS study provides considerable impetus and a worthy model for continued investigation into specific ways in which the computer's coding of CALL can be shown to interact with effective language-learning strategies. In the future, it is hoped that more experiments of this type will be conducted and that they will take the learning task and its related coding element into account. Furthermore, future research should investigate related differences in learning style, learning preference, and aptitude as independent variables in addition to simply controlling for them.

Ethnographic Research

In addition to experimental studies, data are needed that will identify what type of hypotheses should be tested empirically. Ethnographic research on CALL provides insights to that end. The ethnographic researcher usually enters the natural domain of CALL (the classroom or the learning resource center) and through a variety of unobtrusive techniques, including carefully controlled observation and interviewing, gathers data that are then examined as a source of hypotheses concerning the nature of language learning or the effect of materials, strategies, or curricula in place. The ethnographic CALL researcher attempts, as much as possible, to relate learning patterns and variations to previous second-language education research. Furthermore, data are often subjected to quantitative analysis to ensure accuracy and to facilitate interpretation. Rather distinct uses of ethnographic methods have been used in three extensive CALL research projects (Lozano et al., 43; Blomeyer, 7; Robinson et al., 64).

Lozano et al. (43) attempted to discern if a CALL adjunct to a traditional first-year college Spanish curriculum would be more beneficial than using the same amount of time for scheduled language lab practice (see "Comparative Studies" above). In addition to the extensive quantitative data collected from pretests, attitude questionnaires, posttests, learning checks, and attendance records, the researchers decided to enhance their study's design and explanatory power by including ethnographic observations. A single ethnographer was given the task of observing the classes and lab sessions under study at the University of Colorado, interviewing students and instructors to discern attitudes and problems with the procedures and materials, and reporting on tendencies, variations, and patterns. The researchers indicated that the ethnographer's observations during the pilot study were particularly useful in eliminating irregularities in the teaching that occurred in the individual class sections. Of particular interest to the CALL researcher are the observations made during student use of computers and other lab equipment. The data indicated that students using the computer lab had a more positive attitude toward required lab practice than those who used the language lab.

The CLCCS study reported above (64) also incorporated an ethnographic approach. Interviews with students were recorded on videotape in the computer lab and in classroom discussion sessions as were sessions with staff and observers. The transcripts of the interviews provided in the final report revealed information that would probably never have come to the attention of the researchers and teachers, though it was accessed solely through asking people what they were thinking and why. The ethnographic data revealed both positive and negative views toward CALL practice. Overall, five positive general comments emerged: (1) the computer was a forgiving tutor, (2) the computer treated all students the same, (3) self-pacing and individualization were viewed as beneficial, (4) students were more motivated to stay "on task" than in regular classroom activities, and (5) students became more computer-literate. The negative comments referred to the fact that (1) the computer was too inflexible, (2) its novelty wore off after a while, and (3) it was impersonal.

A study by Blomeyer (7) is a third example of ethnographic research. Blomeyer examined the use of CALL as a curricular innovation in two on-site case studies in high schools and through a study of policy analysis in order to make "a preliminary assessment of its [CALL's] impact on the practices common to second language teaching in secondary schools" (p. 5). Data were collected within the classrooms and in microcomputer laboratories, through interviews with teachers, students, and administrators. Some of the most interesting preliminary findings were that no specific characteristics of the CALL software interfered with the educational objective of the material. On the other hand, CALL use did not appear to influence problem solving or other higher-level cognitive strategies. In addition, the ethnographer noted a tendency for students to speak highly of CALL lessons that they knew their own teacher had written (a similar result was observed in the research conducted by Lozano et al. [43]). Such students appeared to have developed a sense of ownership and pride in CALL software that was not exhibited by learners using CALL written by persons unknown to them. Blomeyer's data also indicated no particular characteristic of microcomputer technology that alone led to better gains in learning by any particular sociological grouping (sex, age, social class, value orientation). Finally, the data provide convincing evidence that language teachers must learn how to enter a whole new technological, cultural, and political realm when they begin to implement CALL into the curriculum. The observations from this study indicate that language teachers must develop the ability to make districtwide policies work for them as they attempt to become computer-literate and to procure hardware and software, in an effort to improve their teaching. In short, they must be willing to emerge from the culture of the classroom and enter the culture of the learning center (House, 32); and they must be willing to garner computer time assertively, carefully, and convincingly for their language students.

Countless research questions become immediately apparent upon reading the Blomeyer study: What long-term effects on the quality of teaching might result from continued classroom teacher commitment to software design and programming? What types of rewards are school districts willing to make for such efforts? Do students learn more from CALL materials when the author is their own teacher? The list could go on and on. Suffice it to say, such research provides needed preliminary information for hypothesis generation that would, perhaps, never come to the attention of researchers without the use of ethnographic research methodology.

Formal Surveys

CALL basic research can take the form of formal surveys. Surveys are challenging to construct and require a considerable amount of validation prior to their use. Nevertheless, by sampling just a small percentage of CALL users, formal surveys have the potential of identifying special needs, frustrations, misconceptions, and other useful information.

Two surveys concerning CALL that have been particularly informative are those by Olsen (56) and Stolurow and Cubillos (85). Olson investigated the current or planned use of CALL in departments of foreign languages nationwide, collected the names of faculty presently using CALL, and solicited advice and comments for the neophyte teacher–user. Although Olson acknowledged that the design of the survey lent itself toward response more from CALL users than from nonusers, on a purely descriptive level the structure and content of the survey provided interesting insights and possible impetus for a future effort that would involve more formal data analysis. Results indicated that computer users tend to be enthusiastic about CALL while nonusers tend to express concerns about the dehumanizing influence of machines on language learning. Respondents who employ CALL indicated that students' attitudes toward language study generally improved, and that students learned more material faster than when they used traditional workbooks.

Stolurow and Cubillos (85) conducted a national survey of teachers, authors, administrators, distributors, and publishers to determine their perception of needs and desired opportunities for CALL. Results indicated that the most commonly mentioned need was for more courseware. In addition, teachers expressed the desire for more quality control and improved evaluation of software, and for more effective dissemination of CALL lessons. The most commonly desired opportunity was more training, specifically in the capabilities of CALL and on how to integrate software packages into an existing curriculum. The report concludes with several recommendations of improvements in teacher training and development, in CALL software development, and in professional priorities for the medium.

Conclusion

This chapter has counseled that CALL research should be conducted vigorously, but that the research design chosen for such studies should take into account a number of factors. First, the research itself should be cost-effective; the profession needs to receive the highest possible return for time and effort. Research efforts that stand the best chance of providing explanatory data and adding to the theoretical bases for second-language learning have a greater likelihood of longevity and ecological validity. Second, it has been argued that comparative research that attempts to illustrate the superiority of computers over some other medium for delivering language instruction should forever be abandoned. Finally, encouragement should be given to evaluative research using CALL software that may be widely adopted and may enjoy an extended use over time. Such research helps to ensure a good match between user and software.

Although far too little research on CALL has been conducted, some rather clear foundational tenets are emerging that support previous research in education in general, and in second-language education specifically:

1. Meaningful (as opposed to manipulative) CALL practice is both possible (Schaeffer, 71, 72) and preferable (Pederson, 58, 59; Robinson et al., 64; Schaeffer, 71, 72).
2. The way CALL is designed to encourage the development of language learning skills can result in more learning (Johansen and Tennyson, 37; Pederson, 58, 59; Robinson et al., 64).
3. Learner differences can be documented easily and accurately through computer tally of interactive learning strategies (Jamieson, 35; Pederson, 58).
4. Learner differences can affect learner strategies, learning gains, and attitude in CALL (Chapelle and Jamieson, 11; Pederson, 59).
5. Students tend to demonstrate a more positive attitude toward CALL materials written by their own instructor (Blomeyer, 7; Lozano et al., 43).

6. Language teachers need to develop strategies for maneuvering effectively within the culture of the learning laboratory and the educational institution in order to secure needed computer resources (Blomeyer, 7).

7. Despite the enthusiasm of language teachers who are already using CALL (Olsen, 56), many language teachers are dissatisfied with existent CALL software and desire training on how to integrate CALL into the existing curriculum (Stolurow and Cubillos, 85).

In short, the research clearly indicates that CALL is highly context-bound. The nature of the learners, the task they believe they are supposed to perform, and the way the CALL materials are designed all play individual and interdependent roles in determining learning outcomes. Researchers should continue to investigate all three variables in a variety of contexts in future CALL basic studies.

While classroom teachers cannot be expected to devote their time to grassroots research, there is much they can do. First, they can become critical consumers of research reports and refuse to accept comparative research results as either valid or reliable. Second, they can lend support to basic research on CALL by providing experimenters with insights and potential research questions that emerge as they observe their students using the medium. Third, they can support appropriate research by making their students available as experimental subjects. Fourth, they can encourage more evaluative research by simply demanding such reports from software distributors before investing in major software packages. Finally, they can refuse to be carried away by the current enthusiasm for "proving" that computers are somehow "better" than some other mode of instruction. Rather, teachers should show interest and openness to experimenting with the new technology to discover how it can best benefit the learner, but they should avoid the tendency to make sweeping claims about the computer's effectiveness.

In his description of appropriate second-language research methodologies, Stern (84, p. 63) observes

> language teaching theory has had a strong preference for speculation, the expression of personal opinion, the explanation of practical experience, and participation in controversy—all perfectly legitimate ways of finding directions provided they are balanced by systematic empirical procedures. But in language teaching theory we have tended *to neglect the collection of empirical data* [emphasis added]

Jarvis (36) urges "that we must emphasize and vastly increase subject-matter-specific research knowledge" (p. 396). Such an increased interest in disciplined, dispassionate research that attempts patiently and carefully to add to what is already known about how students learn languages is the best assurance that CALL, unlike the language lab of the 1960s, will be used intelligently.

References, Research on Computer-Assisted Language Learning

1. Abraham, Roberta G. "Field Independence–Dependence and the Teaching of Grammar." *TESOL Quarterly* 19, 4 (1985):689–702.
2. Adams, Edward N., and Peter S. Rosenbaum. *DLI–IBM Joint Feasibility Study in Computer-Assisted Foreign Language Instruction.* Final report. Monterey, CA: Defense Language Institute, 1969. [EDRS: ED 032 542.]
3. Alatis, James. "The Application of Instructional Technology to Language Learning." *CALICO Journal* 1, 1 (1983):9–12,14.
4. Arthurs, J. "The Language Lab: Cybernetics and Self-Interest." *The Canadian Modern Language Review* 36 (1979–80):38–48.
5. Barrutia, Richard. "Two Approaches to Self-Instructional Language Study: Computerized Foreign Language Instruction." *Hispania* 53 (1970):361–71.
6. Belland, John C., William D. Taylor, James Canelos, Francis Dwyer, and Patti Baker. "Is the Self-Paced Instructional Program, via Micro-Computer Based Instruction, the Most Effective Method of Addressing Individual Learning Differences?" *Educational Communications and Technology Journal* 33 (1985):185–98.
7. Blomeyer, Robert L. "The Use of Computer-Based Instruction in Foreign Language Teaching: An Ethnographically-Oriented Study." Unpublished Ph.D. dissertation. Urbana, IL: The University of Illinois, 1985.
8. Bracht, Glenn H., and Gene V. Glass. "The External Validity of Experiments." *American Educational Research Journal* 5 (1968):437–74.
9. Brebner, Ann, Ken Johnson, and Donna Mydlarski. "CAI and Second Language Learning: An Evaluation of Programs for Drill and Practice in Written French." *Computers and Education* 8 (1984):471–74.
10. British Council. *The ESP Teacher: Role, Development, and Prospects.* ELT Documents 112. London, England: British Council, 1981. [EDRS: ED 258 463.]
11. Chapelle, Carol, and Joan Jamieson. "Computer-Assisted Language Learning as a Predictor of Success in Acquiring English as a Second Language." *TESOL Quarterly* 20, 1 (1986):27–46.
12. Clark, Richard E. "Reconsidering Research on Learning from Media." *Review of Educational Research* 53 (1983):445–59.
13. Cronbach, Lee Joseph, and Richard E. Snow. *Aptitudes and Instructional Methods: A Handbook of Research on Interactions.* New York: Irvington, 1977.
14. Curtin, Constance, and Stanley Shinall. "Programing for Learning." *CALICO Journal* 1, 5 (1984):12–16.
15. Dalgish, Gerard M. "Computer-Assisted ESL Research." *CALICO Journal* 2, 2 (1984):32–37.
16. Davies, Norman F. "Foreign/Second Language Education and Technology in the Future." *NALLD Journal* 16, 3, 4 (1982):5–13.
17. Diamond, Robert M. "Instructional Development: One Biased View (Problems, Issues, and the Future)." *Educational Technology* 20, 2 (1980):51–54.
18. Dostert, Leon E. "Tradition and Innovation in Language Teaching: The Changing Times." *The Modern Language Journal* 44 (1960):220.
19. Dursky, Janice. "Comparison of a Computer Assisted Instructional Unit and a Programmed Text Format for Teaching Latin and Greek Derivatives to

Conditionally Enrolled University Students." Unpublished Ph.D. dissertation. Des Moines, IA: The Drake University, 1983.

20. Eisele, James E. "Computers and Learning: Some Needed Research." *Educational Technology* 24, 2 (1984):34–35.

21. Fought, John, Catherine Doughty, Dana Boatman, and Richard Young. "Automated Methods in Foreign Language Training and Instruction." Language Analysis Project, The University of Pennsylvania (Philadelphia), 1986.

22. Gagné, Robert M. "Is Educational Technology in Phase?" *Educational Technology* 20, 2 (1980):7–14.

23. Goodman, H. J. A. "Cognitive Mapping, Learning Styles, and Sensory Preference as Factors in Individualized Instructions: A Position Paper on the As Yet Largely Untapped Research Potential of Integrated Information Systems When Combined with Educational Technology." Paper presented at the Annual Meeting of the American Educational Research Association, Toronto, Canada, March 1978. [EDRS: ED 161 407.]

24. Haas, Werner. "The Potential and Limitation of Computer Assisted Instructions in the Teaching of Foreign Languages." Paper presented at the Annual Meeting of the American Council on the Teaching of Foreign Languages, New Orleans, November 1976. [EDRS: ED 139 269.]

25. Hocking, Elton. "How Far Have the Modern Foreign Languages Progressed since World War II?" *The Modern Language Journal* 43 (1959):168.

26. Holmes, Glyn. "The Computer and Limitations." *Foreign Language Annals* 17 (1984):413–14.

27. _____, and Marilyn E. Kidd. "Second-Language Learning and Computers." *The Canadian Modern Language Review* 38 (1981–82):503–16.

28. Hope, Geoffrey R. "Elementary French Computer-Assisted Instruction." *Foreign Language Annals* 15 (1982):347–53.

29. _____, Heimy F. Taylor, and James P. Pusack. *Using Computers in Teaching Foreign Languages*. Language and Education: Theory and Practice, no. 57. Orlando, FL: Harcourt Brace Jovanovich, 1984. [EDRS: ED 246 695.]

30. Hosenfeld, Carol G. "A Learning-Teaching View of Second-Language Instruction: The Learning Strategies of Second-Language Learners with Reading-Grammar Tasks." Unpublished Ph.D. dissertation. Columbus, OH: The Ohio State University, 1977.

31. _____. "The New Student Role: Individual Differences and Implications for Instruction," pp. 129–67 in Gilbert A. Jarvis, ed., *Perspective: A New Freedom*. The ACTFL Foreign Language Education Series. Lincolnwood, IL: National Textbook Company, 1976.

32. House, Ernest R. *The Politics of Educational Innovation*. Berkeley, CA: McCutcheon, 1974.

33. Huebener, Theodore. *Audio-Visual Techniques in Teaching Foreign Languages*. Rev. ed. New York: New York University Press, 1967.

34. Hurly, Paul, and Denis Hlynka. "Prisoners of the Cave: Can Instructional Technology Improve Education?" Paper presented at the National Conference on Instructional Technology, National Research Council of Canada, Toronto, 1982. [EDRS: ED 244 608.]

35. Jamieson, Joan. "Cognitive Styles, Working Styles on Computers and Second Language Learning." Unpublished Ph.D. dissertation. Urbana, IL: The University of Illinois, 1986.

36. Jarvis, Gilbert A. "The Psychology of Second-Language Learning: A Declaration of Independence." *The Modern Language Journal* 67 (1983):393–402.

37. Johansen, Keith J. and Robert D. Tennyson. "Effect of Adaptive Advisement Perception in Learner-Controlled, Computer-Based Instruction Using a

Rule-Learning Task." *Educational Communication and Technology* 31 (1983):226–36.
38. Keating, Raymond F. *A Study of the Effectiveness of Language Laboratories.* New York: Columbia University Teachers College, Institute of Administrative Research, 1963.
39. Koekkoek, Byron J. "The Advent of the Language Laboratory." *The Modern Language Journal* 43 (1959):4–5.
40. Kyle, Patricia J., Cathy R. Pons, and Marva A. Barnett. "Computer Lesson Design for Elementary French: A Methodological Approach," pp. 68–74 in Patricia B. Westphal, ed., *Strategies for Foreign Language Teaching: Communication, Technology, Culture.* Proceedings of the Central States Conference on the Teaching of Foreign Languages. Lincolnwood, IL: National Textbook Company, 1984.
41. Lesgold, Alan, and Frederick Reif. *Computers in Education: Realizing the Potential.* Chairman's Report of a Research Conference, Pittsburgh, Pennsylvania, November 20–24, 1982. Washington, DC: Office of Educational Research and Improvement (ED), June 1983. [EDRS: ED 235 783.]
42. Lorge, Sarah W. "Language Laboratory Research Studies in New York City High Schools: A Discussion of the Program and the Findings. *The Modern Language Journal* 48 (1964):409–19.
43. Lozano, Anthony G., Beth J. Dublinski, Terry Halwes, Ralph B. Kite, and Sharon Ludwig. *Colorado CAI Spanish Research Project.* Final Report. Boulder, CO: University of Colorado, International Research and Studies Program, 1985.
44. Mathieu, Gustave. "One Answer to Advanced Lab Work." *The Modern Language Journal* 44 (1960):352–54.
45. May, Barbara Ann. "Effective Instruction for Teaching Basic Writing Skills with Computer-Assisted Language Learning in an English as a Second Language Program." Unpublished Ph.D. dissertation. Kingsville, TX: Texas A&I University, 1984.
46. McCoy, Ingeborg H., and David M. Weible. "Foreign Languages and the New Media: The Videodisc and the Microcomputer," pp. 105–52 in Charles J. James, ed., *Practical Applications of Research in Foreign Language Teaching.* The ACTFL Foreign Language Education Series. Lincolnwood, IL: National Textbook Company, 1983.
47. McGraw, Myrtle B. "The Roles of the Teacher and the Student in the Electronic World." *The Modern Language Journal* 43 (1959):218–20.
48. Mellgren, Millie. "Applying Microcomputers in the Foreign Language Classroom: Challenges and Opportunities," pp. 74–78 in Alan Garfinkel, ed., *The Foreign Language Classroom: New Techniques.* Proceedings of the Central States Conference on the Teaching of Foreign Languages. Lincolnwood, IL: National Textbook Company, 1983.
49. Meredith, R. Alan. "Materials and Equipment: The New Generation." *The Modern Language Journal* 67 (1983):424–30.
50. Montague, William E. "Analysis of Cognitive Processes in the Specification of Interactive Instructional Presentations for Computer-Based Instruction." Paper presented at the Annual Meeting of the American Educational Research Association, New York, March 1982. [EDRS: ED 224 476.]
51. Moore, Gary W. *Developing and Evaluating Educational Research.* Boston: Little, Brown, 1983.
52. Morrison, H. W., and E. N. Adams. "Pilot Study of a CAI Laboratory in German." *The Modern Language Journal* 52 (1968): 279–87.
53. Mueller, Gunther A. "Visual Contextual Cues and Listening Comprehension: An Experiment." *The Modern Language Journal* 64 (1980):336–40.

54. Mustard, Helen, and Anthony Tudisco. "The Foreign Language Laboratory in Colleges and Universities: A Partial Survey of Its Instructional Use." *The Modern Language Journal* 43 (1959):332–40.
55. O'Brien, George M. "Siren Songs and a Skeptic." Paper presented at the International Conference on Computers and the Humanities, Los Angeles, April 1985. [EDRS: ED 104 163.]
56. Olsen, Solveig. "Foreign Language Departments and Computer-Assisted Instruction: A Survey." *The Modern Language Journal* 64 (1980):341–49.
57. Omaggio, Alice C. "Pictures and Second Language Comprehension: Do They Help?" *Foreign Language Annals* 12 (1979):107–16.
58. Pederson, Kathleen Marshall. "The Effects of Passage Availability during Adjunct Questioning in Computer-Assisted Reading Practice on Recall Measures of Reading Comprehension in Intermediate College French." Unpublished Ph.D. dissertation. Columbus, OH: The Ohio State University, 1985.
59. _____. "An Experiment in Computer-Assisted Second-Language Reading." *The Modern Language Journal* 70, 1 (1986):36–41.
60. Post, Nancy E. "Microcomputers and Language Training." *Journal of Educational Technology Systems* 11 (1983):277–83.
61. Putnam, Constance E. "Foreign Language Instructional Technology: The State of the Art." *CALICO Journal* 1, 1 (1983):35–41.
62. Ragsdale, Ronald G. "The Computer Threat to Educational Technology." Paper presented at the Annual Meeting of the Association for Educational Communications and Technology, Research and Theory Division, Dallas, 1982. [EDRS: ED 223 231.]
63. Rivers, Wilga M. "Understanding the Learner in the Language Laboratory." *NALLD Journal* 16, 2 (1982):5–13.
64. Robinson, Gail, John Underwood, Wilga Rivers, José Hernández, Carollyn Rudesill, and Clare Malnik Enseñat. "Computer-Assisted Instruction in Foreign Language Education: A Comparison of the Effectiveness of Different Methodologies and Different Forms of Error Correction." San Francisco: Center for Language & Crosscultural Skills, 1985. [EDRS: ED 262 626.]
65. Salomon, Gavriel. "Media and Symbol Systems as Related to Cognition and Learning." *Journal of Educational Psychology* 71 (1979):131–48.
66. _____. "What Is Learned and How It Is Taught: The Interaction between Media, Message, Task, and Learner," pp. 383–406 in David R. Olson, ed., *Media and Symbols: The Forms of Expression, Communication, and Education.* 73rd Yearbook of the National Society for the Study of Education. Chicago: University of Chicago Press, 1974.
67. _____. "Internalization of Filmic Schematic Operations in Interaction with Learners' Aptitudes." *Journal of Educational Research* 66 (1974):499–511.
68. _____. *Interaction of Media, Cognition, and Learning.* Washington, DC: Jossey-Bass, 1979.
69. _____, and Richard E. Clark. "Reexamining the Methodology of Research on Media and Technology in Education." *Review of Educational Research* 47 (1979):99–120.
70. Scanlan, Richard T. "Computer-Assisted Instruction in Latin." *Foreign Language Annals* 13 (1982):53–55.
71. Schaeffer, Reiner H. "Computer-Supplemented Structural Drill Practice versus Computer-Supplemented Semantic Drill Practice by Beginning College German Students: A Comparative Experiment." Unpublished Ph.D. dissertation. Columbus, OH: The Ohio State University, 1979.
72. _____. "Meaningful Practice on the Computer: Is It Possible?" *Foreign Language Annals* 14 (1981):33–37.
73. Scherer, George, and Michael Wertheimer. *A Psycholinguistic Experiment in*

Foreign Language Teaching. New York: McGraw-Hill, 1964.
74. Schramm, Wilbur. *Big Media, Little Media.* Beverly Hills, CA: Sage Publications, 1977.
75. Schrupp, David M., Michael D. Bush, and Gunther A. Mueller. *"Klavier in Haus:* An Interactive Experiment in Foreign Language Instruction," *CALICO Journal* 1, 1 (1983):17–21.
76. Siciliano, Ernest A. "Language Laboratories Develop the Listening Ear." *The Modern Language Journal* 43 (1959):224–25.
77. Simonsen, Sofus E. "Student Approach and Reaction to CAI: An Analysis of Evaluations and Logs." *CALICO Journal* 3, 2 (1985):35–39.
78. Smith, Philip D. and Emanuel Berger. *An Assessment of Three Foreign Language Teaching Strategies Utilizing Three Language Laboratory Systems.* Washington, DC: U.S. Office of Education, 1968.
79. Smith, R. Lorne. "Some Considerations That Seem to Weigh against the Use of Tape Recordings in the Language Laboratory." *The Modern Language Journal* 44 (1960):75–76.
80. Smith, Wm. Flint. Language Learning Laboratory," pp. 191–237 in Dale L. Lange, ed., *Encyclopaedia Britannica Review of Foreign Language Education,* vol. 2. Chicago: Encyclopaedia Britannica, 1972.
81. Spitzer, Dean R., and James P. Kielt. "Technology Assessment: An Antidote for Murphy's Law." *Educational Technology* 17, 7 (1977):20–23.
82. Stack, Edward M. *The Language Laboratory and Modern Language Teaching.* 3rd. ed. New York: Oxford University Press, 1971.
83. Steffin, Sherwin A. "A Suggested Model for Establishing the Validity of Computer-Assisted Instructional Materials." *Educational Technology* 23, 1 (1983):20–22.
84. Stern, H. H. *Fundamental Concepts of Language Teaching.* Toronto: Oxford University Press, 1983.
85. Stolurow, Lawrence, and Enrique M. Cubillos. *Needs and Development Opportunities for Educational Software for Foreign Language Instruction in Schools.* Iowa City, IA: Center for Educational Experimentation, Development, and Evaluation, University of Iowa, June 1983. [EDRS: ED 242 204.]
86. Taylor, Heimtraut F. "Students' Reactions to Computer Assisted Instruction in German." *Foreign Language Annals* 12 (1979):289–91.
87. Teichert, Herman U. "Computer Assisted Instruction in Beginning College German: An Experiment." *CALICO Journal* 3, 2 (1985):18–24.
88. Terry, Robert A. "MONIQUE: The Assistante." Paper presented at the Annual Foreign Language Conference sponsored by the Division of Secondary Education, Richmond, VA, October 1978. [EDRS: ED 145 725.]
89. Underwood, John H. *Linguistics, Computers, and the Language Teacher: A Communicative Approach.* Rowley, MA: Newbury House, 1984.
90. Williams, Roger. "Design, Development, and Testing of Five Computer-Assisted Instruction Lessons in French Grammar. Unpublished Ph.D. dissertation. Athens, GA: The University of Georgia, 1980.
91. Wyatt, David H. *Computers and ESL.* Language and Education: Theory and Practice. no. 56. Orlando, FL: Harcourt Brace Jovanovich, 1984. [EDRS: ED 246 694.]
92. Young, Biloine. "A Do-It-Yourself Language Lab." *The Modern Language Journal* 43 (1959):221–23.

6

Relating Second-Language Acquisition Theory to CALL Research and Application

Catherine Doughty

University of Pennsylvania

Introduction

How students can be brought to learn a second language efficiently is, perhaps, the most compelling question language teachers ask of themselves. Traditionally, there have been two investigatory approaches to an answer: classroom teachers have gained insight into language learning by observation and teaching; and simultaneously, researchers have attempted to formulate theoretical models to explain the complex process of second-language acquisition (SLA). For some time, however, the language teaching field has suffered from a distrust of what theory and research can offer pedagogy because the thinking of theorists is often "loaned" (though unsolicited) from disciplines such as linguistics and cognitive psychology, whose fundamental precepts do not have second-language learning as a primary concern. Bits of information that "seem" useful for the classroom have been passed along as wisdom to be "applied," but little effort has been made to evaluate the relationship between theoretical knowledge and classroom practice (Jarvis, 21); consequently, much of this "wisdom" has been inappropriate for teaching. Recently, however, there has been a renewed determination to remain

Catherine Doughty (M.S., University of Pennsylvania) is a Research Specialist in second-language acquisition and computer-assisted language learning in the Language Analysis Project (John Fought, Director) at the University of Pennsylvania, where she is also a candidate for the Ph.D. in Educational Linguistics. In addition, she is Associate Director of the Ursinus College–Tohoku Gakuin University American Studies Program and a lecturer at Ursinus in Freshman Composition for nonnative writers of English. Her professional affiliations include AAAL, CALICO, TESOL, and the Japan Association of Language Teachers.

focused on theory in order to understand better how students learn a foreign language and how to make teaching more efficient. The key to success in reaching such an understanding is twofold: first, there must be a commitment to develop a specific theory that explains SLA processes; second, there must be a concentrated effort to collect data relevant to *classroom* second-language learning. Instead of relying on knowledge "imported" from other disciplines, the underlying motivation for an understanding of the psycholinguistic processing of second-language learning must now come from within the field of applied linguistics itself (Jarvis, 21). Accordingly, the second-language classroom should be recognized as a vital research milieu and a source of important data for responsible hypothesis formation vis à vis the psycholinguistic processes reflected in what Long (33) calls students' instructed interlanguage development.

Many applied linguists are also classroom foreign or second-language teachers, a qualification that promotes a mutually beneficial relationship between research and pedagogy, and one that has engendered a new concentration on classroom-oriented research. As called for in the early 1980s (Stern and Cummins, 55), and in reaction to the 1970s focus on second-language acquisition in a natural setting, classroom language learning is considered to be an important source of knowledge about SLA, rather than merely to "mirror" untutored, or "naturalistic," language-learning environments (Seliger and Long, 48). As such, classroom research now "counts" as basic theoretical research. Two major benefits derive from this perception: First, as suggested by Pederson in Chapter 5 of this volume, teachers can contribute important insights into the formulation of hypotheses about second-language learning; and second, the potential to improve the quality of classroom teaching through informed materials design and/or the reorganization of classroom activities based on research results is large (Pica and Doughty, 42). Long (29) has suggested that, if these benefits are to be realized in practice, teachers should be trained as researchers in order to interpret reports of empirical findings knowledgeably in relation to their classrooms and in order to contribute their own efforts intelligently to the monumental task of data collection.

Yet even when classroom research and teacher input are seen as equally vital to understanding second-language acquisition, the difficulty of directly observing language acquisition remains a significant problem. To this end the computer has become an important ally in research efforts to collect data detailed enough to shed light on the complex processing and causal variables involved in SLA. Depending on the research aims, computers can be employed in conjunction with or in place of audio and video recorders or human observers and made to follow elaborate and carefully constructed formats for classroom observation. Some advantages of using the computer as a research tool include more control over the collection, examination, and manipulation of data, as well as convenience (and speed) of data recording, storage, and computation within an appropriate experimental design. Since these capabilities promise to facilitate the collection and analysis of behaviors that reflect underlying SLA processes at work, it is clear that CALL research can make an important contribution to the basic research effort "to discover something about the way in which students best learn a language," (Pederson, p. 108 this volume). Moreover, the information discovered in research via the computer can be recycled quickly and easily into the learning environment, thereby improving the quality of everyday classroom instruction.

Since it is clear that neither pedagogy nor theory alone has been able to elucidate the myriad of factors involved in learning a second language, one purpose of this chapter is to discuss the progress theorists have made toward developing models of second-language acquisition. Another purpose is to suggest that researchers pay more attention to classroom data; still another is to underscore that computer-based research on CALL provides an efficient means to accomplish this liaison. To summarize, these important points will be addressed:

1. Second/foreign language pedagogy must be reconnected to theory and empirical research, but the specific motivation to do so must come from a concern for a detailed understanding of SLA shared by researchers and teachers.

2. Classroom-oriented research can make a valuable contribution to understanding SLA processes.

3. The use of the computer as a basic tool in SLA research can provide new and detailed kinds of data.

4. Computers have the capabilities to recycle the results of empirical investigations into the classroom almost at once. Thus, computers make classroom-oriented research methodology accessible to teachers who might not otherwise have time but wish to conduct classroom studies in order to tailor their own instruction to specific individuals or groups of students.

5. Conversely, using the computer in the language classroom offers a convenient means of deriving issues and questions for research that appear in the classroom learning environment.

6. Finally, there is some chance that a reconnection of pedagogy and theory can be further advanced through computer-assisted research into the psycholinguistic processes of language learning.

The extent to which psycholinguistic processing is insufficiently understood will become apparent in the course of examining several SLA models that attempt to describe how language data are integrated into the learner's changing interlanguage grammar (known as interlanguage development) and how such data are accessed and used by the learner under the pressure of communication.

Theoretical Models of Second Language Acquisition _____

A comprehensive model of SLA with explanatory and predictive power has yet to be formulated. While some researchers have concluded that not enough is known to permit the construction of one comprehensive model (Stern, 54), others are more optimistic that the current status of theorizing, together with the body of empirical data amassed to date, indicate that a comprehensive theory is in the offing (Spolsky, 53). Most researchers agree that SLA is too complex a phenomenon to be explained at this stage by a single theory; rather, several models that account for various components of the overall process are thought to be needed to guide future research (Tollefson, et al., 56). To this end, if the purpose of a theoretical model is to facilitate the collection of information about SLA in general, necessary correlates are (1) defining specific research questions that evolve from the componential models themselves and (2) gathering empirical support for each. Ultimately, however, the cognitive processes involved in SLA must be viewed as a unified system (Andersen, 1). Once the empirical data has been collected and conclusions drawn from the research, the component models may be integrated to formulate one coherent theory.

Stern and Cummins (55) have provided a useful framework for the examination of models of second-language learning, as summarized in Figure 1. Within this framework, social context (dominance patterns, integration strategies, and group attitudes), learner characteristics (affective, personality, and cognitive characteristics, as well as age), and learning conditions (objectives, content, treatment, and evaluation) are the variables that affect the second-language learning process (strategies and processes) and its outcomes (interlanguage). Such a componential framework emphasizes an important point: the learning process is central to an understanding of SLA, which must ultimately be seen as an interaction between it as a central process and the variables that affect it, an interaction that then results in learning outcomes. Primarily because learning outcomes are more observable than processes, previous research has been devoted to investigating the effects of numerous variables and conditions on the outcomes of the learning process, thus bypassing the process itself. But, teachers and researchers now recognize the need to examine the learning process as directly as possible. Clearly, the computer is an invaluable tool for observing the variables that affect this process and, by extension, for building a comprehensive SLA theory.

Most research into the educational uses of computers has concentrated on examining the effectiveness of the medium in bringing about more efficient learning, particularly in comparison with traditional classroom instruction, and CALL research has often followed this same line of investigation—the investigation of the learning conditions in the Stern and Cummins (55) perspective. In such research, CALL is seen as a *treat-*

Factors	Attributes
Social Context	dominance patterns integration strategies group attitudes
Learner Characteristics	affective characteristics personality cognitive attributes age
Learning Conditions	objectives context treatment evaluation
SLA Learning Process	strategies processes
Outcomes	interlanguage

Figure 1. Factors That Influence the Learning Process and Their Attributes (adapted from Stern and Cummins, 55).

ment applied to the learner, and the effect of that treatment on learning is then measured. This product-oriented approach to the evaluation of the effectiveness of CALL has proven unsatisfactory primarily due to inattention to the central role of the learning process and the corresponding influence of learner characteristics. Recently, however, a very small amount of basic research implemented on computers has begun to address the learning process issue. Subsequent sections of this chapter relate research on CALL to issues in SLA theory and to the practicalities of connecting classroom teaching and research in general.

Concerns for Theory Construction _____

In any field, theories are formulated by (1) asking important questions, (2) developing models, (3) generating hypotheses therefrom, (4) testing the hypotheses, and (5) revising the models in accordance with the evidence gathered. This five-step process, which may be repeated any number of times taking into account new knowledge gained, defines the relationship between research and theory (Long, 29).

What, then, are the important questions of primary concern to theorists, researchers, and foreign language teachers? Spolsky (53) has put forth the fundamental question researchers must address in order to formulate a comprehensive SLA theory: "Who learns how much of what language under what conditions?" (p. 269). For the classroom language teacher, the language itself and the conditions under which it is studied are perhaps better understood than are the learners or the learning process. Accordingly, the following discussion of SLA models and related CALL research addresses only the "who learns" issues. The five models summarized below outline the many differential effects of learner variables (i.e., individual differences) on the overall SLA process—the *who* component (Bialystok, 2)—but focus primarily on the *process* of SLA—the *learns* part of the question. Taken together, the five theoretical models represent a concise statement of contemporary thinking about many important aspects of SLA theory. Finally, the CALL research reviewed in association with these models reflects some initial computer-based efforts to incorporate classroom data into theoretical considerations of second-language acquisition.

The five models fall within three theoretical frameworks: Monitor Theory, Information-Processing Theory, and Interaction Theory. While Monitor Theory tries to be a comprehensive theory of SLA (but falls short), revisions of it together with constructs from Information-Processing Theory and Interaction Theory may be used to organize efforts in data collection. Once validated empirically, a combination of these theoretical models may explain several important elements of the overall process of SLA and bring applied linguistics closer to a unified theory of second-language acquisition. Some details of the models presented have been omitted so that their relative components may be compared and contrasted. The following template will be used for comparison purposes in conjunction with a graphic interpretation of each model (described at length elsewhere by their proponents).

In general, Monitor Theory à la Krashen attempts to be comprehensive, addressing all five parameters of the template, while Bialystok's revision of Monitor Theory (the Explicit/Implicit Knowledge Representation Model) offers alternative interpretations of the processing, storage, and access-use phases (defined below). The Information-Processing and interactional models seek to explain respectively the access/use and processing phases at a greater level of detail than does Monitor Theory.

Input refers to the language data to which the learner is exposed (i.e., that heard or read).

Processing represents the means by which input available to the learner becomes internalized as part of a developing interlanguage; this psycholinguistic processing has also been referred to as *intake* (Corder, 7), reflecting the distinction between language that is simply available to the learner and that which actually contributes to the growth of the interlanguage grammar.

Storage reflects the memory format, or, in Bialystok's (2) terms, the knowledge representation (i.e., mental organization) of the interlanguage grammar.

Access is another psycholinguistic process, but one by which acquired knowledge may be retrieved from memory and used by the learner.

Output is composed of observable learner behaviors such as comprehension and production. The following discussion of the major components of Monitor Theory, Information-Processing Theory, and Interaction Theory will be delineated by the above template and will address the learning process and learner characteristics components of an overall model of second-language acquisition.

Monitor Theory

Krashen's Version

Monitor Theory (Krashen, 23) is well known to the majority of second-language professionals; its seminal concepts* have been vital stimuli to research. Although the theory as Krashen has proposed it has often been criticized as vague and untestable (Gregg, 18; McLaughlin 37; Pienemann, 44), several of its fundamental notions are valuable and continue to influence the thinking of SLA theoreticians (Long, 30). Figure 2 depicts a simple model of Krashen's Monitor Theory.

Monitor Theory consists of five hypotheses about second-language acquisition: the learning/acquisition hypothesis, the natural order hypothesis, the monitor hypothesis, the input hypothesis, and the affective filter hypothesis. These elements, familiar to readers, have been incorporated into Figure 2. The *learning/acquisition* distinction is made apparent by the separate representation of the two ways in which, according to Monitor Theory, language data may be internalized. Krashen defines "language acquisition" as "a subconscious process; language acquirers are not usually aware of the fact that they are acquiring language, but are only aware of the fact that they are using the language for communication," and Krashen says that "the result of language acquisition, acquired competence, is also subconscious. . . ." "Learning," on the other hand, refers to "conscious knowledge of a second language, knowing

---

*For the complete description of the Monitor Theory, see Stephen D. Krashen, *Second Language Acquisition and Second Language Learning,* Oxford, England: Pergamon Press, 1981 and Stephen D. Krashen, *Principles and Practices in Second Language Acquisition,* Oxford, England: Pergamon Press, 1982.

the rules, being aware of them, and being able to talk about them" (24, p. 10). Moreover, the way in which the input will be internalized is determined by the type of language exposure: only informal language exposure can lead to acquired knowledge, whereas formal exposure results only in learned knowledge (where "knowledge" here and in subsequent comparisons of models refers to information in the learner's developing interlanguage).

Krashen's other hypotheses clearly depend upon the learning/acquisition distinction. Perhaps the most controversial of all is the *monitor hypothesis* from which the theory takes its name and through which Krashen asserts that only acquired knowledge can be utilized to initiate L2 output. The function of learned knowledge, on the other hand, is as a form of editor (the monitor), which evaluates and corrects production from the acquired system. The *natural order hypothesis* states that the acquisition of grammatical structures occurs in a specific, predictable order. As such, this hypothesis relates only to acquisition, and Krashen has claimed that language behaviors mediated by learned knowledge (via the monitor) do not conform to this natural order. The crux of Monitor Theory, however, resides in the *input hypothesis,* which addresses the issue of how language is acquired. Krashen's (24) input hypothesis states that "a necessary . . . condition to move from stage *i* to stage *i* + 1 is that the acquirer understand input that contains *i* + 1 level input, where 'understand' means that the acquirer is focused on the meaning and not the form of the message [and where '*i* + 1' refers to a linguistic structure that is just beyond the current psycholinguistic processing level *(i)* of the acquirer]" (p. 21). Finally, the *affective filter hypothesis,* originally contributed to Monitor Theory by Dulay and Burt (12), states that affective variables, such as attitude, motivation, or personality factors, act either to facilitate or inhibit the psycholinguistic processing through which language data enters into storage in memory.

Several computer-based research studies conducted within a Monitor Theory perspective have attempted to explicate the process by which input is said to become comprehensible to the learner. Krashen (24) has specifically claimed that linguistic structures ("grammar") are acquired while attending to the meaning of an utterance in the input rather than by paying attention to its structure. In a study that postulated practice as important to the internalization of input and sought to determine the relative effectiveness of structured vs. meaningful practice on second-language acquisition (Schaefer, 47), learners were subjected to two sets of computer-based drills reflecting these two kinds of practice. Results indicated that semantic practice (vocabulary) is more effective than structural practice (grammar) in terms of success on semantic measures and that both kinds of practice are equally useful for structural measures (grammar tests). Thus, Schaefer concluded that meaningful practice leads to the acquisition of grammatical structures and further that meaningful con-

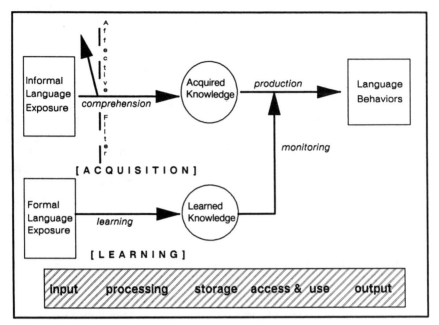

Figure 2. The Monitor Model

tent processing results in better understanding; moreover, since this practice was implemented on computers, Schaefer also concluded that meaningful processing of content is "not dependent upon interaction between people" but "can also take place by interacting with a medium such as a computer" (p. 137).

A study by Robinson et al. (46) at the Center for Language and Crosscultural Skills (CLCCS) in San Francisco investigated the effects of different strategies and different forms of error feedback on achievement. The study also investigated the relationships of various intelligence, motivation, and attitudinal factors (i.e., *learner characteristics*) with the effectiveness of CALL instruction. The questions asked by the researchers on Robinson's team were formulated by taking into consideration the importance of meaning in contrast to form. In their attempt to answer the perplexing question, What is the meaning of 'meaningful'? Robinson et al. utilized the computer primarily to present instruction in a controlled way. Accordingly, one hypothesis of the study was that "Practice in which the student is focused on the meaning of the material will lead to greater learning of structural items than will practice in manipulating the structures themselves, without reference to meaning" (p. 17). This ambitious study probed the above and other important issues and employed the computer to establish control over the presentation of the input. While some of the results were inconclusive (as for example can be seen in the analyses designed to reveal the daily versus cumulative effects of CALL instruction), the CLCCS research effort is noteworthy from two standpoints (Doughty, 8): (1) hypotheses were carefully generated from a base of theoretical considerations, and (2) the study illustrates the convenience of the computer as a tool for such research.

In addition to probing the meaning of "meaning," CALL research has begun to investigate ways to determine a learner's i and $i + 1$ input-processing levels. Parsing algorithms (abstract methods of dissecting and interpreting input to a computer) have been utilized to develop computer programs that analyze the learner's interlanguage. One such research strategy, developed by Markosian and Ager (34), uses a context-free grammar implemented via a computer program to analyze learner responses to computer questions and generates drills according to specifications in accordance with the learner's current vocabulary level. This application conforms to Krashen's input hypothesis in that the program performs some low-level, computer-aided diagnoses to reveal the learner's current level of processing ability (at least in terms of vocabulary items) and generates drills that approximate that level. A logical next step might be to incorporate vocabulary that is just beyond $(i + 1)$ the learner's current level of understanding (i), and to include that vocabulary in computer-mediated activities that provide opportunities to internalize the $i + 1$ input. Such research may make apparent the process through which $i + 1$ input becomes comprehensible. A similar and parallel direction for future research would be to apply the same experimental design to investigate the acquisition of target language syntax, particularly since Krashen's hypothesis intends to account for the acquisition of "grammar" rather than vocabulary.

Krashen has suggested that context provides the key information necessary to allow $i + 1$ input to be comprehended and incorporated into the developing interlanguage system. Recently, and to this end, Johns (22) has described a fascinating classroom application for an existing computational capability, the concordancing program. Concordancing programs search through a document for all the contexts around a specified word and present them in list form with the key words or phrases in their contexts vertically aligned in the center column on the screen. Via a concordancing program called Micro-concord, for example, the computer can offer "both language learners and language teachers a research tool for investigating 'the company that words keep'" (p. 151). Johns reports that the use of concordancing output has already been implemented in the teaching of advanced courses in English, Russian, and German, enabling "advanced learners to take the initiative in carrying out their own research into the variable rules of the language" (p. 151). An obvious connection to this pedagogical application of Micro-concord is the coupling of the concordancing program with the computer's capability for storing records of the students' actions, known as the "learner log." In addition to documenting how learners use the program, the learner log maintains an ongoing evaluation and record of each student's current level of target language ability. Thus, teachers can easily collect valuable and detailed information about student efforts to utilize context as an aid to comprehension, in combination with documentation of the effects of these efforts on interlanguage development.

Three ideas contained in Monitor Theory have generated a great deal of discussion and research: the learning/acquisition distinction, the comprehension of $i + 1$ input as a causative factor in acquisition, and the assertion that acquisition takes place during comprehension rather than production. The first consideration may be referred to as the *knowledge representation problem* while the remaining ideas contribute to considerations about what may be termed the *acquisition problem.* Several revisions and alternatives to the Monitor Model attempt to grapple with both of them, as described below.

Bialystok's Revision of Monitor Theory

In addressing the acquisition problem, Monitor Theory holds that learning and acquisition are two different and entirely separate means of internalizing language, and further indicates that these processes lead to separate sets of language knowledge that, in turn, have different functions as well (i.e., production vs. monitoring). Monitor Theory also states that conditions affecting this input and its internalization determine the route by which the data are processed. Formal, structured conditions, such as those typically found in classrooms, trigger "learning," while a focus on meaning rather than on structure leads to acquisition. Moreover, since these two internalization paths are hypothesized to be separate, to have separate functions, and to lead to different storage formats in memory, Krashen has further asserted that learning cannot lead to acquisition. Alternatively, Bialystok (4) has proposed that these input internalization processes lead to distinct, *but related,* forms of language stored within the developing interlanguage. As evidence of this interrelatedness, Bialystok cites a capacity for the transfer of knowledge from one type of memory storage to another. Figure 3 provides one possible graphic description of Bialystok's Explicit/Implicit Knowledge Representation Model. The suggestion that language knowledge is stored in different forms evolved from the frequent observation that a learner may sometimes "appear to know" (i.e., "use") a particular construction of the target language and other times will seem to have forgotten it. For example, students often demonstrate skill in pattern practice drills, but cannot apply these paradigms in everyday conversation. From this observation, Bialystok draws a conclusion slightly different from Krashen's: while agreeing that there are two entirely separate kinds of language knowledge resulting from two different internalization processes, Bialystok suggests that the two storage formats are not entirely independent of one another.

Because input is not permanently assigned to either explicit and implicit storage in the Bialystok model, this revision of Monitor Theory may be interpreted to state that learning *can* lead to acquisition and vice versa. In other words, while, like Krashen, Bialystok suggests that language knowledge may be stored differently in memory, the Explicit/Implicit Knowledge Representation Model departs from the Monitor Model in providing the insight that the setting (i.e., classroom vs. "natural"), which is the "trigger" for these specific internalization processes, does not necessarily determine the permanent location of the internalized input within memory storage. Moreover, other kinds of processing (such as access and use) may also influence the memory storage format by effecting its reclassification as either implicitly or explicitly organized knowledge.

A more detailed comparison of these two models, both of which find their grounding in Monitor Theory, reveals that Bialystok's revision accepts some elements of Krashen's learning/acquisition distinction but rejects others. As is the case with the Monitor Model, the Explicit/Implicit Knowledge Representation Model accepts that the content of each storage format in memory is determined by the process through which the data were internalized. An example that illustrates this distinction can be found in a comparison between foreign language classrooms, where a great deal of time is spent talking about the language as an object of study ("formal practicing" in Figure 3), and immersion classrooms, where the object of study is a particular content area and the medium of study is the target language ("functional practicing" in Figure 3). In the foreign language classroom, metalinguistic discussions are often accompanied by formal practicing; however, Bialystok cites *functional* practicing as the trigger for internalization along an acquisitional path. (Functional practicing is not clearly defined by Bialystok, but appears to be simply the *use* of the target language during the course of learning content material in immersion settings.) In contrast to Krashen, however, Bialystok postulates that although there are two different forms of storage for internalized language, there is a possibility for transfer of information between the two knowledge stores, which may be activated by any number of constraints on production (situational, interpersonal, task-related, etc.). These constraints on production initiate different psycholinguistic mechanisms for access and use processing which, in turn, affect the organization of the knowledge representation differently.

The two kinds of knowledge representation in Bialystok's model, explicit (or "conscious") and implicit (or "intuitive"), comprise a dichot-

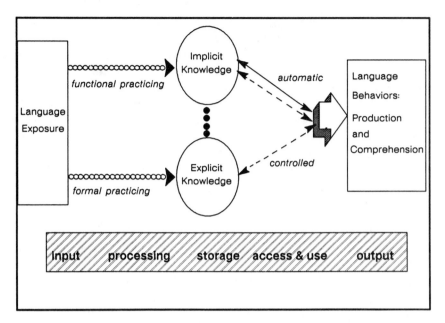

Figure 3. The Explicit/Implicit Knowledge Representation Model

omy from other cognitive models of information of knowledge representation that differentiate analytic and intuitive knowledge. This distinction in cognitive psychology is the *know that* vs. *know how* opposition, which translates in language-learning theory to *know about language* vs. *be able to use language in communication.* As described in detail above, the language stores in memory can be reorganized by the process through which they are accessed, even after having been originally determined by the conditions surrounding the intake process. Bialystok (3) conducted a study designed to document both types of knowledge representation by setting up conditions that facilitated access to each. Results of the non-computer-based investigation revealed that subjects who attested to intuitive judgments of grammaticality could be further induced to provide indications of the kinds of errors they spotted and even to give some form of the rules that governed their decisions about the grammaticality of given constructs or sentences. Such analytical ability indeed points to some kind of interaction between the two forms of knowledge, but more evidence is needed to clarify the nature of the relationship.

A project underway at The Ohio University incorporates the notion of two kinds of processing for the internalization of input, resulting in implicit and explicit storage. The Computer Assisted Simulation of Language Use (CASLU) is a program whose design integrates activities in which students use language as a means to solve problems with a pedagogical component that tracks learner decisions and gives advice to aid problem solving and to influence both the form and appropriateness of the target language that students produce (Soemarmo et al., 52). Thus, CASLU's evaluation of the students' performance is both implicit (because advice is given about choices made in solving the problem) and explicit (because language-specific knowledge is assessed and students are directed to exercises for practice in areas of difficulty).

One member of the CASLU team conducted a small computer-based study that demonstrated that vocabulary can be acquired while the learner focuses on the completion of a CALL problem-solving task rather than on memorizing the vocabulary items themselves (Magoto, 35). Learners were pretested on vocabulary items that were then incorporated into a CASLU problem-solving lesson. After completing the lesson, the students were given a posttest of the same vocabulary. Posttest scores were significantly higher than the pretest scores, suggesting that learning of the vocabulary items had occurred during the course of completing the problem-solving exercises. The posttest score, however, was determined immediately after the treatment, with no follow-up test after a period of time had passed. Another posttest, administered two weeks or one month later, for example, would have strengthened the interpretation of results. Replications of this research are needed along with modifications to the experimental design to determine long-term retention as well as to investigate whether syntax can be acquired during this kind of functional practicing that leads to implicitly organized knowledge.

In addition to departing somewhat from Krashen's notion of how language knowledge is represented in memory, Bialystok has also addressed the *acquisition problem* from a different perspective as well. In order to explain the effects of the various factors that influence learner's production described above (see p. 6), Bialystok has hypothesized that during L2 production, the process of accessing language in storage determines the transfer of information from one storage format to another. This perception details the important distinction between the Bialystok and Krashen versions of Monitor Theory alluded to above. In Bialystok's revised model, production is an important element in the overall acquisition process, whereas in Krashen's version acquisition is restricted to the comprehension process. Generally speaking, for Krashen, the explicit knowledge store is accessed in a controlled manner (with some degree of deliberateness or at some level of consciousness), and implicit knowledge may be reached automatically (or fluently). Currently, it is clear from Bialystok's (4) research that implicit knowledge may also be accessed deliberately and consciously because, when pressed, subjects who originally respond by intuition can identify errors as well as give explanations for them. Nevertheless, it is not yet clear how explicitly learned knowledge can be accessed automatically, and this explanation is crucial support for the claim that learning can lead to acquisition.

The importance of keeping a learner log that records all student actions on a computer and stores all learner responses to CALL programs cannot be overemphasized in the effort to understand how students can be brought to access implicit knowledge automatically. In the CLCCS study by Robinson et al. (46), learner processing strategies were hypothesized to be responsive to error feedback from the computer program. Student responses and program feedback to input errors, together with student responses to error feedback, were stored for analysis and for comparison with achievement scores after the period of instruction had been completed. Further studies that seek to uncover the relationship between error feedback and strategies of learner access/use of language are clearly needed to identify the specific computer-based activities that encourage the kinds of accessing and use strategies that lead to the reorganization of the linguistic material within the learner's memory. Through these strategies, explicitly learned knowledge may become implicit, thus promoting the transition of knowledge from learning to acquisition.

Criticisms of Monitor Theory

While the notions incorporated within Monitor Theory are intuitively appealing and seem consistent with observed evidence, the theory, as stated, has been widely criticized. First, McLaughlin (37) has discounted much of the evidence Krashen has cited in support of the input hypothesis. Secondly, Gregg (18) and Pienemann (44) have pointed independently to an important difficulty with the learning/acquisition (conscious/unconscious) distinction: maintaining a distinction between learning and acquisition rests on providing evidence that the internalization of input may be either conscious or subconscious. While Krashen (23) has provided conceptual definitions of these processes (*learning* conscious grammatical judgments based on rules; *acquisition* subconscious grammatical judgments based on "feel"), both McLaughlin (37) and later Gregg (18) have suggested that it is impossible to distinguish these processes operationally. Operational definitions, the behaviors that reflect hypothesized processes, are standard to research, but following Krashen's definitions, whether subjects who said that they responded by "feel" did so in fact or gave that response because they did not know how to verbalize the rule cannot be determined. Bialystok's methodology is also lacking, to a certain extent, in operational definitions. And, although Bialystok has attempted to link learning and acquisition, there is a conceptual problem with envisioning any division (even with the proposed link) as well as with postulating how the link between the two knowledge stores would operate in memory.

A third reservation about Monitor Theory involves the inadequate explanation of $i + 1$ comprehensibility. Although the input hypothesis claims that acquisition occurs when input slightly beyond the current processing capacity of the learner becomes comprehensible, neither Krashen nor Bialystok describe any specifically defined mechanisms by which input may be comprehended. Rather, Krashen states that learners must "notice the gap" (between their productions and the input around them) and be focused on meaning rather than on form in order to reconcile the differences between their interlanguage and the target language system. "Noticing the gap" is simply too vague a proposal to be tested empirically. Bialystok, on the other hand, postulates distinct practicing strategies to describe the internalization process, but similarly does not explain them.

There appears to be no organized and ongoing effort (directed by Krashen) to gather empirical evidence in support of Monitor Theory. Rather, there are many "restatements of known phenomena in the terminology of the [Monitor] model." (McLaughlin, 37, p. 320). But this is not unexpected in view of the untestable nature of the hypotheses that comprise it. From a pedagogical standpoint as well, Monitor Theory does not offer much hope of enhancing the effectiveness of instruction. If learning cannot lead to acquisition, then the only possible route to success in the classroom is providing comprehensible input, as Krashen has stated. Krashen and Terrell's (25) Natural Approach suggests that the classroom teacher must provide a nonthreatening environment in which input is made comprehensible to each individual learner. However, a specific methodology that creates these learning conditions is in its infancy and is not likely to be developed (or tested) until the operational definitions of the elements of Monitor Theory are described in detail.

Generally, then, Monitor Theory has been criticized on the basis of insufficient evidence in support of its very general hypotheses, which is not to say that Krashen's ideas addressing the acquisition problem and the knowledge representation problem are not worthy of further consideration (Long, 32). SLA models developed within Monitor Theory do not adequately explain the processes by which input enters the developing interlanguage system: thus, there is still a need to address the acquisition problem. Furthermore, although Bialystok has attempted to revise Monitor Theory with respect to the knowledge representation problem, there is no agreement within Monitor Theory about the form that language storage takes in memory. Alternative models have been proposed to resolve some of these difficulties. Information-Processing Theory and Interactional Theory, described below, are theoretical approaches that also address the difficult questions of how language knowledge is internalized and stored and, in combination with some elements of Monitor Theory, may help to provide an overall picture of second-language acquisition. Constructs from these theoretical frameworks should also be incorporated into the design of future CALL research.

Information-Processing Theory

In contrast to Monitor Theory, Information-Processing Theory postulates another format for knowledge representation and the corresponding differences in the psycholinguistic processing of input that determines it (Nation and McLaughlin, 40). McLaughlin (37) emphasizes the significance of the influence of data retrieval on the storage format in memory, as does Bialystok, but succeeds in explaining further its significance. In other words, the ways in which they are accessed and used by the learner, are central concerns of information-processing theory. As can be seen in Figure 4, McLaughlin resolves some of the difficult questions inherent in Bialystok's conceptualization of the knowledge representation problem.

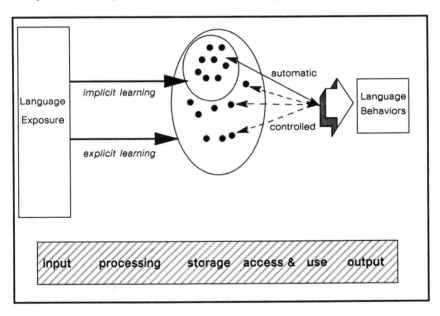

Figure 4. An Information–Processing Model

In place of two forms of knowledge storage in memory (Bialystok's explicit and implicit knowledge), McLaughlin's model hypothesizes one set of language data, which is stored within a system of nodes. These nodes are organized in storage according to the manner by which they entered the memory store *and* according to the processes through which they have been accessed by the learner. Information can enter the interlanguage grammar either as analyzed (separate nodes) or as unanalyzed chunks of data (associated nodes). Grouped nodes are accessed, in their entirety, via automatic retrieval processes, whereas individual nodes must be pieced together slowly when accessed via conscious and controlled processes. But, according to McLaughlin, nodes that have entered storage independently through explicit (conscious) learning may eventually become associated (and, hence access to them may become "automatized") through drilling and rehearsal strategies by the learner (McLaughlin; Rossman, and McLeod, 38). Significantly, McLaughlin's conceptualization of information processing allows for the possibility that explicitly learned knowledge may become implicitly associated and, hence, that learning may lead to acquisition. While in agreement with Bialystok, McLaughlin's information-processing constructs provide an improvement over the "separate but related" notion of storage formats because they explain more about *how* bits of input may become associated during the access and use processing phase of second-language acquisition.

Two vital goals for CALL research are (1) gathering more data for the purpose of understanding the exact nature of the psycholinguistic processing involved in accessing and using a developing interlanguage system and (2) determining how such processing influences the organization of the system in memory. Learner logs that record in tandem the program stimuli (i.e., the screen displays or what the learner sees) and each learner response to it (i.e., what the learner types in or selects from the menu) give both researchers and teachers valuable insight into the strategies and processes students use while completing various language-learning tasks. Doughty and Fought (10) applied the learner log technique to investigate learner reliance on two complementary strategies of language data processing: *hypothesis testing* and *inferencing based on L1* (cognitive processes that may be seen as related to the implicit and explicit knowledge stores, respectively). In this investigation, learners were given complex verb-tense review material presented via an authentic-text format (in this case, a patient's hospital chart) accompanied by various kinds of "extra help" the students could consult by selecting from a screen menu. The kinds of extra help offered were designed to reflect the processing strategies learners might elect. For example, learners employing hypothesis-testing strategies might want to see other contexts containing examples of the verb tense in question, while learners using an inferencing approach might rely heavily on formal rules or examination of the correct answer. Results of the study indicated that students employed various strategies. Two general tendencies seemed to be determined by immediate outcome of the first attempt at a question. If learners were successful on the first try, the overwhelming majority went on to the next question without consulting any of the menu options. After a failed first attempt, learners usually availed themselves of the option to try again. It was when learners were wrong on second, third, or fourth tries that the results of the study revealed a variety of learner strategies in the processing of the linguistic data available via the extra-help selections. Moreover, most learners demonstrated a preference for one type of extra help, indicating a consistent preference for one particular type of strategy.

The same design without computer learner logs would have obscured the important result that learner strategies are constrained by the immediate consequences of their first attempt but that individual preferences for processing strategy prevail under duress (i.e., after repeated wrong answers). However, more information is needed if the effect of the various strategies on interlanguage knowledge representation is to be understood. To this end, an additional benefit of using learner logs is the ability to track how students access and use their interlanguage system by documenting learner responses to computer tasks. For example, Doughty and Fought (10) suggest that consultation with extra-help options parallels Bialystok's notion of controlled access of explicitly learned knowledge and that attempts to complete tasks without any help from the program reflect automatic access to implicit knowledge in memory. An interesting followup study might seek to demonstrate that computer-based practice and drilling of explicitly learned knowledge can lead to the formation of implicitly associated node groups in memory storage that could then be accessed more automatically, as is suggested by McLaughlin (37). The computer's ability to time student responses might also be exploited in order to clarify the distinction between controlled and automatic responses so that the relative effects of different accessing strategies on storage can be determined.

Another investigation into the access and use of the developing interlanguage grammar (Boatman et al., 5) utilized the computer to administer a test designed to examine learner strategies in selecting verb tenses in French as a second language. This CALL study was a partial replication of a non-computer-based experiment (Fayol, 13) with better control over the testing environment provided by the use of the computer as a research tool. The purpose of the original study was to determine what influences native speakers in the process of selecting verb tenses for use in sentences. Extending the work to an investigation of second-language learning, Boatman et al. hypothesized that L2 adult learners of French would exhibit strategies for the selection of verb tense similar to adult native speakers of French rather than like those of children learning French as a first language. The original research showed that native adults rely on context, as determined particularly by the semantic content of adverbs in tense selection, and that children rely on verbal category (in French, verbs can be ranged along a continuum from stative to dynamic aspect). Results of the computer-based L2 study indicated, however, that for most verb tenses adult second-language learners are influenced more by verbal category than by the semantic environment. This study provides a first window into the cognitive organization data within the knowledge representation store in memory and hints at a link between the processing strategies associated with the native language and the developing interlanguage. Furthermore, the detailed results provide data for formulating hypotheses about the exact nature and makeup of controlled and automatic access to language knowledge in memory. It could be that children learning a first language and adults learning their second language rely on explicitly organized knowledge, such as verb classification, to process linguistic phenomena, whereas native adults can intuitively and automatically appeal to the implicit information available in the association between the adverbial context and the verb.

Computerized Models of Information Processing

While the focus of this chapter is primarily on basic research into classroom language learning via CALL, computational abilities of the computer together with parsing algorithms for information processing have also been directed toward developing computerized models of the second-language learner. One such project, the development of a computer model of language production in an adult Japanese learner of English, has resulted in a computer program called CHIE (Gasser, 17). The CHIE project aims to characterize second-language production by examining computer processes that generate responses equivalent to the natural responses of learners on the same task. CHIE's particular emphasis is on the characterization of the causes of learner errors. CHIE may lead to a more detailed understanding of the processes involved in the comprehension of utterances as well as in the production of the target language. CHIE consists of a phrasal lexicon and a network of semantic associations. The phrasal lexicon provides the syntactic and morphological language data and the semantic network simulates the world knowledge needed to interpret and produce syntactic relationships.

CHIE works by first selecting grammatically defined patterns and then combining them according to constraints prescribed by the semantic network to produce surface utterances relevant to the goals that guide plans for language production. The program models several different language strategies that learners employ in the pursuit of a communicative goal but does so in the face of gaps in linguistic knowledge (similar to hypothesized gaps in developing interlanguage systems) that cause errors. (One example of a gap in linguistic knowledge is a phrasal lexicon entry that is not exhaustive enough to enable the program to decide whether a noun is countable or not.) Gasser argues that "characterization of the mental representation of linguistic knowledge and of the cognitive processes involved in language production is crucial to a theory of second language acquisition" (p. 23). Using the technique of incorporating into the program empirical data about actual errors made by second-language learners, Gasser has shown, through computer modeling, that learners err primarily when they must deal with a communicative goal rather than in other circumstances.

Gasser also interprets his results in terms of McLaughlin's notion of processing constraints in order to demonstrate that production is as important to acquisition as is comprehension (as has been noted by both Bialystok and McLaughlin). Suggesting that the association may initially be weak immediately after a particular form has been associated with a function or meaning during comprehension. Gasser hypothesizes that for a given newly associated form to be accessed for production, there is a requirement that few other processing constraints be placed on the speaker. (In other words, the learner must focus on accessing this one form and is thus not capable of simultaneous access of others). Additionally, however, Gasser states that the process of accessing a form has the effect of strengthening the form–function association, thereby making the form more easily accessible at a future time, even under heavier processing constraints. The purpose of CHIE as a model of a second-language learner, thus, is to "explicate the nature of 'processing demands' and reveal under what circumstances the learner can use and strengthen new form–function relationships" (p. 2). The CHIE project has only begun to lay the groundwork for developing a full-scale computer model of second-language production. Current plans are to extend CHIE to a wider range of learner strategies, a system of hierarchical selection strategies, and a characterization of specific points in the process.

The Intake Model

While McLaughlin's proposal that language data is stored in memory in only one format helps to clarify the knowledge representation problem, much is left unsaid about the specific nature of the processes by which input enters the interlanguage system (the acquisition problem). Chaudron (6) suggests, however, that now "the issue for second language research is *precisely* what it is about the learner's language acquisition mechanism that determines intake, [i.e.,] the learner's perception and processing of target language input" (pp. 1–2). Acknowledging the existence of both the knowledge representation problem and the acquisition problem, Chaudron also discusses two independent aspects of second-language learning: (1) the learner's current state of knowledge of the target language (i.e., the internalized interlanguage); and (2) the processes and psychological variables that make up a learner's cognitive apparatus (i.e., the mechanisms for perception and learning).

Chaudron addresses both of these important issues, but seeks to examine in greater detail the psycholinguistic processing by which input becomes internalized. To this end, Chaudron has postulated that the same set of cognitive mechanisms for SLA are at work as in first-language acquisition (Massaro, 36), but suggests that each learner's acquisition process is affected by a different set of interlanguage grammar rules. Moreover, Chaudron has further attempted to factor the internalization of input into several processing stages, proposing that each can be investigated separately to obtain the desired level of detailed analysis (see Figure 5).

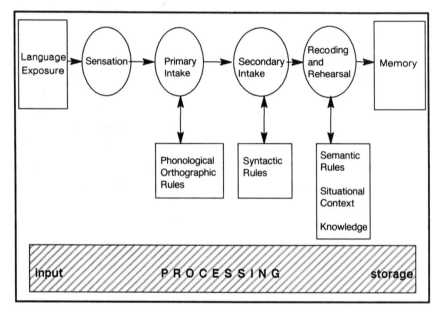

Figure 5. The Intake Model

According to Chaudron's Intake Model, a speech signal is first processed within the primary intake stage. Using phonological and orthographic rules from the existing interlanguage knowledge representation, neural impulses are analyzed partially and stored within short-term memory, which then sends out a filtered signal. Syntactic information is recalled during the temporary storage in memory, thus beginning a secondary stage in the intake processing. Finally, abstract representations of the language data are recoded according to semantic, situation, and world-knowledge information, and the fully decoded information enters the long-term memory store through recoding and rehearsal.

Whether these intake-processing stages are sequential is an important question that remains to be determined. Based on empirical research,

Garrod (16) has argued that the components of the internalization of input are simultaneous rather than sequential and has reported on initial empirical support for this assertion. In Garrod's study, when experimental subjects were interrupted during the processing of sentences, their responses indicated that, from the outset, they had assigned situational and semantic constraints to the interpretation of phonological, morphological, and syntactic information. Chaudron, on the other hand, calls for research to support a detailed model of stage-by-stage psycholinguistic processing and suggests that procedures from first-language acquisition research might be adapted for use in second-language acquisition studies. Chaudron's guidelines for research include the introduction of more control, directions for more standardized measures, and the implementation of a systematic approach to the analysis of each processing stage. Although CALL research has not yet addressed the detailed examination of information processing, Chaudron's suggestions for improving research methodology can be realized by exploiting various applications of the computer as a research tool for this purpose.

Interaction Theory

An alternative but potentially complementary approach to the psycholinguistic investigation of the processes by which input is internalized is offered by an interactional, or conversational, approach to the study of second-language acquisition. Rather than seeking to understand the nature of the psycholinguistic processing, Interaction Theory investigates language production that reflects the underlying internalization process (e.g., as exhibited in conversations). Several researchers who emphasize the importance of comprehensible input to second-language acquisition (Hatch, 20; Long, 26, 27, 28; Doughty and Pica, 11) have speculated on the role of interaction in making input comprehensible. Long, in particular, has claimed that modifications in the interactional structure of conversations between native and nonnative speakers, triggered by the native speaker's reaction to (or anticipation of) a lack of comprehension by nonnative, are what allow nonnative speakers to understand unfamiliar linguistic items they could not otherwise handle (in Krashen's terms, making $i + 1$ input comprehensible). Examples of the kinds of data examined in research motivated by Interaction Theory are modifications to the structure of interaction (seen below in Figure 6—Pica, Doughty, and Young, 43, pp. 5–6) such as (1) confirmation checks, (2) comprehension checks, and (3) clarification requests, as well as (4) repetitions or paraphrases of a previous speaker's or one's own utterances.

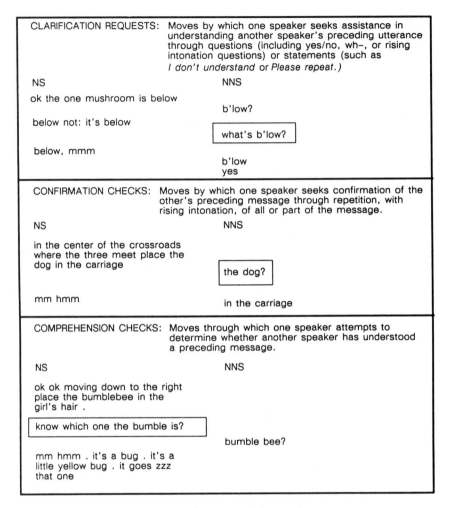

Figure 6. Modifications to the Structure of Interaction

Although these kinds of modifications can be observed when native speakers converse with one another, they have been found to be statistically more numerous when native speakers engage in conversation with nonnatives. Hatch also suggests that the acquisition of syntax is a process parallel to the construction of discourse, and that the teacher acquires the function of different syntactic constituents by observing and utilizing them in conversation. Arguing that the most useful form of conversational interaction for SLA has participants talking creatively about topics that are not planned in advance, Hatch has described this interaction as conversation in which the outcome is negotiated by the participants. This is in contrast to interaction for which the outcome is predetermined (e.g., display questioning in classrooms whereby, for the purpose of providing target language practice, teachers ask questions whose answers they themselves know and suspect that the students know as well). Figure 7 gives an overall indication of the role of interaction in the comprehension of input.

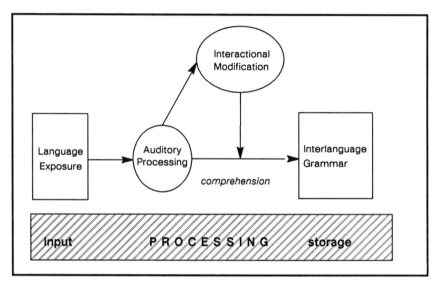

Figure 7. The Interaction Model

As with Information Processing, Interaction Theory also concerns itself with the input internalization phase of the overall language-learning process.

Coupled with an experimental design based on Interaction Theory (and notions from Monitor Theory as well) Doughty (9) has incorporated into a computer-based study at the University of Pennsylvania the CALL research methodology that relies on tracking learner responses in order to determine the effect of instruction on acquisition. In this study, instruction is defined as the presentation of structural material (relative clauses) within a specific framework that varies according to the experimental treatments applied. Rather than asking whether computer instruction is better than other forms of instruction, the primary aim of this study is to add empirical evidence in support of the beneficial effects of instruction on acquisition (see Long, 31, for a review). Whereas early studies investigating the role of the computer in instruction erroneously sought to establish the computer as a superior teaching tool, for Doughty the computer provides the medium for data collection and analysis.

Doughty relies upon SLA theory for determining the nature of the "extra help" material by using a program that provides branching via menu selection, thus enabling learners to select carefully controlled aids to the processing of language data. Learners are presented with the following reading activities while engaged in a computer L2 reading lesson: skimming, scanning (the treatment phase of the experiment), and recall. In the skimming phase, learners are instructed to glean the overall meaning of a passage and are guided by a highlighting of the topic sentences of each paragraph and a timing option that only allows a brief period of skimming time per page. During the scanning phase, one of three experimental treatments is presented: (1) presentation of the passage with extra reading time but no extra help provided (unstructured, unaided, but continuous processing), (2) presentation of the passage in chunks with formal rules available through the menu for the analysis of each chunk (a treatment parallel to traditional form-based approaches to instruction provided by calling up another program called Animated Grammar— Soemarmo and Graney, 51); and (3) presentation of the passage in chunks with information about the meaning of each chunk available by learner request through interaction with the menu (*please repeat; please say that again another way; please give the meaning of* [a specific word]). In this third condition, learners must obtain keys to the meaning of the passage chunks in much the same way as partners in a conversation interact to understand each other by clarifying, confirming, or checking comprehension (Doughty and Pica, 11). Doughty has hypothesized that the experimental condition based on Interaction Theory (condition 3 above), will lead to the greatest amount of comprehension as documented by reading recall tasks administered at the end of the session. Learners are to be pretested and posttested in an attempt to measure the effects of the three instructional treatments on acquisition. Because of its beneficial effects on comprehension, Doughty has hypothesized that the treatment that derives from Interaction Theory will have a greater effect on acquisition than will the extended processing format for the structure-oriented treatment.

Two recently completed studies that have also examined the learning process from an interactional perspective are those of Young (58) and Piper (45). Both researchers have noted the potential benefits of a frequent "spinoff" from text-based CALL activities: conversational interaction in the target language is often stimulated when learners work in groups on computer tasks. Both researchers tape-recorded and described the conversations of second-language learners as they cooperated in the completion of CALL program tasks; both assessed this interaction with regard to its potential influence on language learning as suggested by Hatch (20) and Long (30); and both aimed to examine whether the nature of the CALL software would determine differences in the kinds of conversation that occurred among learners engaged in these CALL activities.

Young's study, for example, was conducted within an Interaction Theory framework and asked specifically whether CALL activities that allow a negotiated outcome (primarily language-learning-oriented adventure games or simulations) vs. those for which the outcome is predetermined (i.e., word sequencing and cloze testing programs) would generate different kinds of conversational interaction among learners. Young reported that the task determined the kind of conversation generated; programs that allowed for the negotiation of outcome produced more creative language than tasks for which the outcome is predetermined by the program itself. Young interpreted the results of this study from the perspective of an interactional model of language learning and observed that open-ended activities that allow for creative learner conversations (1) are promising for CALL software development and (2) indicate an important direction for empirical research.

Piper (45) similarly examined CALL conversations according to a number of categories of conversation types, including several of Sinclair and Coulthard's (50) well-known observational categories, and noted that three kinds of language are typical of the conversations among students who are working in groups on computer tasks: (1) *repeating* language from the screen, (2) *managing* the computer and the task, and (3) *discussing* the language task itself while working towards a solution or the completion of the task. Not surprisingly, the type of CALL program used was found to determine the nature of the exchange. Cloze tasks primarily produced management language, word-ordering tasks resulted in a large amount of repetition, and none of these tasks caused much discussion. While the results of both Young's and Piper's studies provide a good deal of descriptive, empirical data about the nature of learner conversations generated during CALL activities, Piper suggests some reasons for restraining the enthusiasm for the direct-application interactional CALL in the classroom, pending more investigation. Upon detailed examination "CALL tasks . . . appear to give rise to two types of discourse—an apparently incoherent one where learners are thinking aloud and a more coherent one where they are exchanging information" (p. 194). Furthermore, "CALL tasks appear to provide no opportunity for language learners to develop the more demanding ability to construct 'long turns'" (p. 194). And, moreover, when the range of language and variety of language functions generated by CALL activities are analyzed, "the discourse [is] impoverished" (p. 196). Obviously, more investigation like that of Young and Piper is needed in order to determine whether the inter-learner conversations around CALL tasks are representative of those that have been theorized to be beneficial to the development of syntax in second-language acquisition, according to the interactional framework. Furthermore, efforts toward developing CALL materials that foster such useful interaction must be initiated.

Connections between Research and Classroom Teaching ___

Much research into classroom language learning has reflected a "person-oriented approach that examines characteristics of the supposed good language learner: intelligence, personality, cognitive style, motivation and attitude" (Nation and McLaughlin, 40, p. 41). However, the problems of "person" or learner-oriented research are numerous: (1) valid measures of learner variables not subject to interaction with other variables are difficult to obtain, (2) the collection of data uncontaminated by factors outside of the design of the study is virtually impossible, and (3) the generation of empirical evidence of these kinds of factors is cumbersome at best.

Building the computer into a research design for the investigation of learner characteristics offers these advantages: (1) better control over other cognitive variables, (2) the capability to isolate a particular learner variable, (3) the control necessary for understanding the interaction between learning conditions and the learning process, and (4) a more direct and connected way to evaluate learning outcomes. All these advantages combine to provide a firmer foundation for making inferences about and gaining insight into the central learning process. One example of a computer-based approach to research is the investigation of the role of the cognitive variable "field-dependence" (involving the relationship between the ability to differentiate the small parts from complex wholes) in language learning. Several non-computer-based studies (Naiman et al., 39; Hamayan et al., 19) have supported the hypotheses that the field-independent individual (who can see the smaller parts) is a better language learner. These studies failed, however, to control for other equally essential cognitive variables such as IQ and aptitude, known to be highly interactive (Stern and Cummins, 55), and gave no consideration to the possible interaction between learning conditions and learner characteristics. As such, the field-dependence variable under consideration could not be isolated and any conclusions drawn about learning outcomes were too general to be supported by the data.

Mellgren (41) conducted a computer-based study that attempted to measure the combined effects of relative field dependence (other cognitive factors were controlled for) and a clearly defined instructional context, computer homework. Mellgren used the computer as a medium for out-of-class practice and thus greater control was maintained over the learning conditions. Learner characteristics were identified and partialled out by means of rigorous pretesting so that only the cognitive variable under investigation was considered in the final analysis. Results indicated that the cognitive trait of field independence could consistently predict success on computer homework, whereas students who were field dependent could be counted on not to do as well. While not an investigation of the learning process, as with the majority of the studies reviewed above, Mellgren's study presents important implications for the appropriate use of the computer in foreign language instruction with respect to the combined effects of learning characteristics and learning conditions. Mellgren's work also demonstrates that the amount of *control* offered by computer-mediated research is one possible solution in the effort to conduct "cleaner" studies. For example, using the computer as a research medium, time of exposure to the language data as well as the nature of the linguistic material itself can be strictly controlled, environmental factors can be standardized, and learner responses can be monitored and, more importantly, recorded in detail.

In the majority of the studies mentioned above, the computer is either an instrument that collects data or is medium of instruction. Both roles are useful in classroom-oriented research because information is generated about what learners actually do in lessons. Interestingly, this often turns out to be different from what they think they are doing, and also from what they have been trained to do. Garrett (15) has called this "getting at what is going on inside students' heads" while they are learning a foreign language. Using a methodology that combines classroom observation, teacher "hunches," and the computer as a data-collection instrument, Garrett (Chapter 7 in this volume) proposes a system of conducting ongoing classroom research that feeds directly and immediately back into classroom teaching and learning. Specifically, Garrett suggests that the computer makes classroom observation convenient and precise through the simultaneous collection of data from several individual students. The computer feeds directly into teaching hypotheses generated from global classroom observations that can then be tested directly via the computer medium with the very students on whom the original observations were made. Production data (learner output) is the kind most frequently gathered on the computer, but with the audio components now readily available to computer instruction, listening comprehension data may also be collected in a similar fashion. Garrett suggests that classroom research is important because the questions that teachers feel are worth following up in the classroom can be the first questions to be investigated. In this way, the benefits of CALL research are threefold: (1) there is immediate feedback to teaching, (2) benefits accrue in the classroom, and, (3) there is an overall benefit to the field of applied linguistics. Garrett further notes that it is important to find out what learners actually learn—as opposed to what they are taught—and why and to what extent learning is affected by teaching. Once there is some sense of what idiosyncrasies students hypothesize about language, then, for one applied example, the true individualization of foreign language instruction can come into place.

The dissertation work of Garrett (14) applied the system of cyclical observation and hypothesis generation to the investigation of the development of complex grammatical structure in German as a second language (GSL). Garrett's study sought to provide empirical support, from the classroom, for the Interlanguage Hypothesis, which, as originally put forth by Corder (7) and Selinker (49), asserts that the development of complex structure in L2 proceeds through a series of grammars that approximate its grammar. The Interlanguage Hypothesis stresses, however, that each approximative grammar is a system on its own and, therefore, the interlanguage grammar should not be seen merely as an imperfect reflection of the target language grammar. In terms of learner output, the Interlanguage Hypothesis emphasizes the importance of viewing learner errors as windows into the systematic development of the interlanguage grammar rather than as "mistakes" in the target language. Of specific interest to Garrett was the systematic relationship between the dative case and indirect objects in the development of GSL interlanguage grammars and a relevant hypothesis based on a classroom observation about how students learn (or fail to learn) the details of the relationship. Garrett reasoned that students typically did not add dative case endings to indirect objects because they did not understand what a direct object was rather than because they did not understand the dative case. All students were pretested to see if they knew the dative paradigm and only those students who did were included in the study, which focused on this grammar point in drill-and-practice exercises. Student production data collected on dative case vs. accusative case on indirect vs. direct objects revealed a number of interesting observations about the interlanguage grammars of GSL students:

1). Students distinguished between dative and accusative on the basis of whether the objects were animate or inanimate, a "rule" that generates the right answer 90 percent of the time but is not the actual rule.

2). Students only have trouble with dative case when the dative is required of a pronoun, a paradigm that is considered to be the hardest to learn in German.

3). Students get case endings right when both objects are nouns, but when the indirect object is a clause, it is always marked in the accusative; this again is a rule that almost always produces the right answer but is not the native one.

Garrett also discovered interesting strategies adopted by students when they got a wrong-answer markup from the computer program and were asked to do an immediate second try:

4). Some students routinely changed the ending to a different case. From this strategy, Garrett gleaned that they had no idea of what "case" really does in a language; in other words, they know case exists, they know how to form the endings, but they do not know its function.

5). Other students left the ending unchanged in favor of changing the root of the word; when asked why, students said that they assumed they had gotten the stem wrong.

From these two kinds of data, Garrett has concluded that the ability to correct grammar mistakes is not always an indication that the original error was some kind of performance error (as has often been suggested). In light of the relevance of Garrett's data to the Interlanguage Hypothesis, this result is a very important notion that merits further investigation.

Conclusion

This review of the connections between SLA theory and CALL research has emphasized the necessity for re-establishing the link between theory, research, and classroom methodology. Cooperative research efforts are necessary if the complex process of second-language acquisition is to be understood and if any of the progress in theory building is ever to be useful to classroom language teachers. Moreover, in this chapter, classroom-oriented research (particularly involving hypotheses generated from classroom data together with the recycling of the research results back into the classroom) has been suggested as a very promising source of empirical knowledge about the language learning process. Equally important, the chapter has underscored the role of the computer as an indispensible research tool and revealed its potential in contemporary CALL research. Still, however, there is a need for an integrated effort toward understanding second-language acquisition, starting with theoretical frameworks that are motivated by the concerns of teachers and researchers and resulting in large amounts of data collected under classroom conditions.

At present there are some research efforts that seek to establish and develop such a unified approach. One group currently forming proposes to design an intelligent tutorial called the Plus One System (Yao and Ross, 57). The researchers hope to enhance the design of Plus One by considering both the SLA literature and the experiences (and intuitions) of language teachers and learners. Plus One will be developed in stages in order to accommodate any progress made by SLA theoreticians in addition to any advances in the technology of computers and will have capabilities for incorporating a number of teaching methodologies. Although named for Krashen's Input Hypothesis, the designers of Plus One have noted some of the difficulties with Monitor Theory and, thus, have adopted a modular and flexible approach that is not strictly tied to any one theoretical model. Plus One also will maintain a database for the purpose of modeling each student's current interlanguage. Such information will be useful both for the collection of empirical data and for including a computer-diagnositic component in the system. Yao and Ross have identified the need for a cooperative effort by teachers, researchers, and CALL designers; accordingly, they have set a time framework of five to ten years for completing the Plus One intelligent tutoring system for TESOL.

Another long-term project is the establishment of a cooperative research effort among leading researchers in applied linguistics at the National Foreign Language Resource Center (R. Lambert, Director). The center, to be located at Johns Hopkins University, will be staffed by researchers and teachers from universities across the nation. The goal of cooperative research at the National Foreign Language Resource Center is to investigate a number of important and related issues in second-language acquisition and language teaching. Some of the important research areas are to be classroom research, the measurement of proficiency, comparisons of methodology, individual learning differences, and the special considerations of very complex and uncommonly taught languages such as Japanese and Chinese. The computer as a research and data-sharing tool is a central link in this cooperative effort. Using a network of computers, data will be circulated among researchers, analytical tools will be developed, and databases will be created.

Efforts such as the cooperative work on the Plus One system and the establishment of the National Foreign Language Resource Center—which encourage the collaboration of researchers and teachers in developing a theory specifically oriented toward SLA—in time may bring the field of applied linguistics closer to understanding all elements of Spolsky's (53) question: "Who learns how much of what language under what conditions?" In the interim, the computer and CALL remain important instruments to help clarify the process of second-language acquisition, and, as such, promise to facilitate a new connection between pedagogy and SLA theory.

References, Second Language Acquisition Theory and CALL Research

1. Andersen, Roger. "Introduction: A Language Acquisition Interpretation of Pidginization and Creolization," pp. 1–63 in Roger Andersen, ed., *Pidginization and Creolization as Language Acquisition.* Rowley, MA: Newbury House, 1983.
2. Bialystok, Ellen. "A Theoretical Model of Second Language Learning." *Language Learning* 28, 1 (1978):69–83.
3. _____. "Explicit and Implicit Judgements of L2 Grammaticality." *Language Learning* 29, 1 (1979):81–103.
4. _____. "The Role of Linguistic Knowledge in Second Language Use." *Studies in Second Language Acquisition* 4, 1 (1981):31–45.
5. Boatman, Dana, Christopher Cierri, and Nadine O'Connor. "The Role of the PC in Researching Learning Behavior." Paper presented at CALICO Conference. U.S. Naval Academy, Annapolis, MD, 1986.
6. Chaudron, Craig. "On Models and Methods for Discovering Learner's Processing of Input." *Studies in Second Language Acquisition* 7, 1 (1985):1–14.
7. Corder, S. Pit. "The Significance of Learners' Errors." *International Review of Applied Linguistics* 5, 4 (November 1967):161–70.
8. Doughty, Catherine. "A Response to Robinson," pp. 47–55 in John Fought and Catherine Doughty, eds., *Second Language Teaching and Educational Technology: A State of the Art Symposium.* Washington, DC: Defense Intelligence Agency, 1986.

9. _____. "The Effects of Instruction on the Acquisition of Relative Clauses in English as a Second Language." Ph.D. dissertation in progress. University of Pennsylvania (Philadelphia), 1987.

10. _____, and John Fought. "On Investigating Variable Learner Response: Toward Achieving Better CALL Courseware Design." Report from the Language Analysis Project, The University of Pennsylvania (Philadelphia), 1984.

11. _____, and Teresa Pica. "Information-Gap Tasks: Do They Facilitate Second Language Acquisition?" *TESOL Quarterly* 20, 2 (1986):305–25.

12. Dulay, Heidi, and Marina Burt. "Some Remarks on Creativity in Language Acquisition," pp. 65–90 in William C. Ritchie, ed., *Second Language Acquisition Research*. New York: Academic Press, 1978.

13. Fayol, Michel. "Les Temps verbaux: influence du type et du contexte: Une étude développementale." Unpublished manuscript. Laboratoire de Psychologie, Université de Dijon, 1981.

14. Garrett, Cornelia B. [Nina]. "In Search of Interlanguage: A Study of Second Language Acquisition of German Syntax." Unpublished Ph.D. dissertation. University of Illinois (Urbana-Champaign), 1982.

15. _____. "Computers and Classroom Research." Paper presented at the Northeast Conference on Foreign Language Teaching. Washington, DC, 1986.

16. Garrod, Simon. "Language Comprehension in Context: A Psycholinguistic Perspective." *Applied Linguistics* 7, 3 (1986):226–38.

17. Gasser, Michael. "Second Language Production: Coping with Gaps in Linguistic Knowledge." Technical Report UCLA-AI-85-18, Los Angeles: UCLA Artificial Intelligence Laboratory, 1985.

18. Gregg, Kevin. "Krashen's Monitor and Occam's Razor." *Applied Linguistics* 5, 2 (1984):79–101.

19. Hamayan, Elsie, Fred Genesee, and G. Richard Tucker. "Affective Factors and Language Exposure in Second Language Learning." *Language Learning* 27, 2 (1977):225–41.

20. Hatch, Evelyn. "Simplified Input and Second Language Acquisition," pp. 64–86 in Roger Andersen, ed., *Pidginization and Creolization as Language Acquisition*. Rowley, MA: Newbury House, 1983.

21. Jarvis, Gilbert A. "The Psychology of Second Language Learning: A Declaration of Independence." *The Modern Language Journal* 67 (1983):393–402.

22. Johns, Tim. "Micro-Concord: A Language Learner's Research Tool." *System* 14, 2 (1986):151–62.

23. Krashen, Stephen. "The Monitor Model for Adult Second Language Performance," pp. 152–61 in Maria Burt, Heide Dulay, and Mary Finocchiaro, eds., *Viewpoints on English as a Second Language: Trends in Research and Practice*. New York: Regents, 1977.

24. _____. "Some Issues Relating to the Monitor Model," pp. 144–58 in H. Douglas Brown, Carlos Yorio, and Ruth Crymes, eds., *Teaching and Learning English as a Second Language: Trends in Research and Practice*. Washington, DC: TESOL, 1977.

25. _____, and Tracy D. Terrell. *The Natural Approach: Language Acquisition in the Classroom*. San Francisco: Alemany Press, 1983.

26. Long, Michael H. "Input, Interaction and Second Language Acquisition." Unpublished Ph.D. dissertation. Los Angeles: UCLA, 1980.

27. _____. "Questions in Foreigner Talk Discourse." *Language Learning* 31, 1 (1981):135–58.

28. _____. "Native Speaker/Nonnative Speaker Conversation in the ESL Classroom," pp. 281–97 in Mark Clarke and Jean Handscombe, eds., *On TESOL '82*. Washington, DC: TESOL, 1983.

29. _____. "Training the Second Language Teacher as a Classroom

Researcher." pp. 281–87, in James Alatis, H. H. Stern, and P. Stevens, eds., *Applied Linguistics and the Preparation of Second Language Teachers: Toward a Rationale.* Washington, DC: Georgetown University, 1983.

30. _____. "Native Speaker/Nonnative Speaker Conversation and the Negotiation of Comprehensible Input." *Applied Linguistics* 4, 2 (1983):177–93.

31. _____. "Does Second-Language Instruction Make a Difference? A Review of Research" *TESOL Quarterly* 17, 3 (1983):359–82.

32. _____. "A Role for Instruction in Second Language Acquisition," pp. 77–99 in Kenneth Hyltenstam and Manfred Pienemann, eds., *Modeling and Assessing Second Language Acquisition.* Clevedon, Avon, England: Multilingual Matters, 1985.

33. _____. "Instructed Interlanguage Development." In Leslie Beebe, ed., *Issues in Second Language Acquisition.* Rowley, MA: Newbury House, forthcoming.

34. Markosian, Lawrence, and Tryg Ager. "Applications of Parsing Theory to Computer-Assisted Instruction," pp. 65–77 in David Wyatt, ed., *Computer-Assisted Language Instruction.* Oxford, England: Pergamon, 1983.

35. Magoto, Jeffrey. "CALL, Task-Based Learning and Vocabulary Learned in Context," pp. 63–82 in Ohio University Working Papers in Language and Linguistics, no. 8. Ohio University, Department of Linguistics, 1986.

36. Massaro, Dominick. *Understanding Language: An Information-Processing Analysis of Speech Perception, Reading and Psycholinguistics.* New York: Academic Press, 1975.

37. McLaughlin, Barry. "The Monitor Model: Some Methodological Considerations." *Language Learning* 28, 2 (1978):309–32.

38. _____, Tammi Rossman, and Beverly McLeod. "Second Language Learning: An Information Processing Perspective." *Language Learning* 33, 2 (1983):135–58.

39. Naiman, Neil, Maria Frölich, H. H. Stern, and Angela Todesco. *The Good Language Learner.* Toronto: The Ontario Institute for Studies in Education, 1978.

40. Nation, Robert, and Barry McLaughlin. "Novices and Experts: An Information-Processing Approach to the 'Good Language Learner' Problem." *Applied Psycholinguistics* 7, 1 (1986):41–56.

41. Mellgren, Millie P. "The Effect of Supplemental Computer Instruction on Achievement in Spanish." Unpublished Ph.D. dissertation. University of Nebraska (Lincoln), 1984.

42. Pica, Teresa, and Catherine Doughty. "Input and Interaction in the Communicative Language Classroom: A Comparison of Teacher-Fronted and Group Activities," pp. 115–32 in Susan Gass and Carolyn Madden, eds., *Input and Second Language Acquisition.* Rowley, MA: Newbury House, 1985.

43. _____, _____, and Richard Young. "The Impact of Interaction on Input Comprehension." Paper presented at the 20th Annual TESOL Convention, Anaheim, California, 1986.

44. Pienemann, Manfred. "Learnability and Syllabus Construction," pp. 23–75 in Kenneth Hyltenstam and Manfred Pienemann, eds., *Modeling and Assessing Second Language Acquisition.* Clevedon, Avon, England: Multilingual Matters, 1985.

45. Piper, Allison. "Conversation and the Computer: A Study of Conversational Spin-off Generated among Learners of English as a Foreign Language Working in Groups." *System* 14, 2 (1986):187–98.

46. Robinson, Gail, John Underwood, Wilga Rivers, José Hernández, Carollyn Rudesill, and Clare Malnik Enseñat. "Computer-Assisted Instruction in Foreign Language Education: A Comparison of the Effectiveness of Different

Methodologies and Different Forms of Error Correction." San Francisco: Center for Language & Crosscultural Skills, 1985. [EDRS: ED 262 626.]

47. Schaefer, Reiner. "Meaningful Practice on the Computer: Is It Possible?" *Foreign Language Annals* 14, 2 (1981):133–37.

48. Seliger, Herbert, and Michael Long. *Classroom Oriented Research in Second Language Acquisition.* Rowley, MA: Newbury House, 1983.

49. Selinker, Larry, "Interlanguage." *International Review of Applied Linguistics* 10, 2 (1972):219–31.

50. Sinclair, John M., and Richard M. Coulthard. *Towards an Analysis of Discourse: The English Used by Teachers and Pupils.* Oxford, England: Oxford University Press, 1975.

51. Soemarmo, Marmo, and John Graney. *Animated Grammar.* Public Domain Computer Program, Ohio University, Department of Linguistics, n.d.

52. Soemarmo, Marmo, Jeffrey Magoto, Giovanni Bennardo, and Kitty Franklin. "Project CASLU (Computer-Assisted Simulation of Language Use)." Paper presented at the Champaign-Urbana Conference on Computers in Language Research and Language Learning, University of Illinois at Urbana-Champaign, October, 1986.

53. Spolsky, Bernard. "Formulating a Theory of Second Language Learning." *Studies in Second Language Acquisition* 7, 3 (1985):269–88.

54. Stern, H. H. "Language Research and the Classroom Practitioner." *Canadian Modern Language Review* 34, 4 (1978):680–87.

55. _____, and James Cummins. "Language Teaching/Learning Research: A Canadian Perspective on Status and Directions," pp. 195–248 in June K. Phillips, ed., *Action for the '80s: A Political, Professional, and Public Program for Foreign Language Education.* The ACTFL Foreign Language Education Series. Lincolnwood, IL: National Textbook Company, 1981.

56. Tollefson, James, Bob Jacobs, and Elaine Selipsky. "The Monitor Model and Neurofunctional Theory: An Integrated View." *Studies in Second Language Acquisition* 6, 2 (1983):1–16.

57. Yao, Fuseng, and Ruth Ross. "The Design of the Plus One System." Paper presented at the Champaign-Urbana Conference on Computers in Language Research and Language Learning, University of Illinois at Urbana-Champaign, October 1986.

58. Young, Richard. "Computer-Assisted Language Learning Conversations." Paper presented at CALICO Conference. U.S. Naval Academy, Annapolis, MD, 1986.

7

A Psycholinguistic Perspective on Grammar and CALL

Nina Garrett
University of Illinois

Introduction

The purpose of this chapter is to discuss the potential of the computer in helping foreign language students learn to use the grammatical principles of the target language for communicative purposes. There is considerable disagreement in the field of foreign language education about whether grammar should be explicitly taught, because of the general feeling that learning grammar rules, or even learning to manipulate grammatical forms, does not contribute directly to learning to speak grammatically in spontaneous communication. This chapter suggests that a psycholinguistic rather than a linguistic notion of grammar is essential to the organization of such language learning, and will show how the computer is ideally—perhaps uniquely—suited to assist learners in that effort.

The argument necessarily involves theoretical considerations and exploration of general pedagogical concerns in order to establish a psycholinguistic perspective on grammar before ways to implement that perspective in computer materials can be suggested. The first part of the chapter will briefly propose a philosophical contrast between the terms CAI (computer-assisted instruction) and CALL (computer-assisted language learning). The second part will deal with current approaches to grammar, discussing (a) pedagogical attitudes toward grammar in general, (b) how current software represents those attitudes, and (c) ongoing efforts

Nina Garrett (Ph.D., University of Illinois) is Research Associate and Project Coordinator at the Language Learning Laboratory, University of Illinois at Urbana-Champaign, where she pursues theoretical issues in classroom second-language acquisition, organizes basic research projects, and consults on the integration of CALL into instructional and research programs. She is a member of ACTFL, AAAL, AERA, and co-editor of a regular column, "Foreign Language Teaching and the Computer" in *Foreign Language Annals*.

to improve error analysis and feedback within that CAI paradigm. The third section introduces a different way of thinking about grammar, suggesting a psycholinguistic perspective as a possible solution to theoretical and pedagogical problems. The fourth section then develops this notion into a framework for the design of CALL materials for grammar, and addresses the problems of error analysis and feedback from this psycholinguistic perspective. The chapter will close with a brief discussion of the implications of this psycholinguistic approach for classroom practice and for related research in mediated second-language learning.

CAI and CALL

Early attempts at developing computer-assisted instruction in foreign languages were understandably constrained by limits on what the technology could do; to use the computer idiom, the earliest foreign language computer-assisted instruction (FL CAI) was *machine-driven.* Limits on the amount of machine memory, on the ability to produce foreign language accents and special characters, on flexibility in judging student responses, etc., all required that software developers stay within a narrow range of possible exercise types, most commonly vocabulary and drill-and-practice grammar lessons. In the early days, many of the lessons being marketed were developed not by teachers but by programmers who had only a superficial knowledge of the foreign language and little if any idea of language pedagogy. At that point, the general perception of the computer's role in language teaching (that it only provided expensive ways to undertake already commonplace activities) was similar to that of many new technological media: it has often been said that television entertainment began by doing in its flashy new way essentially the same kinds of shows as had been popular on radio.

More recently, the increasing sophistication and power of computer technology has reduced the extent to which machine limitations control the design of materials, so that pedagogical considerations have come to the fore. As a consequence, FL CAI is now *teacher-driven,* both practically and conceptually—practically because foreign language teachers are participating in the design and production of software, and conceptually because current developments in FL software are increasingly dominated by the notion that the computer should act as much as possible like a good teacher.

It is time for FL CAI to become *learner-driven.* The computer's full potential for interaction with the individual learner cannot be exploited until decisions about the kinds of materials to be used and their design are based on theoretically motivated and research-based insights into the language-*learning* process rather than on traditional precepts about the language-*teaching* process.

Increasing use of the acronym CALL instead of CAI seems to suggest that this change of perspective has already taken place, but the terms are not always contrasted to the same purpose. Underwood (8), for example, implies that the term CAI in a strict sense should refer to lessons that actually present new instruction (i.e., tutorials), and seems to consider drill and practice as CALL, although of the most prosaic kind (p. 38). Another possible distinction has CAI referring to computer activities that replicate and extend classroom explanations and drill on grammar and vocabulary, and CALL referring to software that engages students in using the target language (TL) for interesting purposes without focusing attention explicitly on the formal aspects of the language they produce.

In this chapter, the terms CAI and CALL are not used to represent different types of lessons, but rather to connote different orientations in foreign language education. An exploration of current language-education philosophy and experience suggests that what is conventionally *taught* under the label of grammar is not what students need to *learn* in order to communicate grammatically. In this chapter, CAI thus refers to the use of computer materials designed to extend the role of teacher and/or workbook, to present or drill grammar as it is thought of traditionally in materials organized according to analyses of the target language. CALL, on the other hand, refers to uses of the computer developed on the basis of hypotheses about the process by which learners come to be able to communicate grammatically in that language. *Computer-assisted instruction in grammar,* from this perspective, is one extension of applied linguistics, since that is the discipline that concerns itself (among other things) with the generalizations that describe the abstract system of a given language. In contrast, to promote *computer-assisted learning of grammatical processing,* it is necessary to conceive of foreign language education as applied *psycho*linguistics, which concerns itself (among other things) with the way the human mind uses language.

Helping the student to learn grammar from any perspective is not necessarily the most important role for the computer. There are computer activities that assist the learning of vocabulary and cultural material, and more and more foreign language software is appearing in which the second language is used for content learning, problem solving, and recreational purposes. Many are excellent programs (although many are not), and having a variety of computer activities is obviously important in helping students develop the wide range of capabilities that is crucial to communicative language use, as well as in holding their interest. One purpose of this chapter, however, is to suggest that the learning of psycholinguistic processing of grammar underlies and is more involved in the general effort of learning a TL than the learning of "grammar" in its current restricted sense. From this perspective, therefore, the development of CALL materials focusing on grammatical processing may be one of the most important concerns for FL education.

Grammar and Language Learning _____

Teaching Grammar vs. Learning to Speak

To talk of teaching a language is to imply that there is a body of information, a subject matter, that teachers know and transmit to students. For centuries foreign language education accepted without question that the subject matter to be taught is the language, a set of vocabulary items, and a set of grammar rules based on the description of the target language furnished by linguists. In this view, it was the teacher's responsibility to select, simplify, and order these rules and transmit them to the students; it was the learners' responsibility to "know" these rules and practice "using" them until they could be "applied" accurately in translating and parsing sentences.

In recent years, however, most teachers have come to agree that the goal of language education should be not the learning of "the language"—an intellectually mastered body of material—but rather the learning of "how to speak the language," that is, a complex skill. But a complex skill cannot in fact be taught the way a body of information can; teachers can describe and demonstrate the behavior that constitutes the skill, but memorizing or understanding that description is not the same as learning the skill itself. In short, "teachers" of a complex skill cannot really teach it; they can only assist the learning by providing learners with structured opportunities for practice.

Speaking a language is arguably the most complex skill human beings ever acquire, and so, appropriately, most good language teaching these days is designed precisely along the lines of assisting learning. Teachers use most of their class time to model the TL and provide students with authentic situations for interaction. Students must undertake to express their own ideas on the TL, developing their language skill primarily on the basis of feedback on the success of that interaction. Given a certain amount of motivation, intelligence, and goodwill, students typically learn a great deal of language with this kind of help.

But there is still one component of language thought to be a teachable subject matter, a body of information to be mastered, and that is the grammar of the TL. Grammar is conventionally presented in foreign language textbooks as a set of descriptions of the formal features of the target language codified as rules for its correct production. Nowadays students are not required to recite the rules, but they are still expected to be able to "use" them—not in order to translate and parse, but to give correct TL form to the expression of their own ideas. Grammar rules thus seem to constitute a body of information to be transmitted to students, and mastery is supposedly achieved through drill and practice, although it is, ideally, demonstrated finally in spontaneous grammatical communication, not on discrete-point tests.

The problem is that although "the rules" of the language are taken for granted as defining grammaticality, the connection between *teaching grammar* and *learning to produce language grammatically* seems unreliable at best. Students and teachers alike feel that learning and/or practicing grammar rules is of little help in the effort to communicate one's own meaning accurately (let alone appropriately) in authentic spontaneous conversations. As a consequence, the grammar explanations in language textbooks have dwindled over the years, and methodology textbooks too have devoted less and less attention to training teachers to explain grammar. Nonetheless, most teachers still cannot help but feel that students must somehow be brought to some degree of demonstrable accuracy in the grammar of the TL through an understanding of how grammaticality is achieved. In a word, more or less reluctantly, teachers continue to teach *grammar,* hoping that students will learn *grammaticality.*

Grammar on the Computer

It is this complex of attitudes that has made many teachers feel that grammar work is exactly the right task to be relegated to the computer. Since the current philosophy of language teaching demands much heavier emphasis on the communication of meaning than on form, teachers feel that classroom time should be devoted as much as possible to authentic spontaneous interaction in the TL. Chastain (1), for example, says, "The goal of second-language educators should be to seek ways and means to expand the proportion of class time spent on the exchange of meaning in the second language" (p. 345). Of those teachers who favor the use of the computer at all, many feel that the machine can serve them best by taking over the tedium of drilling the student in the mechanical manipulation of language form, which is what grammar connotes.

It should be noted that still other teachers feel that grammar drill in any medium is incompatible with a focus on communicative competence and should be avoided entirely. They argue that the power of the computer, like that of the teacher, should be devoted entirely to communicatively oriented exercises, simulated communicative situations, etc., and they regard drill lessons as less worthy of attention either by the student or the programmer. Conflicting convictions about the value of teaching grammar thus undermine the effort in the classroom and on the computer. The result is a vicious circle: this grudging and negative attitude toward grammar inevitably prevents the development of innovative and exciting grammar software, and the fact that most computer grammar lessons have been mechanical and organized around discrete points of grammar increases teachers' sense that even on the computer grammar is boring or pointless.

Nonetheless, grammar has been the focus of a fairly high proportion of the foreign language software developed so far. In the "machine-driven" stage of CAI, grammar lessons were considered second only to vocabulary drills in ease of programming because the surface grammaticality of student input on discrete-point items can be checked by a mechanical comparison of letters or words to the correct TL version. In the "teacher-driven" stage, grammar software is popular not only because it relieves teachers of a burdensome task but also because the computer imposes no radical change in the way the chore is handled and therefore poses them no threat. Classroom explanations of grammar often add little to the textbook presentation, which can thus be presented just as effectively on a screen. And computers, like workbooks, provide answers by which students can correct their own work, so using the computer for this purpose does not change the overall approach. For the most part, grammar lessons on the computer have been developed along exactly the same lines as grammar lessons in any other medium and, in effect, many of them are simply the same lessons "computerized" with varying degrees of attention to "user friendliness." Programs have focused on the same "subject matter to be transmitted" and have been flawed by the same uncertainty about whether, or how, learning grammar fits into learning to communicate grammatically. The one real advantage in doing grammar on the computer rather than in a workbook (as most grammar software is now designed) is that the computer can give students immediate feedback on the correctness of their input.

Feedback and Error Analysis in CAI

But even in the task of "teaching grammar" (i.e., promoting student mastery of a body of rules) current software is not notably successful except perhaps with very able students. Most students learn no more from grammar on the computer than they do from grammar in the workbooks, because much of the commercially available offerings are of the "wrong, try again" model, which only indicates *whether* student-produced bits of language match the TL model stored in computer memory (sometimes also showing the correct answer) without indicating *how* or *why* the student input does not match. The ability to provide immediate and supposedly helpful feedback on student FL production has always been claimed as a major advantage for CAI, although the reasons offered are sometimes given in behaviorist terms (feedback gives positive/negative reinforcement) and sometimes in a cognitive framework (feedback provides confirmation/disconfirmation in hypothesis testing). Current efforts to improve grammar software therefore tend to focus on different ways of giving students better feedback, which is often said to be based on "error analysis."

One technique offers a feedback message that is in fact not based on analysis of the student's error at all, but presents an analysis of the *correct* answer; no matter what wrong answer the student types in, the feedback message is the same, explaining what it should have been. Teachers tend to feel that this restricted feedback severely constrains the usefulness of computer grammar lessons because students cannot always analyze how the "rule" they were using to produce their incorrect response differs from the correct one merely on being told "wrong," or even on seeing the correct answer after one or more unsuccessful attempts. Only in the most mechanical of drills, such as those that require students to choose among forms in the same paradigm, is this limited feedback message likely to be sufficient. Furthermore, students who have made only typing or spelling errors may resent grammar explanations.

In another technique, the computer indicates which specific letters of the student response do not match the correct answer. DASHER, for example, replaces incorrect letters with dashes, while TUTOR (the language of the mainframe PLATO system) and TUTOR-like languages for the microcomputer such as EnBASIC, TenCORE, and TEL, put symbols indicating a variety of error messages beneath the student's response (see Figure 1). Again, no *analysis* of the error takes place; the *location* of the error is pinpointed on the basis of the computer's letter-by-letter comparison of the student's input with the machine-stored correct version. This type of error markup has the advantage of allowing students to recognize their typing mistakes without having them labeled as grammar errors; the more detailed specification of the location and nature of the error (word missing, extra word, word belongs here, misspelling in ending, misspelling in root, etc.) can help the student to analyze the problem. But the machine looks only at the surface characteristics of the input; students must still derive for themselves the appropriate grammatical explanations for their errors, for example that the particular "misspelling" represents a wrong case choice as opposed to wrong gender.

A further level of feedback accuracy can be achieved if a CAI lesson author draws up a list of anticipated wrong answers for every item and programs the computer to give an appropriate message in response to whichever one the student enters. This technique allows the computer to give highly grammar-specific feedback if the author so desires. The disadvantages of this approach are that it is extremely time-consuming for the author to prepare and uses a great deal of machine memory; furthermore, unless the target student audience is relatively able and motivated, teachers will often find it difficult to anticipate all the wrong answers that may be produced. Similarly, they may find it even more difficult to establish unambiguous connections between certain wrong letters in the response and an appropriate explanation.

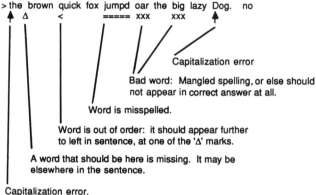

For example, suppose the correct answer and your response look this way:

The quick brown fox jumped over the lazy dog.

> the brown quick fox jumpd oar the big lazy Dog.   no

Capitalization error

Bad word: Mangled spelling, or else should not appear in correct answer at all.

Word is misspelled.

Word is out of order: it should appear further to left in sentence, at one of the 'Δ' marks.

A word that should be here is missing. It may be elsewhere in the sentence.

Capitalization error.

Figure 1. Answer mark-up on the PLATO system

The most sophisticated technique for providing "intelligent" feedback to student errors is based on current efforts to develop machine parsing, by which the computer is programmed to do a linguistic analysis of the student's response, comparing it to a stored analysis of the relevant grammar rules of the TL and returning a feedback message based on that comparison. The lesson author does not need to specify anticipated wrong answers, because the program can identify them. The development of computer parsing is still in its infancy (see Chapter 8 by Underwood in this volume) and no commercially available foreign language software incorporates such feedback mechanisms, but some linguists working in the area of artificial intelligence believe that limited parsing techniques will be available before too long. If so, it will be possible for the machine to analyze student errors in terms of linguistic units such as roots and endings, to check for concordance between adjectives and nouns or subjects and verbs, for example, and to give feedback in terms of grammatical categories and rules.

All these efforts to enable the computer to inform the student with greater precision of the particular grammatical rules being violated by an erroneous response will certainly constitute an improvement in the instructional component of CAI vis à vis grammar. But such refinements do not address the issue of whether grammar should be explicitly taught at all (cf. Krashen, 6, ch. IV), because they do not concern themselves with the question of how the learning of linguistic rules (cognitive mastery of a body of material) can be made to contribute to learning how to speak a language or how to communicate in spontaneous interaction (development of a complex skill).

The question of whether to use the computer to help students learn grammar, and of how that might be done, cannot be separated from this larger issue. The following section will suggest that a different perspective on grammar might provide a better basis for understanding how it functions in communication.

Psycholinguistic Processing

Linguistic vs. Psycholinguistic Rules

A Psycholinguistic Notion of Grammar.   How do "grammar" rules function in the act of speaking and comprehending language? Speakers do not begin with grammar rules and proceed from them to construct an utterance: they begin rather with an idea to communicate. To express one's own meaning is to *encode* it in grammatical and appropriate linguistic form; to understand someone else's utterance is to *decode* its form so as to arrive at the meaning. Speakers of a language must follow the same rules for encoding and decoding if their ideas are to be mutually comprehensible. To learn how to speak and understand a second language is therefore to learn how to do that encoding and decoding by the rules of its speakers rather than the rules of one's own native language community. *But the rules "used" by speakers for encoding or decoding meaning are not the rules common to foreign language textbooks.* The linguistic rules describe how the grammatical utterances of a language are related in its abstract system, and they describe the constraints on the surface form of an utterance, thus dictating its final form, but they do not describe the psycholinguistic process by which a speaker constructs the utterance.

The formulation of such a description, of the processing rules of a language (i.e., the rules by which its speakers process meaning into form and vice versa) is one of the goals of the field of psycholinguistics. The domain of psycholinguistics may overlap in some areas with the domain of psychology, but there are many psychological dimensions to language learning that cannot usefully be called *psycholinguistic.* Individual learners bring to the task complex and different sets of psychological characteristics that influence language learning in ways psycholinguists are only beginning to explore. For example, psychological factors such as motivation, cognitive style, and preferences for perceptual mode all influence the student's approach to second-language learning (and may influence individual students' ability to profit from using the computer), but there is as yet no clear evidence that these factors have a variable influence on how the learner structures language psycholinguistically. That is to say, there is no reason to believe that integrative motivation or field-independant cognitive style, for example, have a direct effect on learners' ability to use subordinate clauses or the dative case to encode meaning.

The interaction of these various individual characteristics with the process of language learning is not yet clearly understood, but it seems more useful to regard them as variables that affect the way the learner's mind comes to grips with the *general* task of language learning, long before the actual processing of meaning comes into play.

The following sections will explore the implications of a psycholinguistic notion of grammar with regard to the way grammar might be learned. These implications must be made explicit before the computer implementation of this perspective can be suggested.

The Processing of Meaning. In principle, a grammar in the psycholinguistic sense includes specifications for the relationships between the meanings human beings might want to express in language and the forms agreed upon by a given language community to express those meanings. Ideally, then, one would want a foreign language textbook to give learners a description of the native speakers' processing rules, starting with some prelinguistic specification of (1) a meaning to be conveyed, proceeding step-by-step through (2) the encoding operations, and ending with a specification of (3) the surface linguistic form. (The comprehension model would describe the reverse.) Unfortunately, this psycholinguistic processing happens so automatically and so fast in one's native language that introspection into the act is virtually impossible, and psycholinguists are far from able to supply sets of processing rules as linguists have supplied system rules. But it is not impossible to construct a simplified model of how a language conveys meaning—and, in fact, fluent educated nonnative speakers, such as language teachers, may be best able to make such an analysis.

None of the three components in the processing can be taken for granted. It is often assumed that the *kinds* of meaning (the first component) human beings want to express are universal (although the content words for a topic like the theory of relativity are not), but that assumption overlooks the fact that of the infinite number of bits of meaning available for expression, each particular language has a different subset of concepts that must be marked *grammatically* rather than by choice of vocabulary. To speak a language, one must "know" which bits these are, although for native speakers and naturalistic learners this knowledge is not conscious or explicit. This point is seldom made with any generality in textbooks, despite the fact that certain forms such as grammatical gender are presented on this basis. It is crucial that language learners understand that not only the kinds of grammatical marking but also the concepts they mark vary from one language to another. For example, the *shape* of an object is not a bit of meaning that must be grammatically indicated in English (it can be implied by the name of an object, as in "sphere," or by an adjective such as "round") but in Navajo a verb of handling must be given a grammatical marker to indicate the shape of its direct object. In some languages the *purposefulness* of an action must be marked on a verb; in some languages nouns must be marked for their position on a scale of *animacy,* and so on.

The second component of processing is the set of coding systems that handle the marking of meaning. Human languages have a small number of systems: (1) function words, (2) ways of changing lexical form such as prefixes, suffixes, infixes, vowel changes, etc., (3) word order, and (4) suprasegmental features such as stress and tone. Each language uses some subset of these systems, and different languages may use different coding properties to convey the same bit of meaning. For example, location may be indicated by a preposition or function word in one language, but by a noun suffix in another. Traditional grammar explanations give such scanty attention to this important component of processing that students often have no idea of the differences in kinds of meaning conveyed by verb endings and noun phrase endings (regardless of whether textbooks use technical grammatical terminology or not).

Speakers must also know how to choose the right form from the paradigm of that coding system for a particular context. For example, a German speaker needs to "know" that endings on noun modifiers mark case relations and that it is the accusative case that marks transitivity. Further, the speaker needs to "know" that there are different accusative forms marking the three grammatical genders and yet another marking plurality. Traditional grammar presentations, however, tend to present only the latter part of the processing.

It is important to note, on the other hand, that not all of the bits of code in a language are directly related to a specific bit of meaning. Some forms may once have had meaning that has since been eroded in historical changes. Moreover, some forms may carry information that is also, and more clearly, represented elsewhere. For example, personal endings on verbs are said to indicate which noun is the subject, but in languages like English and German, which require a sentence to have an explicit subject, the verb ending is actually redundant, because nominative case forms or the position of a noun phrase indicate the subject much more clearly. In Russian or Spanish, in contrast, the subject is often omitted and the verb ending is correspondingly more important. In another example, although the dative case on sentence objects in German often carries the meaning "recipient," the dative case on objects of the prepositions *aus, bei, mit,* and several others carries no discernible meaning. Those prepositions always take the dative, that's all, just as some others always take the accusative. When learners get the case wrong after these prepositions, the error causes no confusion about meaning, but the sentence is ungrammatical. Some of the formal requirements in a language, therefore, cannot be explained in terms of meaning but can only be stated as arbitrary surface structure constraints, as Higgs (5) points out in his hierarchy of explainability.

The term "meaning" usually refers to semantic information. But many grammatical structures encode syntactic information, clues about the organization of the utterance. For example, a relative pronoun encodes the syntactic information that a separate sentence has been embedded to modify one of the main sentence's nouns. Several semantic categories may be merged into a single syntactic one: the semantic roles of both agent (as in "I warm the coffee") and experiencer (as in "I am cold") are represented by the syntactic subject in English. These combinations too may differ across languages; in German, for example, the experiencer is not rendered in the nominative case as the agent is, but in the dative case as the recipient is.

This psycholinguistic perspective on what grammar is and how it operates in the mind of a speaker provides a basis for understanding why the learning of traditional or linguistic grammar has not been of much use to students. Because textbook explanations of grammar are based on linguistic rules, they describe the required final form of an utterance, focusing almost exclusively on the third component of the three discussed above, the required surface form, rather than on the psycholinguistic process that leads to it. Most textbook grammar rules "explain" a structure in terms of its relationship to other structures in the system as a whole (for example, the passive is usually explained in terms of its structural relationship to the active, and the negative and interrogative in terms of the positive and declarative). In other cases, structures may be explained by reference to other elements in the sentence. ("If a clause begins with one of this list of conjunctions, the finite verb must come last.") Most rules describing grammatical structures make only indirect reference to the meaning they encode, and even then this meaning is often given in terms of grammatical labels. These labels are supposed to be familiar to students who have studied English grammar, and the assumption is that the labels remind them of the way meaning is processed in English. So, for example, "explaining" that the dative case in German is used for the indirect object is supposed to evoke in students the knowledge that that term refers to the recipient of an action so that they will use the dative case in German to encode that notion. The vast majority of grammar points in most foreign language textbooks receive only such surface-based explanations.

There are, of course, structures that can only be explained in terms of the distinctions in meaning they convey, where the explanation ties to function like a processing rule. For example, in prepositional phrases of place in German that use one of nine prepositions, the dative case specifies the meaning "place where" and the accusative "place to which." But even though textbooks explain that the concept of directionality is the crucial determiner of case, students are routinely diverted from the concept by being told that the presence of a verb of motion is the easy clue to the need for the accusative—which will lead them to make errors in sentences like "We drove around in the city for two hours" (dative) or "The teacher wrote the grades in his notebook" (accusative). Still worse, explanations for many structures are short-circuited when the meaning is defined in terms of traditional grammatical labels, which are often misleading or outright wrong: the difference between the imperfect and the present perfect is routinely labeled as one of tense, but it is in fact a difference of aspect, a term that almost never appears in French or German textbooks.

Can Psycholinguistic Processing Be "Taught"? Even if speakers do use psycholinguistic or processing rules rather than linguistic ones in constructing or comprehending utterances, that is not of itself an argument for teaching processing rules to language learners. Knowing what the processing rules of a language are is still not the same thing as being able to use them. Students will not learn to speak solely on the basis of cognitive mastery of processing rules (via CALL or otherwise) any more than they do solely on the basis of mastery of linguistic rules. In learning any complex skill, understanding why and how the behaviors work is only one way of organizing the learning, making it more efficient, reducing confusion and misdirected hypothesis testing. The skill itself can only be developed as the learner practices it. Explanations of processing rules will be of use to classroom learners only if they are thought of as organizing principles to assist ongoing active efforts to communicate in the target language. The understanding and the doing must be connected; teaching students to understand linguistic rules has not assisted the doing, because the rules do not describe how processing is done.

The argument advanced here is thus twofold. (1) If students are to be given any explicit explanations of grammar, an understanding of processing rules will serve them better in learning to communicate in a new language than will a knowledge of linguistic rules. (2) Beyond elementary school levels classroom learners need some organizing principles for their learning. The first assertion is based on the examination of the function of both kinds of rules in the preceding sections of this chapter. The second is a topic of serious disagreement among foreign language teachers, some of whom are convinced that classroom learners need only to be psychologically receptive to large amounts of comprehensible input without any explicit discussion of grammar (cf. Krashen, 6, ch. III).

The theoretical backgrounds for these opposing positions need not be rehashed here; the point is that the claim forms a testable hypothesis (and the computer provides an appropriate medium for testing it, as is suggested at the conclusion of this chapter). Research studies could compare the communicative skills of three groups of students, all in communicatively oriented classrooms: (1) those who receive no explanations of grammar at all, (2) those who receive traditional grammar explanations like those common to communicatively oriented textbooks, and (3) those who receive explanations of processing. The research instrument might be the ACTFL/ETS Oral Proficiency Interview or any reliable and valid test of communicative abilities. Such research cannot be undertaken, however, until the processing approach has been implemented. (For a more detailed discussion of the theoretical basis for conceiving of grammar in psycholinguistic terms and of the pedagogical implications of this approach, see Garret, 4.)

Why Implement the Processing Approach via CALL

This discussion of the differences between the traditional approach to grammar and the psycholinguistic perspective should not be taken to imply that the latter represents a total change from current practice. Many teachers intuitively use a psycholinguistic perspective to elaborate on textbook rules so as to help students use structures accurately in spontaneous speech. (Perhaps the ability to do this is one of the characteristics that makes a good teacher.) But teachers have not been trained from this perspective, and most feel that they should not spend much class time discussing grammar. Although the desirability of using class time for personal and group interaction and spontaneous communication is unarguable, the corollary is the need to provide students outside of class with access to the processing principles that will help them organize their learning and the means to practice them efficiently and individually in the absence of a teacher or tutor.

The computer has advantages, including its ability to individualize instruction. It is the ideal medium both for helping students understand the psycholinguistic perspective on language and for helping them to use it to develop their own processing in the TL.

Individualization is claimed to be one of the major advantages of CAI, but so far individualized instruction has meant little except allowing students to control some of the conditions under which they proceed through the material. Pace is controlled by the learner in virtually all lessons except in game formats, and even there the learner can usually choose among several pace settings. In other attempts at individualization, some CAI lessons allow students to choose whether they want audio, or in which order they enter lessons, or whether to review missed items. All these options accomplish a certain amount of psychological individualization in allowing students to impose their learning-style preferences on the lesson, but the *material* being taught is still the same for all students, and it is being taught in the same *way.*

There is much more to individualization than student control over superficial details of an instructional presentation. Individualizing learning assistance for psycholinguistic processing requires an assessment of the learner's unconscious language processing and the use of that assessment to design the learning needed. Yet it would be impossible for classroom teachers to collect the detailed data needed to assess each student's processing of each grammatical structure. Even when teaching one-on-one, a teacher cannot store the student's every utterance and constantly analyze the patterns of errors, combined with the patterns of correct use, needed to hypothesize the individual's idiosyncratic interlanguage rule for "when this form is used." Interlanguage research has shown that even learners with the same native language and the same amount and kind of input in the target language may still develop very different interlanguage rules for any given structure, so the teacher cannot assume that one kind of idiosyncratic processing will be common to all students in the class (Garrett, 3). Since neither methodology nor foreign language textbooks have as yet adopted the notion of processing as an organizing principle, teachers have no training in applying this approach to their analyses and no support for it in their materials.

The computer, on the other hand, can be programmed not only to present instructional material but also to elicit student response to it, collect information about student performance, analyze that information for evidence of idiosyncratic processing, and give feedback based on that analysis to the learners. Finally, the computer can, if teachers desire, use the analysis to control the choice of the next instructional material offered to help the learner reshape the processing. Used in this way, CALL offers major advantages to students over CAI. At the same time, this kind of CALL fills another frequent demand, that the computer be used to do things that cannot be done otherwise, rather than provide an expensive electronic version of other media.

How to Implement the Processing Approach via CALL ____

Having explored the reasons foreign language education should conceive of grammar in psycholinguistic rather than in linguistic terms and why this approach should be implemented on the computer, this section will suggest a framework for designing CALL activities that will help students use this perspective on grammar in organizing their own language learning.

Topics for CALL grammar lessons can be roughly divided into four groups, which will be discussed separately below: (1) consciousness raising, (2) major grammatical topics in the TL, (3) particular structures, and (4) the surface structure. It should be clearly understood at the outset, however, that the order in which they are discussed herein does not represent some absolute order of presentation to the student; these do not constitute a syllabus, but are conceptual groupings. The best order of lessons or topics from among these groups needs to be determined empirically according to pedagogical principles and to the nature of the TL.

Consciousness Raising

The first topic, a general prerequisite to helping the learner understand and make use of the processing approach, could be called consciousness raising. Students must be brought to think about language and about language learning in terms of the acquisition of processing. They will almost certainly never have thought about "how language works" in any terms other than traditional grammar labels, and they generally approach the task of learning a second language with a very negative attitude toward "grammar" as they have always conceived it.

Consciousness-raising lessons should lead students to understand the concept of processing itself and the variety of ways in which any language's forms encode a variety of different kinds of information—semantic, syntactic, pragmatic, discourse, and sociolinguistic. The purpose of these lessons is not to teach the terminology for discussing all this, but to give students a way of thinking about processing that will help when they come to processing problems in the TL. The material should take the form of highly interactive tutorials with many examples in the native language—but "highly interactive" should not be allowed to mean only that students often press NEXT or ENTER. (Many lessons called tutorials are nothing more than page-turning exercises.) Students' attention must be engaged constantly; after the presentation of any concept or set of examples they can be asked for their intuitions or asked to respond so as to show that they have understood the material. Once they have developed some insight into the bits of meaning that must be grammatically encoded in English, the general concept of processing can be extended to show that other languages require grammatical marking for quite other bits of meaning. A wide variety of examples in other languages, translated literally, usually intrigues students. Even those who resent "the language requirement" and feel no motivation to learn a foreign language can be fascinated by insights into "how language works."

Another set of consciousness-raising CALL tutorials can help students establish a framework for understanding certain major grammatical concepts. It cannot be assumed that even those students who have "learned English grammar" have any conceptual grasp of what the labels, categories of analysis, and explanations actually mean in terms of expressing one's own thought in language. Among the most important topics might be:

- What does grammatical case mean? What are the differences between a language that marks case with word order and one that uses inflections? What is the relationship between semantic roles, such as agent, patient, recipient, and grammatical notions such as subject, direct object, indirect object?
- What is the difference between tense and aspect? How do the concepts interact in verb expressions?
- What is the difference between main or coordinate clauses and sub-

ordinate ones? Why do languages have subordinate clauses?
- What is the difference between finite and nonfinite verb forms? What are the various nonfinite forms used for?
- Which grammatical structures operate mostly on a sentence level, and which are used to organize meaning in larger units, such as paragraphs or conversations?

Major Grammatical Topics in the TL

A second category of CALL lessons is needed to organize the major grammatical topics of the TL. A few lessons giving a general overview might be introduced at the beginning of the language course, but it will be more important to establish a piece of the conceptual framework at each point in the syllabus when a new kind of TL structure is introduced. (For example, the first time a verb tense is explicitly presented, a general discussion of the TL tense system is appropriate, and so on.) The number, scope, and nature of the major organizing topics will of course vary from one language to another. Here again, multiple examples are vital, but it will probably be more efficient to limit them to the native and the target language, so as to provide a contrastive analysis of processing. (Most of the examples that have made their way into textbooks are based on contrastive analysis of *linguistic* rules, not on contrastive processing.)

Even at these first two levels of CALL materials, the lessons can be individualized. Some students have an intuitive understanding of psycholinguistic processing, without having thought about it in those terms, or can grasp the explanations very quickly and may need only a little help to make their understanding conscious and generalizable. Others may have a thorough grounding in the terminology and the surface structures to which it refers but little grasp of communicative uses. Still others will have neither. These tutorials on grammar should include a fairly small set of questions after an introduction of the topic to allow students who do understand it to bypass unnecessary explanations or exercises and proceed to more relevant sections. Those who find later that they have not grasped the material well enough can always return to it; students can be encouraged to go back to these general lessons whenever they find themselves confused about the way a particular structure fits into the processing system of the TL.

Particular Structures of the TL

The third and most complex group of CALL lessons must address the processing of particular grammatical structures in the TL. It cannot be taken for granted that reference to apparently analogous structures in English will be helpful. Contrastive analysis of *structures* will not necessarily provide clues to contrasts in *processing*. The discussion of how similar meaning is processed in English may be helpful, but lesson designers must be on their guard against assuming that a structure encodes the same meaning in two languages just because the grammatical label for the structure is the same (the subjunctive encodes a quite different meaning in French than in German).

Lessons on particular structures must allow students to focus separately on three parts of the learning: (1) understanding the concept to be marked, (2) knowing the form of the marking, and (3) developing fluency and semiautomaticity in connecting them.

The first part of this type of CALL lesson establishes the conceptual groundwork of the structure. Students practice recognizing those bits of meaning that dictate the need for the structure in question in contrast to those that do not. For example, when the accusative case is being introduced, students need help in distinguishing direct objects from predicate nominatives or other objectlike noun phrases that come after verbs (such as "I'm going home"), because in English it is word order that encodes direct-objecthood and so they may think that any noun phrase after the verb is a direct object. Students should practice on a wide variety of English sentences, indicating whether they contain a direct object, until they demonstrate a reliable sense of transitivity, whether it is labeled as such or not. (If after they respond to the English sentence the TL translation is provided automatically, with the relevant form highlighted, they will receive extra input.) If the TL notion of transitivity (or whatever) differs significantly from English, the next step is to offer a selection of TL sentences, again with the relevant form highlighted, showing the contrast and explaining it; these can also be followed by literal translation to point up the contrast. Curtin's (2) lesson on aspect in Russian is an excellent example of this kind of exercise, as is Shinall's (7) presentation of the perfect/imperfect difference in French.

In the early part of tutorials of this type, the meaning should be unambiguous and easy for students to recognize, but in time it will be especially important to offer as examples sentences in which the distinguishing features are less clear—in order to fine-tune their grasp of the concept. For example, in presenting those nine prepositions in German mentioned above following which the choice of case marks "place where" or "place to which," it is the *apparently* anomalous sentences that most clearly point up the fact that the case choice marks the concept of directionality, whether the verb expresses it explicitly or not.

The second part of the tutorial focuses on the purely formal character of the structure, the other end of the meaning–form continuum. Drills are set up so that no conceptual decisions are required; students know what category of form they need (i.e., which paradigm they are working from), and the point of the exercise is to practice using the correct bit of the paradigm in given sentence environments. (This kind of drill makes up the bulk of traditional grammar lessons both in workbooks and in software.)

While the processing perspective makes it clear why drilling form alone will not help students to use a structure, even learning to make conceptual distinctions in additional CALL exercises will not of itself solve the problem, because the explicit focus of both conceptual and formal exercises is entirely different from the communicative situation. In spontaneous communication, a speaker's mind is not focused explicitly either on analyzed bit of meaning or on form. In virtually all conventional grammar exercises and tests, either the pattern of blanks to be filled or the drill instructions make the student aware of the particular "rule" that is supposed to apply, the particular structure being called for. Students' ability to perform well on such a test is no guarantee whatsoever that they will be able to produce the structure in communicative situations, where no such indication is provided. Students must therefore be given practice in bridging the gap between language-producing situations that make too explicitly focused a demand (drills on either meaning or form) and situations in which the demand is entirely unfocused (spontaneous communication). Only "open" (rather than discrete-point) exercises offer this opportunity—and it is in these CALL lessons that the transition is made between learning the components of processing and learning to do it.

Open exercises are ones in which the student's attention is not directed to one particular structure, either its meaning or its form. One type of open exercise is translation from English into the target language. Translation exercises have been out of favor for many years because teachers fear that they encourage students to attempt word-for-word renditions of the native language sentence. Although this might tend to be true in the context of the conventional approach to grammar, in which explanations are routinely given in terms of surface equivalences, under the processing approach it is much easier to train students not to translate word for word but to think about the different kinds of meaning in a sentence and work out the parallel processing required to render them in the TL.

In designing CALL translation exercises it is important to prevent students from making many extraneous errors, such as typos and misspellings or the choice of an unanticipated vocabulary item, since computer response to them can distract attention from the particular problem that needs work, and can be discouraging as well. One partial solution, which helps prevent extraneous errors but still avoids focusing conscious attention on a particular structure, is to supply with each sentence the vocabulary needed and other information appropriate to the task—gender of nouns, verb class, tense required, etc.—whatever information does *not* contribute directly to the production of the structure in question. This information can be given at the bottom of the screen for each sentence.

The same effect can be obtained with the "scrambled and dehydrated sentence" format, in which the student is given a series of words or phrases in the TL and told to combine them to make a sentence. If the concept to be practiced is word order, then after the student has indicated the correct order of words or phrases the computer can automatically insert the necessary function words and inflections. If the exercise requires the student to supply inflections, the computer can take care of the word order on its own. At an advanced level the student might be given only a series of nouns and a verb and instructed to add any necessary function words and inflections.

These open exercises need not be used extensively for every structure to be learned, but they must occur regularly to prevent the gap between the students' ability to produce a certain form when they know it is required and their ability to realize unconsciously (or rapidly enough to seem so) when that form is required for the thought they want to express.

Checking Surface Structure

So far this chapter's suggestions for designing CALL lessons to help students understand processing and learn how to do it in a foreign language have dealt only with the connection between meaning and form. However, there are grammatical structures in every language for which some particular uses cannot be "explained" in terms of the meaning they convey; certain forms must be used in an utterance just because it would otherwise be considered ungrammatical. In other words, descriptive grammar rules impose a set of final constraints on utterances. The fourth level of grammatical processing, therefore, is checking the surface structure of what one is about to say against the template of grammaticality provided by the linguistic rules. Native speakers do not consciously use explicit normative grammatical rules to monitor production, except in deliberate attempts to speak "correctly" (as for example by remembering to use "whom," or not to split infinitives); usually this monitoring is entirely intuitive. But it is common for native speakers as well as second-language learners to self-correct, to back up in an utterance and repair it because of the feeling "it's going to come out wrong."

It has been argued here that linguistic rules do not themselves function as processing rules because generalizations about the nature of the product do not necessarily describe the process. Nonetheless, the end result of the psycholinguistic processing (the utterance itself) must be describable by the rules of the linguistic system in order to be grammatical, and it is in this way that psycholinguistic and linguistic rules intersect.

The ability to monitor successfully, in this psycholinguistic sense, depends on having an underlying set of intuitions about whether an utterance is grammatical, i.e., having the relevant competence in the Chomskyan sense. (It is not a matter of having a conscious knowledge of the relevant learned rule.) It is these intuitions that provide the template against which to check the outcome of the processing; for the native or near-native speaker, the intuitions are established through years of interactions with a stable speech community whose norms are unconsciously analyzed and followed to ensure membership. Students, however, have fragmentary and unreliable intuitions about the TL (or about their own interlanguage version of it), and so they have inadequate templates for monitoring surface structure. It is sometimes said that the goal of language learning is to develop a competence as similar as possible to that of the native speaker, i.e., the same intuitions. Part of the task of language learning, then, is to build something like the native speaker's template, and that is accomplished by letting students submit their output to a model of the native speaker's template and helping them to understand how that template operates, so as to promote the building of their own.

CALL exercises on formally required surface structures are essentially no different form the form-focused exercises described in the discussion of the processing of grammatical structures where a meaning-form connection does need to be made. It is helpful to students, however, to be made aware that though the exercises are similar the processing is different.

Feedback and Error Analysis in CALL

Feedback in conventional grammar CAI is designed, ideally, to make students aware of the mismatch between their input and the required form in terms of linguistic rules. But even when students can correct a wrong answer after getting the standard "wrong—try again" feedback, their doing so does not guarantee that they understand anything about why they made the error in the first place, or why the "alternate" answer is the correct one, or what the error message (or even the exercise itself) is supposed to help them learn. Instead, they often revise their answers on the basis of a "binary correction strategy" ("If it isn't X, it must by Y.") Even when the TL paradigm for a structure includes three or four logically possible forms, students often adopt a rule of thumb for choosing between just two. For example, although in German there are four cases, students who make a case error in marking sentence objects and objects of prepositions usually correct it as if the choice were limited to dative and accusative. Though there are three genders, students confronted with a gender error often lump masculine and neuter together in contrast to the feminine. True, in many of the processing choices to be made, such a binary strategy does fit "the facts" of German: with few exceptions, if a verb isn't strong it's weak; if "nicht" is the wrong negative form it must be "kein"; if the article isn't definite it's indefinite; if the second-person pronoun isn't familiar it must be formal, and so on. (Other binary sets will obtain in other languages.) The issue for the teacher or CALL lesson designer who wants to supply appropriate feedback is not whether the binary correction strategy invoked by students is inaccurate; knowing that it *is* invoked should make it clear that giving feedback that indicates an error and requiring that the error be corrected will not assure that students have been assisted in any learning at all.

Most of the feedback-design recommendations in discussions of computer-based instruction in any field are predicated on hypotheses from learning psychology—the advisability of "personalizing" the feedback with the student's name, or of varying it (or making it more palatable) by using responses like "fantastic/sorry" instead of "yes/no" or "right/wrong," etc. Discussions of feedback in FL software tend to focus on questions such as whether the response should be in the target language or not, whether students should automatically see (or should have the option of seeing) the correct answer and, if so, at what point in the sequence of correction attempts, whether hints should be given, whether students should be made to type the correct answer in, etc.

Unfortunately, none of these questions can be answered in the abstract or for the learner population as a whole. Some students prefer to figure out the right answer for themselves and will not accept the option of on-line helps even when they are offered and even when the responses they make indicate that they are far from understanding their own problems. They become disaffected or angry if the right answer is provided automatically, and learn little from it. Other students, in contrast, want to make minimal effort, and always choose to see the answer as soon as possible so as to be able to get to the next item, learning little from seeing it. Hints and selective response to errors (either surface responses such as the standard PLATO markup or DASHER's substitution of dashes for incorrect characters) may be helpful to students who know the material and only need practice in making their production more fluent, but markup or analysis may be perceived as frustrating or even mocking by students who don't understand their problems. These are important affective issues, and they must be taken into account in continuing attempts to individualize CALL. Nonetheless, they are only indirectly related to the issue of concern in this chapter, the learning of TL grammatical processing. The kind of CALL feedback required will vary according to the level of processing being addressed.

As was discussed above, current attempts to improve the feedback offered in conventional grammar CAI are based on the assumption that, to correct errors, the learner needs a reminder of the required final shape of the utterance, whether that reminder is an indication of which characters are wrong or a hint about the reasons one form or another is appropriate in terms of grammatical labels or the presence of other structures in the sentence. In some cases this assumption may be correct. If the error in question is simply a violation of a surface-structure constraint, resulting from the student's forgetting something that need not be understood but only memorized, or if the learner has grasped the concept but has not had enough practice in choosing paradigmatic forms, then it is appropriate to supply such a reminder of the linguistic template.

When, however, the use of the grammatical structure in question is controlled by the presence of some kind of meaning, when the choice between the forms is dictated by conceptual considerations, then the feedback message should not assume that the error was made because of a formal problem; the student may not have understood or recognized the relevant meaning. For example, when students of German mark an indirect object with the accusative case instead of the dative, teachers commonly assume that the error is due to forgetting either the dative endings or the fact that indirect objects take the dative. In any particular instance, either of these may be the problem, but it is very often the case that students have no real sense of why the noun or pronoun is an indirect object; they have never been made aware that the *grammatical* notion "indirect object" is specifically constituted by the *semantic* relation of recipient. (The fact that many German textbooks also use the phrase "indirect object" to refer to any noun phrases in the dative, even those that represent the semantic role of experiencer, is not particularly helpful either.) Obviously if students have no underlying sense of what an indirect object is, a feedback message to the effect that they have forgotten what the dative endings are will be of no real assistance to their learning even if it does clue them in to the right answer. This circumstance is the basis for the prevalent belief that correcting errors does very little good.

How is one to know at which level of processing the student is going wrong? In sentences taken at random from students' TL production, it is virtually impossible to be certain; linguistic parsers, and error-analysis algorithms based on them, are becoming increasingly sophisticated in pinpointing the linguistic rules being violated, but they cannot determine whether the error was purely formal or was motivated by processing problems. The more spontaneous and authentic and communicative the utterance the more difficult the analysis. Even an observant and linguistically sensitive teacher listening to classroom interchanges cannot do more than develop hunches about why a particular student seems to be making particular errors, and students themselves are notoriously incapable of reliable introspection. It is possible to analyze students' TL data for patterns of errors and correct production, but a discouragingly large amount of data is needed to allow the postulation of idiosyncratic processing rules—far more, and far more complex, than can be generated by the conventional grammar exercises commonly assigned. The computer can play an important role in such research, as will be described briefly below.

It is clearly crucial to CALL that feedback address students' processing problems, but this does not pose an impossible demand on error-analysis programming. If the teaching of grammar is conceived in psycholinguistic terms from the beginning, then there will be no need for error-analysis techniques capable of analyzing all levels of processing simultaneously.

CALL exercises that focus student attention explicitly on one or another stage of processing—the conceptual distinctions to be marked, the interaction of one kind of meaning with another, the choice of grammatical structure, the choice of paradigmatic form, etc.—require that feedback address only that stage.

CALL lessons devoted to consciousness raising about psycholinguistic processing and to the exploration of major grammatical topics in the TL can ask for simple responses—yes/no, multiple choice—to check on understanding of the concept. In such lessons "incorrect" responses demonstrate lack of conceptual recognition, and the lesson should not respond as if the student should have known something but didn't. Rather it should show some understanding of why learners might have thought what they did, and explain how and why the processing of the language is different. Curtin's Russian aspect tutorial gives a one-sentence explanation as part of the feedback to both correct *and* incorrect responses in the exercises, whereas most drills that give any explanatory feedback do so only after a wrong answer. Curtin (personal communication) explains that she has found in drilling conceptually challenging material that students will sometimes deliberately give wrong answers in order to call forth explanatory feedback; giving it for correct responses as well helps the students by corroborating what might have been only a guess. Beginning this way helps to make students capable of more useful introspection into their own processing, and it also provides an explicit anchor for TL forms, which otherwise often float around in confusion.

The CALL exercises focusing on form then temporarily set aside considerations of meaning; in these, as has already been indicated, the feedback too can ignore the processing of meaning and can rest on the best available linguistic analysis, reminding students of the language system requirements.

In meaning-focused and form-focused CALL lessons, only one component of the processing of a given structure is dealt with at a time; each can thus be mastered before it is confused with the other. Then in later higher-order CALL exercises that demand that students process form and meaning together, it will seldom be difficult to ascertain whether an error is due to formal or conceptual problems. If students have been required to achieve consistently high performance on the purely formal drills, then errors on the open exercises can reasonably be assumed to be conceptual in origin. Even without referring back to earlier work, a CALL lesson can move back and forth between levels of processing to help students find the source of difficulty. Suppose that a student's score on an open exercise is unsatisfactory. The lesson can remind the student of the formal requirements, perhaps displaying the paradigm at the bottom of the screen, and can offer all the items again or present a new set of similar ones. If performance is then entirely accurate (or almost so) the student can be advised to work on learning the forms better. If, on the other hand, the score improves only a little or not at all, then the program can suggest that the student may be having difficulties with the conceptual distinctions required and should review the earlier part of the lesson that dealt with them. If the exercise has a large enough selection of sentences, the lesson can continue to present unfamiliar items that require the same processing, so that students do not simply learn to produce the sentences they have learned how to correct.

In advanced-level open exercises where students construct sentences out of supplied elements, the program will have to be able to check the input against a stored list of several different correct sentences. The teacher/author is unlikely to be able to think up as many possible responses as the students, so rather than reject bizarre but grammatical answers the feedback might offer the stored list together with questions to help students decide whether their sentence is as good as the ones suggested.

If CALL exercises are designed to *diagnose* students' level of comprehension of a concept, or their mastery of a formal category, it may be appropriate to defer feedback until the end in order not to affect performance. Students should be told that the purpose of the exercise is to allow the computer to develop a basis for guiding them on the most efficient learning path. The diagnosis should then be given at the end, with a brief explanation of the criteria for the recommendation to review, proceed through the lesson, review a tutorial, or skip to another segment.

It is possible to design such diagnostic exercises to allow the computer to analyze students' errors for evidence of some particular processing problem. For example, since English-speaking students often have difficulty in recognizing indirect objects, one could put together a translation exercise containing indirect objects in a variety of sentence environments: in some of the English sentences it might be indicated with "to" (as in "I gave the money to my brother") and in others with word order ("I gave my brother the money"). If the program keeps tabs on the percentage of errors made on each of these two types of sentences, and if the percentage is significantly higher on the former type, then the program can provide a feedback message such as "You seem to have more trouble recognizing the indirect object when it has the preposition 'to' in front of it; remember it's the notion of recipient that counts—English can encode it two ways but German only with the dative case." It is up to the teacher-author to design these analyses on the basis of experience in understanding students' most common problems.

Integration of CALL and Classroom Activities

If adequate materials and an adequate number of computers were available, it would in principle be possible for teachers to assign explicit work on grammar entirely to the computer so that they could, if they wished, devote all their class time to communicative and proficiency-oriented activities. It seems likely, however, that once the concept of processing is familiar, both teachers and students will feel more comfortable if the study of grammar is not entirely segregated. More important, the integration of CALL and classroom activities can be mutually supportive and result in more efficient learning. Processing exercises can be assigned as homework, following up on some classroom explanations or practice of new forms or functions, just as linguistic exercises always have been assigned. In addition, however, many of the CALL activities proposed here could be carried out *in preparation for* the classroom activities they relate to. The CALL work can serve as an advance organizer: a firm grasp of the relevant conceptual material should prepare students to understand much more of the near-native-speed language heard in class. Preparatory work of this kind can thus help turn much more of the input of the classroom into *intake.*

Summary

To sum up, then, the psycholinguistic perspective on grammar as processing suggests several different kinds of second-language learning tasks.

1). Learners must develop the ability to recognize the kinds of semantic and syntactic meaning that are obligatorily represented in grammatical form in the TL, and they must know what formal elements encode those meanings.

2). They must know the surface structure constraints of the TL well enough to be able to monitor the output of their processing so that it fits the TL linguistic template; that is, they must develop the intuitions about grammaticality that make up TL linguistic competence.

3). They must develop facility in actually carrying out TL processing, not just know how it works; they must learn a skill, not just master a body of material.

It has been argued in this chapter that CALL activities can be uniquely helpful (and may be essential) in organizing students' learning. CALL lessons can tailor the presentation of conceptual material to the level of understanding of individual students and allow each one the amount of practice he or she needs (1) to recognize the meanings that must receive grammatical form, (2) to master the required forms, and (3) to develop reasonable fluency in *using* that recognition and mastery in language production—in other words, students are individually assisted to learn the components of the complex skill of speaking the TL in preparation for doing so in spontaneous communication.

Many teachers intuitively use a psycholinguistic perspective on grammar to assist language learning in class. Most teachers, however, are neither trained nor inclined to think this way about grammar. No textbooks are yet written from this perspective or designed to offer teachers the necessary support for it, and FL textbook publishers are understandably reluctant, given the limited market, to invest in radically new approaches.

This means that those who are interested in developing CALL materials along the lines suggested in this chapter have a unique opportunity to effect a significant change in the way students learn a foreign language. Software development is enormously time-consuming, but for those experienced both in lesson design and programming it still takes less time than getting a new textbook written, printed, and into the hands of a significant number of teachers; moreover, software is inherently amenable to pilot-testing and revision.

The development of even limited programs to address the psycholinguistic processing of particularly problematic grammatical structures in a given language would allow empirical research on the claim that students will be able to make use of this kind of lesson better than conventional grammar teaching. But the research possibilities are not limited to studies of the efficacy of CALL. (Such evaluative studies cannot answer the general question "Do computers improve language learning?" but they can assess its usefulness to various kinds of learners, under various circumstances.) Computer-assisted *basic* research in classroom FL learning could be of enormous significance to the related fields of second-language acquisition and foreign language education. Studies using the diagnostic error-analysis techniques discussed above (and much more complex versions of them) could explore a host of important questions about how the classroom learner's processing resembles or differs from that of the native TL speaker and that of a naturalistic learner, questions with both pedagogical and theoretical implications. (See Garret [3] for a report on one such research project.) To pick a few at random: Are semantic concepts more likely to be transferred from the native language than syntactic ones? If structures are explained in processing terms, does that reduce the likelihood of transfer? Are there "natural" or "good" interlanguage rules (i.e., idiosyncratic ways of processing a meaning–form relationship) that are not the TL rules but do work as a step in the right direction, as opposed to unnatural or counterproductive ones? Is there a qualitative difference between the interlanguage rules or "good" language learners and "hopeless" ones? And if so, can the latter be explicitly helped to learn like the former? Are there universals in processing rules? Do students' processing rules always fit within a range of processing rules of natural languages, and if not how and why do they violate those universals?

The implications of such research can hardly be overestimated, and it must be carried out by foreign language teachers. Most teachers, however, have never been able to undertake research because they cannot possibly make the time to collect and analyze data within their already overburdened teaching schedules. The computer makes it possible. A collaboration of teachers, CALL lesson designers, and programmers could develop the instrumentation to undertake second-language acquisition research hitherto undreamed of.

Until teachers and students try to bring the psycholinguistic perspective to bear, the hypothesis that doing so will make a difference cannot be tested, but theory, research, and common sense supply ample reason to believe that it will. In this effort the computer's role will be crucial.

References, A Psycholinguistic Perspective on Grammar and CALL

1. Chastain, Kenneth. *Developing Second-Language Skills: Theory to Practice.* Skokie, IL: Rand McNally, 1976.
2. Curtin, Constance. *Russian Review Packet.* Wentworth, NH: COMPRess, 1983.
3. Garrett, Cornelia B. [Nina] *In Search of Interlanguage: A Study of Second-Language Acquisition of German Syntax.* Unpublished Ph.D. dissertation. Urbana-Champaign: University of Illinois, 1982.
4. Garrett, Nina. "The Problem with Grammar: What Kind Can the Language Learner Use?" *The Modern Language Journal* 70 (1986):133–48.
5. Higgs, Theodore V. "Language Acquisition and Language Learning: A Plea for Syncretism." *The Modern Language Journal* 69 (1985):8–14.
6. Krashen, Stephen D. *Principles and Practice in Second Language Acquisition.* Oxford, England: Pergamon Press, 1982.
7. Shinall, Stanley L. *French Review Packet.* Wentworth, NH: COMPRess, 1983.
8. Underwood, John H. *Linguistics, Computers, and the Language Teacher: A Communicative Approach.* Rowley, MA: Newbury House, 1984.

8

Artificial Intelligence and CALL

John H. Underwood
Mills College

Artificial Intelligence and Natural Language _____

Artificial Intelligence: An Overview

In using computers for language practice, one runs the risk of merely mechanizing the least attractive aspects of what we already do. The "wrong—try-again" approach, in which the computer asks all the questions, knows all the answers, and tosses students an occasional verbal reward to keep them going, will probably not go far toward helping them achieve real proficiency in the language. What is needed is practice that more closely resembles natural contextualized use of the language and that makes fuller application of the computer's capability for flexible and personalized interaction. It can be done. Researchers in the branch of computer science known as "artificial intelligence" (AI) have for years been experimenting with just such ways of using computers—flexible, natural, humanlike responses to human input.

Artificial intelligence is not without its controversy, starting with the very name by which it is known. It is doubtful that non–computer scientists would have paid much attention to the term coined by McCarthy thirty years ago if instead of "artificial intelligence" he had used "complex symbolic processing" or "heuristic programming." But McCarthy's

John H. Underwood (Ph.D., University of California, Los Angeles) is Assistant Professor of Hispanic Studies and Linguistics at Mills College in Oakland, California. He is a member of ACTFL, CALICO, MLA, and TESOL, author of the widely acclaimed *Linguistics, Computers, and the Language Teacher: A Communicative Approach* (Newbury House) for which he won the Kenneth W. Mildenberger Award in 1984, and co-author (with Richard Bassein) of *Juegos Comunicativos* published by Random House.

catchy phrase stirs up passions. In one (extreme) view, artificial intelligence is nothing less than a contradiction in terms: intelligence is uniquely human. On the other side are the optimistic AI researchers who argue that intelligent behavior is independent of the medium in which it occurs: "Neurons or silicon—the difference is irrelevant" (Patrick Winston, quoted in Marback, 12).

Although the first image that comes to mind when one hears of "intelligent machines" may be something akin to R2-D2, robotics is actually only a small part of AI work. Artificial intelligence ranges from programs that play chess or prove mathematical theorems to those that aid in the diagnosis of mainframe computer failure or help prospectors find new oil deposits. The key in each case is that the computer is programmed to do things that would require intelligence if accomplished by a human. Artificial intelligence is thus a science somewhere on the border between psychology and computer programming, dedicated to developing techniques for solving intellectual problems. Some scientists like to think of AI as "scuba gear for the mind—it enables the mind to go places it hasn't been before" (Feigenbaum and McCorduck, 6, p. 44).

There are others who define AI in a slightly narrower way, using the term "intelligent" to refer only to those applications in which the program can be said to either draw inferences or to "learn" from the input it receives. Such programs are considered truly "intelligent" because they can internalize new knowledge and formulate conclusions not programmed into them. For the purposes of this chapter, however, the term artificial intelligence will encompass programs that range from the simple application of stored rules to simulated intelligent behavior. Topics not included are the murky—though admittedly fascinating—philosophical questions such as "Can machines think?" and "What is intelligence?"; rather, the principal focus is on the application, or potential application, of AI to computer-assisted language-learning (CALL) programs, and on guidelines for the creation of some clever, indeed even "intelligent," tools for language practice.

Knowledge Representation and Expert Systems

Two areas of AI are of particular interest to those who deal with language and meaning: knowledge representation and natural-language processing. Knowledge representation refers to the challenge of encoding in machine-readable form the kind of knowledge that is needed to solve problems, which can be very complex (the design of semiconductor chips) or seemingly trivial and commonsense problems (how to lead a robot to find its way around a coffee table). Much of current AI work is involved with coding this kind of knowledge in order to create so-called "expert systems." To accomplish this coding, a team of systems designers first studies a human expert's process of reasoning through some narrowly defined problem, then programs this process into the system as a set of "if-then" rules. For example, in designing MYCIN, a Stanford system that can diagnose bacterial infections, doctors were consulted and their collective expertise was programmed into the system. The program is then able to reproduce the steps a doctor would go through in the process of analyzing symptomatic data and suggest a probable diagnosis. In one test of the system, MYCIN outperformed all of the medical experts evaluating it (Winograd, 27).

A project at the University of California (Berkeley) offers a good example of both the direction of current work on these systems and attendant problems. Known as the UNIX Consultant, the intent is to provide an on-line consulting service for users who have problems with UNIX, the principal operating system at UC Berkeley (and many other academic institutions). Once this expert system is operational, users' queries will be written in ordinary English to be processed by several different modules which, in turn, will parse the input (i.e., analyze its grammatical structure; see below) and symbolize its meaning in a manner that could then be interpreted by the knowledge base, a storehouse of information about UNIX. When a response is formulated, another program will generate an answer in English to represent this information to the user.

Key problems in the project have been concerned largely with meaning: how to represent a great deal of technical knowledge about UNIX, how to determine the meaning of the user's input sentence and infer from it the user's actual intent, plus the additional problem of generating an answer to the question in an intelligible manner. Another type of problem—the need for a wide and varied lexicon—was revealed when the Consultant was demonstrated to a group of UNIX users not familiar with the project and who used terms the system hadn't been programmed to expect. Those working on the project concluded that it may have been "overambitious" in scope.

Natural-Language Processing

Natural-language processing (NLP) involves all those areas in which the computer is programmed to deal with natural (human) language as meaningful symbols rather than just strings of characters. Unlike word processing, where the computer knows the text only as letters, NLP seeks to find ways for computers to "understand" language, albeit in some limited sense. This includes (1) work on "natural-language interfaces" or "natural-language front ends," which allow users to communicate with computers in ordinary English (or French, etc.); (2) machine translation, which attempts to understand the text enough to come up with an equivalent version rather than just a word-for-word mish-mash; (3) the particularly thorny problem of understanding speech, which requires identifying the salient acoustic features of the human voice. Computer experts now often refer to NLP efforts as "amateur systems," since, unlike expert systems, NLP programs are designed to be used by laymen. Although much progress has been made in this area in the last few years, the real breakthroughs in NLP have yet to appear; the Japanese push to be first with the "Fifth Generation" supercomputers, may—some say—be the eventual catalyst for genuine advances.

Computers and Natural Language

Understanding Natural Language

There are basically two ways in which humans can communicate with a computer: (1) through a set of written instructions in a programming language such as BASIC or Pascal and (2) through an existing program, which serves as an interpreter—providing one follows its rules ("Enter name here: "). (A third possibility for the technically minded is to write the instructions in the computer's own language, known as machine language—a string of ones and zeros.) Clearly there would be many advantages if, as an alternative, one could give instructions to the computer in everyday English or some other natural language. The problems, however, are not straightforward. Human language is highly complex, redundant, and more often than not ambiguous. Computers, on the other hand, are basically symbol manipulators—the only thing they "know" is that a given symbol is or is not the same as another. A very complicated and cleverly designed program is required to enable a computer even to approximate an understanding of natural language.

Consider the problem this way: It is a fairly trivial task to program a computer to recognize written words (spoken words are another matter entirely), since a word, after all, is just a string of characters. Each of these words can have associated with it certain information that enables the system to "know" what it means, a sort of dictionary in which it can look up definitions. Less trivial, though still manageable, is to parse the sentence in which the word is found, i.e., analyze its structure and perhaps identify the parts of speech. But human understanding is many times more complex than word recognition and parsing sentence structure. Consider, for example, the kinds of knowledge needed to figure out the antecedent of *it* in "She dropped the plate on the table and broke it." Human listeners can look for a clue in the attendant discourse, perhaps something like "Remember that glass coffee table I told you about?" Context will also help straighten out cases of simple lexical ambiguity, such as "She cannot bear children" or "The rabbi married my sister." Likewise, idiomatic expressions such as "run up" as in "He ran up a big bill" can be distinguished from the literal "He ran up a big hill" only because of our knowledge of the real world and the kinds of things one can truly "run up." In summary, natural language is "context-sensitive," i.e., meanings of words or phrases are sensitive to the context in which they appear. Conversely, programming languages are "context-free": in BASIC, for example, "run" is always a verb and it always means the same thing: "start the program."

In addition to what is known about a natural language and the world it symbolizes, part of everyday, commonsense knowledge deals with the way conversation works. This enables one to infer, for example, a logical relationship between two otherwise unconnected utterances:

Student 1:   Did he say anything about the exam?

Student 2:   I just got here.

Humans know the rules of conversation and assume a connection rather than a non sequitur. In the above case, common sense predicts a relationship between one's having just arrived in a class and an awareness of what had been said before entering. Speakers are normally not aware how much of what is understood depends on just such implicit connections.

One of the more humbling discoveries in natural-language processing is that language cannot be separated from pragmatic knowledge associated with common sense. The result is a curious paradox with respect to the success of natural-language programs. Machines do much better at tasks that require large amounts of highly specialized knowledge than at simple, everyday tasks: "the more highly structured knowledge is, the easier it is for us to codify it for computer use. On the other hand, getting around in the real world is not a highly structured task—the average house pet can manage it easily, but machines cannot" (Feigenbaum and McCorduck, 6, p. 59).

A complete system to understand language, even if the problem of recognizing speech sounds is ignored, then, must be capable of all of the following procedures: (1) lexical analysis (matching words to entries in the system's dictionary), (2) morphological analysis ("peeling off" and identifying affixes that may appear on words), (3) syntactic analysis (identifying parts of speech, phrase grouping, and overall structure), (4) semantic analysis (the dictionary meaning of the words) and pragmatic analysis (what the words mean in this context), and (5) enough real-world knowledge to make some sense of what is going on. The pitfalls are many, and subtle. The outlook, according to Winograd (27), is guarded: "software that mimics the full human understanding of language is simply not in prospect" (p. 144).

The following sections contain a discussion of subcomponents of natural-language processing of particular interest to foreign language teachers: parsing, machine translation, speech recognition, and speech synthesis.

Mechanical Parsing

Parsing a sentence, mechanically or otherwise, means identifying its structure, a process that on a computer requires storing the words according to their syntactic categories (parts of speech) and specifying rules for forming possible sentences. The parser then proceeds word by word through the sentence, identifying the syntactic category of each while checking sequences of categories against those allowed by the rules, and assigning appropriate phrase structures to the sequences.

Suppose, for example, the input sentence is "The boy ate the pizza." The program "knows" that *the* is an article, *boy* and *pizza* are nouns, and *ate* is the past of *eat*, a verb. When the program recognizes *the* followed by a noun, it successfully matches this combination with a rule it has been given for forming noun phrases (NP → det N; i.e., "the noun phrase consists of a determiner and a noun"). The verb together with the other noun phrase (the pizza), matches the rule for the verb phrase (VP → V + NP). Finally, the noun phrase and the verb phrase together successfully match the rule for sentence (S → NP + VP), and the parse is complete.

The rules given here are simplified greatly for the sake of example. In actual practice, the biggest problem in programming such a parser is describing these rules correctly, i.e., the system's grammar. A simple phrase-structure grammar can deal with a fairly large subset of English sentences. For more complex sentences, parsers have used so-called "extended grammars" as in, for example, the augmented transition net grammar (ATN) used in SHRDLU, described in a later section. A full description of an extended grammar is beyond the scope of the present article; use of similar parsing programs in CALL software, however, is considered below.

Machine Translation

Some of the earliest work in AI attempted to develop translation programs that could somehow scan technical journals written in foreign languages and produce English versions automatically. The project turned out to be considerably more complicated than anticipated, and results were often absurd, if not unintelligible. One of the problems was that developers underestimated the need to parse the structure of the text they were dealing with. In an early paper, two pioneers in machine translation offered examples of word-for-word translations that their computer had produced

(Richens and Boothe, 15). These examples, according to the authors, "illustrate the relative unimportance of syntax . . . ":

Finnish: muut neljä ulkomaista kantaa ovat osoittautuneet viljelysarvoltaan kovin epävarmoiksi

English output: other [plural] four foreign country [out of] standpoint [partitive] bear [partitive] are show oneself [past plural] cultivation value [genitive accusative] very insecure [become]

The program has added lexical and structural clues to give the reader a more complete picture of the original. But when the English output is compared with a standard English equivalent, it is clear that syntax is anything but unimportant in understanding natural language:

Edited English: The other four standard varieties from abroad have proved reliable as regards cultivation value.

What such work did demonstrate was the feasibility of using computers to generate a first draft of a translation to speed up the work of the human translator who, in turn, could concentrate on editing and polishing the translation. Most "machine translation" is thus more accurately described, at least at present, as "machine-assisted translation."

Several machine-translation programs (both for mainframes and for micros) are now available commercially, with prices ranging from a few tens of thousands of dollars to ten times that number. Some produce so-called "high-quality" translations of scientific documents, i.e., with an accuracy of at least 90 percent, but depend heavily on pre- and/or postediting.

Current work on machine translation is centered on developing more sophisticated syntactic and semantic representations of language that can aid the program to understand more fully the material being translated. The Japanese Fifth Generation project has a goal of developing a system that would be perhaps 95 percent accurate and yet cost one-third less than human translators. Such a machine would need the help of an expert system—a set of programs that could represent a high level of different kinds of human knowledge, in this case syntactic, conceptual, and commonsense knowledge.

Speech Recognition

The full understanding of even written natural language requires the recognition of morphological, syntactic, and semantic elements. When the phonological information necessary to recognize speech is added, it is of little surprise that automated speech-recognition systems are still relatively primitive. We have not yet duplicated the virtuosity of Hal, the on-board computer in *2001: A Space Odyssey* (Clarke, 4), who understood everything Dave said and could also detect overtones in his voice:

Hal: Look, Dave, you've got a lot of things to do. I suggest you leave this to me.

Dave: Hal, switch to manual hibernation control.

Hal: I can tell from your voice harmonics, Dave, that you're very upset. Why don't you take a stress pill and get some rest?

Speech recognition adds one more level of analysis to the list of steps described earlier for language understanding. At this initial level, the input is nothing more than sound waves, which first must be converted to waves of electrical current, then sampled thousands of times per second to determine their shape. The combined pattern of shapes gives an electrical "picture" of the sound: the picture in turn must be matched against a library of stored pictures in the system. When a match is found, the sound is recognized, and the system can report with some confidence, "That was a /p/".

In actual practice, however, much can go wrong. Human voices are all different, and no one pronounces the same word exactly the same way twice. In addition, strange things happen to sounds when combined. "Did you give the cat your dinner?" comes out like "Did you give the catcher dinner?" and so forth. Humans are helped by the context in which sounds are uttered and can make reasonably good guesses about what the speaker is trying to say. It appears that accurate speech recognition ultimately will have to use this same strategy: consult syntactic and semantic information to help the system determine what was probably said, given an assumed pragmatic environment.

Speech Synthesis

Speech synthesis is in many ways a simpler matter than speech recognition. The problem is one of simulating those same patterns of acoustic signals—i.e., phonemes—that humans recognize as part of the system of our language. There are now relatively inexpensive systems to accomplish this end. The user merely types an English sentence on the screen and the program voices it through its built-in speaker. A system now available for the IBM PC has an acceptable (if somewhat Swedish-sounding) accent in English (8). The so-called SMOOTHTALKER for the Apple Macintosh is not yet quite as elegant (18). The author has in his office a Spanish-speaking version of DECTalk, which pronounces typed-in sentences with any of a number of different voices, ranging from "Beautiful Betty" (soprano) to "Huge Harry" (baritone). The system, still in production, is being developed by the Digital Equipment Corporation for RENFE, the

Spanish national railroad, in order to synthesize constantly updated train information for those who call in.

Classic Experiments in Natural-Language Understanding —

Computer scientists have been experimenting for at least twenty years with programs that can carry on a conversation with humans. Boden (3) describes early programs that could "talk" about baseball ("Who won the World Series in 1927?") or the weather ("What is the high today in Des Moines?"). The best-known are ELIZA (or DOCTOR) the sympathetic therapist, and SHRDLU, the expert in the world of toy blocks.

ELIZA

ELIZA (Weizenbaum, 23) was named after the woman in Shaw's "Pygmalion" who was taught to talk "right." Developed in 1966 at MIT, ELIZA can carry on a plausible conversation with a human typing at a terminal. The topic of conversation depends on the nature of ELIZA's "script," or programmed role. The most famous of these is DOCTOR, designed to simulate ("parody," says Weizenbaum) the role of a psychotherapist in a consultation by responding to the patient's "complaints" as below (ELIZA's responses are given in uppercase):

PLEASE TELL ME YOUR PROBLEM
I'm very unhappy these days
I AM SORRY TO HEAR YOU ARE UNHAPPY
The problem is my father
TELL ME MORE ABOUT YOUR FATHER
Last night I dreamt he spanked me
WHAT WOULD IT MEAN TO YOU IF HE SPANKED YOU?
Didn't you ever get spanked?
WE WERE TALKING ABOUT YOU, NOT ME

ELIZA creates the illusion of understanding through the use of a technique known as "pattern matching." For example, "I am X" is a pattern that causes the computer to respond with a prefabricated pattern of its own, such as "How long have you been X?" If X contains one of the words identified in the script as negative, such as *unhappy* or *depressed*, the response can then be "I am sorry to hear you are X." When the user types in something ELIZA doesn't recognize, the computer either hedges ("Why do you say that?" "Please go on," etc.) or it recycles a sentence the user typed earlier ("Earlier you mentioned that your brother has been picking on you"). Since ELIZA contains a large number of response patterns, the program is able to carry on a fairly lengthy dialog without repeating itself.

It should be obvious, however, that ELIZA has no real knowledge of what the user is saying. In fact, it is precisely because of this innocence that Weizenbaum chose to use the psychotherapist format: it is one of the few situations in human discourse in which, if the speaker mentions "boats," for example, one can naively respond, "What do boats mean to you?" or "Tell me more about boats." Another difficulty with ELIZA is that the program has very little knowledge of the structure of the sentences it receives, and can easily be misled. If the user happens to type a slightly more complex sentence such as "Thinking about what I am doing always upsets me," the program blindly applies the pattern " . . .I am X . . ." and responds with something like "How long have you been doing always upsets you?"

Nevertheless, ELIZA does manage to recreate much of the naturalness and spontaneity of real conversation. For this reason, a number of CALL researchers have experimented with foreign language versions of the program, which are described below.

SHRDLU

What is most glaringly missing in ELIZA, then, is any real knowledge about sentence structure or the subject at hand. The solution to the first problem is to build in a parser. The second is more complicated. One could either attempt to provide the program with an encyclopedia of knowledge about the world, or try to limit the topic of discussion to some micro-world it can handle. In a project known as SHRDLU, Winograd (24, 26) opted for the second approach. The micro-world in this case was limited to a set of a dozen or so toy blocks appearing on the screen. SHRDLU was programmed to understand everything that was typed in with respect to the position of these blocks, and could move them according to ordinary English instructions given by the person at the console. The following is part of a longer dialog with the system (Winograd, 25, p. 57); SHRDLU is in caps:

How many blocks are in the box?
FOUR OF THEM.
Is at least one of them narrower than the one which I told you to pick up?
YES, THE RED CUBE.
Can the table pick up blocks?
NO.
Can a pyramid be supported by a block?
YES.
Will you please stack up both of the red blocks and either a green cube or a pyramid?
OK. [Carries out command]
Which cube is sitting on the table?

THE LARGE GREEN ONE WHICH SUPPORTS THE RED
PYRAMID.
Had you touched any pyramid before you put the green one on the lit-
tle cube?
YES, THE GREEN ONE.
When did you pick it up?
WHILE I WAS STACKING UP THE RED CUBE, A LARGE RED
BLOCK, AND A LARGE GREEN CUBE.
Why?
TO GET RID OF IT.
Why did you do that?
TO CLEAN OFF THE RED CUBE.

SHRDLU is not actually a single program, but a set of subprograms working together. Some of the subprograms are responsible for parsing the
input sentences and determining how their parts are related. Others use
the information from the parser to determine the meaning of the sentences. Still others are specialists at knowing about blocks and using this
knowledge to reason about the intended meaning of the sentences. To do
this, they must use information about the context, about the current state
of the set of blocks. And they must have very specific knowledge about
structural signals in English. For example, if instructed "Pick up a red
block," the computer may pick up any of the red blocks; "Pick up the red
block" signals that the speaker has a particular one in mind.

For all its sophistication, SHRDLU also has its limits—even within its
own domain of expertise. As Winograd (27) points out, its grammar cannot handle phrases such as "three blocks high" or "a three-block stack."
Nor can its reasoning program carry out one command while keeping
track of another ("Build a stack without touching any pyramids"). And the
program has only begun to address the problem of inference, of figuring
out what the speaker really meant. Finally, Winograd cautions that
expanding the program's world could create as many problems as it would
solve. In an expanded world, the system would then have to face the problem of determining which information might be relevant to the question
at hand; in the micro-world, everything is relevant.

Applications of AI to Language Learning ──────────

Computer-assisted language learning (CALL) offers a rich opportunity for
employing many, if not all, of the techniques of natural-language processing in a useful and productive application. Yet it is curious that much of
CALL exists in a world all its own. For the most part, CALL software
shows little awareness of current thinking about how people learn language or how language teaching is best accomplished. Nor does CALL

seem to make use of the interesting techniques (parsing, semantic analysis, etc.) that have been developed in natural-language processing by computer. One could argue reasonably that the application of any technology in education should attempt to employ the best and most effective techniques currently known. In the case of CALL, this would mean considering, at least in part, artificial intelligence.

Natural-language systems can be developed to "understand" language on many different levels, from simple recognition of words to full syntactic and semantic parsing. Each of these concepts has been the subject of experimentation in the context of computer-assisted language instruction. One way of categorizing these efforts is in terms of the basic strategies they employ. Three groups define themselves: (1) conversational programs that employ keyword matching in the style of ELIZA, (2) programs that use syntactic parsing, with or without a knowledge base, and (3) intelligent or semi-intelligent adventure games, which generally incorporate some of the features of both (1) and (2).

Keyword Matching: ELIZA as Tutor _____

LIESL

Kossuth (9) describes her experiments with a German version of ELIZA, dubbed LIESL, adapted from an English version (in BASIC) published in a book of BASIC computer games (Ahl, 1). German faculty at Pomona College have developed ten different scripts for student use; topics of conversation range from discussion of stories in a reader used in class to everyday subjects such as the German class, weekend activities, etc. LIESL is updated every other week with a new script. The following is a sample of a conversation using the "Wochenende" (weekend) script:

TAG, LIESL HIER. WIE WAR DAS WOCHENENDE?
Super!   (keyword: super)
TOLL, ERZÄHL MAL DAVON!
Ich war auf einer schönen Party.   (Party)
WO WAR DIE PARTY? ICH HABE NICTS DAVON GEHÖRT.
Die Party war im Studentenheim.   (Party)
HAST DU NETTE LEUTE KENNENGELERNT?
Nein, ich war mit meinem Freund da.   '   (Freund)

Translation:
HI, THIS IS LIESL. HOW WAS YOUR WEEKEND?
Super!
TERRIFIC, TELL ME ABOUT IT!
I went to a great party.
WHERE WAS THE PARTY? I DIDN'T HEAR ABOUT IT.

The party was at a friend's house.
DID YOU MEET ANYONE NICE?
No, I went with my friend.

German instructors keep track of student use of these programs by requiring them to turn in a printout each week of a conversation with LIESL. Student use is aided by an on-line dictionary that students can call up for any word that LIESL uses by typing that word preceded by a question mark.

One advantage of an implementation such as LIESL is that it is built on a program in BASIC that can be adapted to run on virtually any microcomputer. One disadvantage of the BASIC version, however, is that it cannot offer the range of answer processing that is possible in the larger and more complex LISP version, such as the DOCTOR game available on most mainframe computers running the UNIX operating system. The principal strategy in the BASIC version is the matching of simple keywords, as in the example above. For each such keyword, there is a set of responses or response frames ("Why do you say that you are ___?"). The original LISP version, and versions adapted from it, allow the script to specify not only keywords, but different contexts in which these words may be found, thus determining more about what is being said. For example, different contexts could be given for the pronoun *you* (let X stand for whatever words might occur in that position):

you X me
I X you
I think you X
I want you to X

The response could thus be more exactly keyed to the input; for "I want you to X," ELIZA could respond with "Why do you want me to X," etc.

FAMILIA

Underwood (19, 20) describes an experimental simulated Spanish conversation program, FAMILIA, based on ELIZA. Adapted from the original LISP ELIZA, FAMILIA consists of two separate parts: (1) the original LISP language analyzer, which contains language-independent input routines for analyzing the user's sentences, and (2) a Spanish version of the script. In FAMILIA, the script was designed around the type of conversation one might have about one's family members, who they are, and what they are like.

One additional feature was added to the FAMILIA script—rules that allow the program to detect syntactic errors of certain types. Thus, prior to generating a response sentence, the program can check the syntax of the input sentence for a recognizable error and type out an appropriate message. The key error FAMILIA anticipated was confusion in the use of the two verbs for "to be" in Spanish, *ser* and *estar*, since most of the input would consist of descriptive statements. Thus if the student volunteered, "My father is [está] very tall," the program could respond with "Do you mean your father is [es] tall?" and so forth. Evaluative feedback is accomplished by marking adjectives in the script as requiring one or other of the two verbs. FAMILIA also allows the student to ask questions about unfamiliar family terms the program might use, as in the following conversation (computer output is in upper case):

Hola
HOLA--VAMOS A HABLAR DE TU FAMILIA
Mi familia está en Colorado
¿ENTONCES UDS. SON DE COLORADO?
Bueno, mi madre está de Boston
¿QUIERES DECIR QUE TU MADRE ES DE BOSTON?
Mi madre es de Boston
¿Y TUS ABUELOS?
Mis abuelos están en Colorado también
¿TIENES TIOS?
No entiendo
¿SI USO UNA PALABRA QUE NO ENTIENDES, ESCRIBE: "QUE ES UN---?"
¿Qué es un tío?
¿TU TIO ES EL HERMANO DE UNO DE TUS PADRES
Sí, mi tía está profesora en Berkeley
¿QUIERES DECIR QUE TU TIA ES PROFESORA EN BERKELEY?
Mi tía es profesora
¿ALGUIEN MAS EN TU FAMILIA ES PROFESORA?

There is much to be said in favor of student practice with programs like LIESL and FAMILIA. They provide contextualized practice focused more on meaning than on form. The material is related to the student and hence interesting and motivating. And it is a form of comprehension-based practice, since the student cannot proceed without understanding what the program has said.

There are, however, obvious drawbacks. The main problem is simply that the program, for the most part, has no notion of the grammaticality or meaningfulness of the students' sentences, and looks merely for certain strings of letters (keywords) to which to respond with other strings of letters. The "conversation," then, is ultimately superficial. Although these programs allow for some amusing CALL activities, they can never know enough about what the student is doing to be engaged in any serious teaching. A further shortcoming in the keyword approach is that it works much better in a relatively uninflected language such as English since the keyword can usually be listed in only one form. In contrast, in German or Spanish, keywords must have several different forms depending on tense inflections, gender, and so forth, each of which must be listed separately.

Parsing and Knowledge-Based Systems

In a review of different strategies for processing students' answers in CALL, Pusack (14) concludes that "the only real hope for truly effective foreign-language CAI" is through rule-based parsing (p. 63). Yet, as Pusack points out, to be successful such programs must be limited to a highly restricted domain, i.e., a small subset of the possible utterances in the language. It is unreasonable to expect a parser to handle all the sentences in a natural language; moreover, it simply is not necessary—the language that students can be expected to use in most CALL activities is limited to a relatively few lexical items and standard structures.

All the CALL programs that have incorporated some sort of parser successfully have in fact been quite limited in both structures and vocabulary. Four such programs, offered as examples of what can be done with parsing in the CALL environment, are considered below.

JOHN AND MARY

This experimental program (Higgins and Johns, 7) is part of a group of programs known as GRAMMARLAND, which the authors characterize as an attempt to use SHRDLU's principles for CALL "to create a miniature universe of discourse and a program that will manipulate things in that universe, answer questions about it, ask questions, or do any of these things at random if the user merely wants a demonstration" (p. 75). JOHN AND MARY creates a mini-world consisting of a room, a door, and two stick figures visible on the screen. The student manipulates this world with language, asking where the people are, or instructing the program to send them out or bring them in. The program can parse sentences such as the following:

Is Mary here?
Where is Mary?
Bring Mary in.
Send Mary out.
Shut the door.
Are John and Mary together?

The response to a question is a verbal answer; in the case of a command, there is a change in the graphics. Higgins and Johns give a complete

BASIC listing of a somewhat skeletal version of the program in the appendix to their book (7, pp. 177–87).

JUEGOS COMUNICATIVOS

JUEGOS COMUNICATIVOS, developed for publication in connection with a college Spanish textbook, consists of a set of problem-solving games designed for communicative practice in Spanish (Underwood and Bassein, 21; French and German versions are in production). JUEGOS actually consists of two rather separate components: a language-independent parsing program, and a set of language-specific data files in which word classes, morphological rules, and syntactic patterns are all specified for any particular environment. As noted above, the program's ability to parse intelligently depends on an environment limited to that of the mini-world displayed on the screen.

An example of one of the activities from JUEGOS is the game "Las cinco diferencias." Two almost identical pictures are displayed.

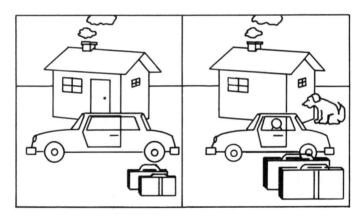

Fig. 1: On-screen Graphics for "Las cinco diferencias" (JUEGOS COMUNICATIVOS)

The student is instructed to describe the five things that are different in the picture on the right. With each input sentence, the program parses to see if it can recognize a structure. If so, the parser then checks the elements in that structure for problems of gender or concordance, missing elements, etc. When problems are detected, the questioned words are highlighted and some message is displayed to give the student a hint about the nature of the problem (¿Masculino o femenino? etc.). If no syntactic problems are found, the program checks the semantic content of the input sentence to see if it agrees with the picture. The following is a sample dialog about the picture above:

No hay puerta en la casa
TIENES RAZON
Las maletas son más grande
¿SINGULAR O PLURAL?   [highlights "grande"]
Las maletas son más grandes
TIENES RAZON
Hay una ventana
¿COMO. . .?
Hay una ventana en la casa
SI, PERO NO ES UNA DIFERENCIA
Hay perro   [highlights "perro"]
FALTA EL ARTICULO
Hay dos perros
YO NO VEO MAS QUE UNO

One reason the parser can be this accurate is that it does not have to attempt to handle vocabulary or structures beyond those needed to describe the picture on the screen. The few basic structures allowed are spelled out in the instructions (although many times there are half a dozen structural variations, all of which describe the picture correctly).

What enables the program to recognize these words and structures is the information given in the data file. This includes a lexicon in which root words are grouped by syntactic classes and subclasses (masculine nouns, feminine nouns, etc.). Morphological rules explain how plurals, etc., are formed from these roots (and hence recognized, by using the same rule to "peel off" the affix). Finally, rules are given for possible sentence patterns, in terms of syntactic units such as noun phrase (NP), prepositional phrase (PP), adjective phrase (AP), etc.; as a result, "Las cinco diferencias" requires only three basic patterns, with variations depending on choice of optional elements (indicated in parentheses):

(1) (no) hay   NP   (PP)
(2) NP   (no) ser   AP
(3) NP   (no) tener NP   (PP)

It should be clear, however, that syntactic parsing is not enough, since it only allows the program to comment on the structure of the student's sentences, while remaining oblivious to their meaning. JUEGOS thus adds an element known as "semantic attributes," which amounts to declaring that there is a logical relationship between certain items that may be found in the input sentences. In the above picture, for example, there is a negative relationship between "house" and "door." This can be expressed in a number of syntactically different ways ("There is no door on the house," "The house doesn't have a door," etc.), which can be reduced to relating "house" and "door" in one of a number of possible negative structures. Since the program has first parsed for syntactic structure, it knows that these words occur together in the sentence; furthermore, it knows where they occur, and that the sentence is negative. Based on that information, the program can safely assume that the correct assertion has or has not been made.

The suitcases in the picture above provide an example of this attribute relationship. In the semantic section of the lexical file, the following statement appears:

maletas = grandes largas
maletas ≠ pequeñas cortas.

This means there is a positive relationship between *maletas* and *grandes* or *largas*, and a negative relationship between *maletas* and *pequeñas* or *cortas*. Given this statement, all of the following sentences will be true:

Las maletas son grandes
Las maletas son largas
Las maletas no son pequeñas
Las maletas no son cortas

And, conversely, the following sentences will automatically be false:

Las maletas no son grandes
Las maletas no son largas
Las maletas son pequeñas
Las maletas son cortas

STATION

In a similar manner, Cook (5) describes programs in which syntactic parsing is complemented by some sort of knowledge representation that allows the program to "know" and recover essential information about the environment at hand. In an ESL program called STATION, students simulate dialogs with the local railway station in Colchester (England), inquiring when trains leave, which platform they leave from, how much the tickets cost, etc.:

HELLO. BRITISH RAIL, COLCHESTER.
Could you be telling me the train to Harwich?
SORRY, I DON'T UNDERSTAND
When is the next train to Harwich?
IT LEAVES AT THREE O'CLOCK
What platform is it?
IT LEAVES FROM PLATFORM 4
When does he arrive?
WHEN DOES WHAT?
When does it arrive?
IT ARRIVES AT HALF PAST THREE
How much is it?

IT COSTS TWO POUNDS.
Thank you. Goodbye.

As with the "semantic attributes" in JUEGOS, STATION stores information in terms of the relationship between items; here, this relationship is expressed in a manner that can be understood by a computer language known as PROLOG designed for the declaration of logical relationships:

leave(harwich,three)
ticket(harwich,two)
arrive(harwich,four)
platform(harwich,four)

"Leave(harwich,three)" means that there is a relationship called "leave" with two items "Harwich" and "three," that is, "The Harwich train leaves at three o'clock." If enough such information were programmed, the result would be in effect an expert system for students to consult in order to practice using language to accomplish one of its most important functions: get information.

A Computerized German Essay Processor

One application of parsing strategies is an aid to students who are writing sentences in a foreign language. The parser can help students with any errors that are detected to the extent that it can read these sentences and recognize their grammatical structure. Ruth and Alton Sanders (17) of Miami University (Oxford, Ohio) and Wright State University (Dayton, Ohio), respectively, have together received a major grant from the U.S. Department of Education to design a computerized essay processor for intermediate and advanced students of German.

The essay processor will be based on an expanded version of the parser used in the tutorial-game prototype, SPION (see below). Although the original parser was designed to recognize only WH-questions and command forms, and contains a lexicon limited to that needed for the game, the expanded version will be designed to parse all the basic syntactic structures of German (including word-order variants) and will contain a lexicon equivalent to the contents of a standard paperback German–English dictionary. In addition to syntactic parsing, the program will check for both spelling problems and morphological anomalies (wrong case, wrong gender, etc.) in student input.

The authors do not anticipate creating an infallible system, but one that will provide the student with a useful and comprehensive check on the material written. The program will not attempt to correct errors, but will simply flag them; the authors believe it is more useful (and safer) pedagogically to help the students find errors than to try to help edit them.

Given the wide range of vocabulary and structures the essay processor will accept, it was considered unrealistic to attempt to include a semantic component. As a result, the program will be purposefully oblivious to the meaning of what the student has written, and will be unable to detect semantic errors of the "Sincerity admires John" type. Students who intentionally write nonsense to fool the system (as students tend to do) will have to be content with having the system help them write grammatically correct nonsense.

The essay processor is being developed in LISP and PROLOG, and uses an augmented phrase-structure grammar for syntactic parsing. When completed, it will be implemented in IBM PC format and will be made available without charge for field testing to interested college and university foreign language departments.

Intelligent Games

There are many computer adventure games with which the reader may be familiar (not video games of the joystick variety, but those that require the player to type in responses). Most operate on the same principle: The computer describes the situation ("There is an open door on your right, stairs on your left," etc.), and asks what the player wants to do next. In an intelligent game, this is an open choice, not just "pick one of the following." Allowing the player to input a somewhat free response means, of course, that there must be at least a certain amount of parsing involved in order to find out what has been typed in. In actual practice, this parsing is usually fairly primitive, often allowing the player to respond with nothing more than "Open door" or even, in some cases "door open" (in the latter case, the "parser" is actually only looking for a word match, and ignores word order).

ZORK

The best-selling game, ZORK, a product of MIT graduate students of the 1970s, is available in commercial versions (28) and as part of mainframe operating systems such as UNIX. The following represents the opening dialogue:

ZORK: You are standing in an open field west of a white house
       with a boarded front door. There is a small mailbox here.
User: Look in the mailbox.
ZORK: The mailbox is closed.
User: Open it.
ZORK: Opening the mailbox reveals a leaflet.
User: Read the leaflet.
ZORK: "Welcome to ZORK . . . ."

The interchange that takes place when using such a game can be genuinely meaningful, an example of true reading for meaning, since "the user does not think about the language in use, but only about the action and where it might lead next . . . . [This] creates an optimal setting for language acquisition" (Kossuth, 10, p. 13). And the natural motivation to play games means that students will use them in earnest and will repeat adventures in order to find a better way to "beat the game." Because of the multiple branching possibilities of such programs, the user will never read through the same sequence twice. Student users, Kossuth claims, "voluntarily read more than they would if assigned a linear text, and their comprehension can be expected to increase with each repetition" (ibid).

MYSTERY HOUSE

Any adventure game of the type just described can be improved with the addition of computer graphics so that the scene can actually be viewed by the user. One game that does in fact include pictures is MYSTERY HOUSE (13), a program in which a series of murders must be solved. As the scenes unfold, the graphics change. When the user instructs the program to open the door, the picture of a closed door is replaced by one of an open door. The addition of relevant visual material adds to the screen an important element of redundancy, with the result that the language used is potentially more meaningful to the user.

The French version of this program, however, is a classic example of doing things in a hurry. Intended for language practice rather than game-playing, the program has serious flaws in design, the most glaring of which is a lack of sensitivity to the structure of French. For example, not only does it accept "ouvrez porte" in place of "ouvrez la porte," the language generator that produces responses, alas, comes back frequently with ungrammatical French. The original strategy for dealing with unrecognized commands was to insert the input verb into a canned response frame: "I don't know how to (verb)." The strategy is a safe one in English, for all command forms are the same as infinitive forms. But command forms and infinitives in French are always different. The "solution" in the French version of MYSTERY HOUSE is to convert all input commands to one form of the infinitive (and even then to the least common, the one ending in -re). The result is some very disconcerting French: "*Je ne sais pas cherchre," instead of "Je ne sais pas chercher," etc.

This "goof" is given as an example of artificial intelligence gone bad. An adventure game in which student input must be "understood" and responded to in a natural communicative fashion is clearly an excellent opportunity for using at least some natural-language processing techniques. The French version of MYSTERY HOUSE, then, can best be described as an unfortunate "occasion manquée."

SPION

SPION (Sanders and Sanders, 16) is a German spy game that takes the student through a world of German airports and hotels. Unlike the two games described above, SPION was written with language learning in mind and therefore attempts to provide a somewhat more useful set of situations than haunted houses and dungeons. SPION also incorporates a certain number of on-line aids for the student.

SPION allows the student to respond with either commands or Wh-questions. If students are puzzled over a word the program has used, they can instead type in "?", which takes them to a dictionary containing most of the vocabulary used in the program. Responses to situations are given as a choice: "Should I read the note, take the plane, go into the café, take the bus . . .?" (which simplifies the parsing problem when the student types a choice). The program also insists that each German sentence be spelled correctly and that the words be in the right order. If the input is lexically and grammatically correct it is sent to the "semantic interpreter" to check which of the possible choices the student has intended. If a grammatical problem is detected, as when a student uses an incorrect verb form, a generic message is typed out:

> User: Gene . . . [for Gehen, "Go . . ."]
> SPION: Das scheint mir nicht richtig. Versüchen Sie noch einmal! ["That doesn't look right to me. Please try again!"]

The feedback, although not specific to the error, signals to the student that there is a problem with the form of the statement. Sanders and Sanders claim to have avoided more analytical error feedback deliberately, mainly so that the program will be perceived more as a game than as a language exercise, and because they believe it is not helpful to tell students exactly what is wrong. As in the case of JUEGOS, however, it is clearly possible to give feedback that hints at error and still forces the student to think about and discover where the problem lies.

Current Major Projects Using AI in CALL _____

Project Athena

Potentially the most interesting project in which AI strategies are being applied directly to CALL is Project Athena, currently underway in the Foreign Languages and Literatures Section at MIT. Part of a five-year campuswide experiment in integrating computers into the curriculum, the MIT/CALL project makes full use of one of the best AI facilities in the world. The goal is to develop materials for teaching a four-course sequence in French, Spanish, Russian, German, and ESL. The materials are intended to supplement but not replace classroom time or the teacher; they will, however, replace both the textbook and the audio lab.

Part of the Athena project will incorporate interactive video. Of more interest here are the plans for the natural-language processing of typed-in sentences. This component of the system will make use of a parser connected to a system for knowledge representation that will enable the computer to understand the meaning of the sentences. The program will thus be able to detect the student's semantically incoherent or culturally inappropriate statements, in addition to flagging spelling mistakes, typos, and grammatical errors.

As of this writing, none of the work on Project Athena has been demonstrated or described in any detail. However, published descriptions of planned programs are found in Kramsch, Morgenstern, and Murray (11), and include three distinct programs: LINGO, Topicks, and what is tentatively called Reverse Eliza (named for the ELIZA discussed above). One of these, LINGO, is described as follows:

> A student is shown a picture of a dorm room with some representative German objects in it and is introduced to a poltergeist with whom the student is invited to converse. The poltergeist will mess up the room following the student's orders, but in order to talk with the spirit the student must follow certain rules of conversation. Our parser and knowledge representation system are powerful enough so that we can accept sentences of much greater complexity than the "kill troll with sword" variety . . . . The messed up room picture will be stored to be retrieved by another student who will be given the task of cleaning up the room (p. 32).

The student learns to interact with the ghost in a manner resembling natural discourse. For example, the computer may not understand the student's directions and may ask for clarification, or it may suggest ways in which to improve the language being used.

"Reverse ELIZA" is a curious variation on the "standard" ELIZA. Instead of answering ELIZA's questions or comments, the student must obtain information from a rather terse and laconic conversation partner, one who knows the answers but must in effect be coaxed to give them up. The point is to learn those communicative skills necessary to "pry information out of a reluctant informant, using tactful questioning techniques" (ibid). If standard Wh- questions are used, Reverse ELIZA will give only scanty information; the user will find it more successful to employ indirect approaches, such as "reactions (Oh, really?), commentaries (That's too bad!), repetitions and paraphrases (You were sick?), interpretations and inferences (So you mean you had to stay at home)." The student thus learns very much the same strategies the original ELIZA (as DOCTOR) employed to keep the conversation going.

University of Rochester's TALK Project

A team of language teachers and programmers in AI at the University of Rochester are developing a parser-based authoring system for CALL materials (2). Called TALK (Teacher's Authoring Language Kit), the system will allow instructors to produce materials with built-in error-analysis capabilities. Rather than match answers literally as strings of characters (in the manner of authoring systems such as DASHER or EnBASIC), TALK will parse the student's input and check for syntactic category, morphological problems, etc. The program is being developed in a combination of LISP and the C programming language.

A unique feature of TALK will be the ability of the system to actually talk to the student by reproducing segments of stored speech at appropriate places in the program. "Speaking to the student" will be accomplished by means of digitized rather than synthesized speech (human voice segments recorded and stored in digital form—in a manner similar to compact disk recordings for music—on the same data disk that contains the program information), an arrangement that has the advantage of providing high-quality authentic speech segments that can be accessed by the program at random when needed. The TALK system will be designed so that the author using it can easily include commands for playback of these segments in the instructional program.

Project Alexis (Mills College)

The Foreign Language Department at Mills College (California) has begun initial planning and development of Alexis, a multifunction language-learning system for the VAX computer. Alexis is intended for first- and second-year students in French, German, and Spanish who will have access to VAX terminals located at various points on campus, including dormitories and the language lab. A unique feature of the system is the variety of activities it offers the student: exercises in reading comprehension, grammar (featuring an "intelligent" authoring system), compositions mailed to the instructor through foreign-language electronic mail systems, conversation (different versions of ELIZA), and games.

All activities in the Alexis system will also have access to several help features, including a full "helpscreen" to allow the student to move to any point in the system, complete on-line instructions, and on-line dictionaries for all three languages. When complete, the latter will contain the full first- and second-year lexicon corresponding to the contents of textbooks used at that level; definitions will be given in the foreign language.

Development work on Alexis is quite advanced, in part due to the strategy of the team charged with developing software. Wherever possible, the system incorporates existing programs that can be adapted to the purposes of the project. The reading program, for example, is an exercise developed by a Mills graduate student as a thesis project; the grammar authoring system is being developed by a computer-science professor as a by-product of another project; the electronic mail was already in place; the ELIZA program, and one of the games (ZORK), is available to UNIX users as public-domain software on most versions of the operating system; the remaining games were developed by two of the team members on contract to Random House Publishers, Inc., who have given permission for the incorporation of their product into this noncommercial system. When complete, Alexis promises to be a model for using mainframe academic computers (of which the VAX is the most common) for language practice.

Intelligent Grammar Tutor (University of Pittsburgh)

Vernick and Levin (22) describe work in progress in the design of an intelligent grammar tutoring system for ESL. Their instructional model extends the notion of an "intelligent" CALL system to include three different kinds of information they feel the system should possess: (1) knowledge of the subject matter (i.e., the lexicon and grammar of the items in the exercise), (2) knowledge the system acquires about the types of errors the student makes, and (3) knowledge of the most appropriate pedagogical strategies for the handling of specific types of errors. The addition of components (2) and (3) will enable the system to decide on the kinds of feedback to provide the student, as well as how much and when to provide it. Taking into account the learner's past and present performance, as well as the types of errors made, this feedback may consist of advice to the student in the form of suggestions for further practice and testing.

The ESL system described by Vernick and Levin will also possess intelligence of the type described in this chapter: knowledge of the structure of the language, more specifically that part of the language being practiced. In this case the structures involved include the passive and relative clauses in English. Using a limited lexicon and a set of grammar rules, the parsing component will compare student input with the instructor's model and note any morphological or syntactic problems. (Spelling, since it is not the point of the exercise, will be corrected automatically by a routine that compares misspelled words with a list of correctly spelled words.)

Getting Started in Intelligent CALL

Much of what is described above is clearly beyond the reach of the average language teacher who has an Apple IIe and a little knowledge of BASIC.

Some of the techniques described herein may be incorporated only partially into one's CALL efforts; perhaps they suggest no more than a basic approach—an attitude toward using, or trying to use, computers in a better way.

The more ambitious may wish to explore ways to try out some of the techniques described. As should be clear from the description of the less complex programs (e.g., SPION), there is much that can be accomplished even on a small scale. This section is devoted to outlining ways to experiment with building better mousetraps.

The artificial intelligentsia's favorite programming language is LISP. Although it is a fascinating language to puzzle through, a LISP program is usually far from transparent. LISP functions, for example, can be somewhat cryptic: (setq 'verb (car (cdr sentence)) is LISP for "let 'verb' be equal to the first element [= car] of everything but the first element [= cdr] of 'sentence'."

A more accessible language, and one undoubtedly more available to users of the typical school microcomputer, is LOGO. Although popular in schools for the teaching of geometrical reasoning through what is known as "turtle graphics" (making an object called the turtle move on the screen according to student instructions), LOGO, like LISP, is actually a powerful string-handling language, i.e., a language for manipulating words and sentences. Most versions of LOGO can be adapted to the kind of natural-language techniques that go into a good interactive program. And LOGO commands tend to be considerably more mnemonic and straightforward; the instruction given above in LISP would in LOGO read something like "MAKE 'VERB [FIRST BUTFIRST SENTENCE]."

How does one begin? As with everything else, start with something small. Play with writing LOGO routines that manipulate sentences or parts of sentences successfully. Most LOGO manuals give examples of short language programs or routines, such as a procedure for converting normal English sentences to Pig Latin ("igpay atinlay"). Most users have found that trying out such programs gives them ideas for going on to something more relevant to their interests. The teacher/programmer is limited only by the boundaries of his or her creativity.

One alternative to this do-it-yourself approach is to purchase either a ready-made adventure game or one of the new adventure-game authoring systems now available, and adapt to it to one's one language and tastes. Kossuth (10) describes such systems and her experiments with adapting such programs. The results might be described as instant AI. This author's experimentation with ELIZA similarly amounted to taking an existing (and complicated) program, translating it into Spanish, and reworking it to meet his own structural and pedagogical goals (19, 20).

Conclusions

What We Know

When one takes a close look at what natural-language processing can (and cannot) do, one gets a better sense of both the limitations in, and the possibilities for, developing a more "intelligent" CALL. It is clear that full language understanding by computer is not within the range of current possibilities. One must recognize, as did Weizenbaum and Winograd, that even the most clever of programs does not approach the understanding of the human speaker in normal language use; says Winograd (25) of SHRDLU, "the heuristics in our system touch only the tiniest bit of the relevant knowledge" (p. 191).

Yet it is equally clear that it is unnecessary for a CALL system to achieve anything approaching full understanding in order to be useful. Even the "semi-intelligent" system, endowed with partial understanding of language structure and/or meaning, can provide a rich and meaningful form of interaction with the student. A grammar exercise can use parsing strategies to provide a much more specific form of feedback. A game program can be programmed with certain simple semantic rules that allow it to judge the appropriateness of the student's input for the situation at hand. In each instance the success of the program will depend on its having a carefully restricted domain, i.e., a limited range of lexicon and structures it must "understand."

What the Future Holds

It is probably much too early to try to speculate where this experimentation will lead, particularly since artificial intelligence itself is, some say, still in the horse-and-buggy stage. But it seems safe to say that CALL is beginning to move in a much more interesting direction, and that perhaps the emphasis on drill-and-practice programs will shortly become a thing of the past. As with any new technology, the language lab included, initial efforts tend to copy the kinds of things one has been used to doing. CALL initially looked suspiciously like "programmed instruction," a logical, if unfortunate, model for using what appeared at first to be yet another "teaching machine." But it should be clear that today's computers are a far cry from mere teaching machines. What they can do is virtually endless, bounded not so much by the mechanical limits of the machines themselves as by our own imagination.

References: Artificial Intelligence and CALL

1. Ahl, David H. *More BASIC Computer Games*. New York: Workman, 1979.

2. Blake, Robert. "CALL and the Language Lab of the Future." Paper in preparation, 1986.
3. Boden, Margaret A. *Artificial Intelligence and Natural Man.* New York: Basic Books, 1977.
4. Clarke, Arthur C. *2001: A Space Odyssey.* New York: New American Library, 1968.
5. Cook, Vivian. "Designing CALL Programs for Communicative Teaching." Paper in preparation, 1986.
6. Feigenbaum, Edward A., and Pamela McCorduck. *The Fifth Generation: Artificial Intelligence and Japan's Computer Challenge to the World.* New York: New American Library, 1984.
7. Higgins, John, and Tim Johns. *Computers in Language Learning.* Reading, MA: Addison-Wesley, 1984.
8. IBM PC Voice Communications Option. White Plains, NY: IBM, 1985.
9. Kossuth, Karen C. "Suggestions for Comprehension-Based Computer-Assisted Instruction in German." *Die Unterrichtspraxis,* 17, 1 (1984):109–15.
10. _____. "Using the Adventure Formats for CALI." *CALICO Journal* 3, 2 (1985):13–17.
11. Kramsch, Claire, Douglas Morgenstern, and Janet H. Murray. "An Overview of the MIT Athena Language Learning Project." *CALICO Journal* 2, 4 (1985):31–34.
12. Marbach, William D. "The Smarter Computer." *Newsweek,* 3 December 1984, pp. 89–91b.
13. Mystery House. Program for the Apple II Computer. Coarsegold, CA:Sierra On-Line Systems, 1980.
14. Pusack, James P. "Answer-Processing and Error Correction in Foreign Language CAI." *System* 11, 1 (1983):53–64.
15. Richens, R. H., and A. D. Boothe, eds. *Machine Translation of Languages,* New York: Wiley, 1955.
16. Sanders, Ruth H., and Alton F. Sanders. "'Intelligent' Games for German Language Teaching," pp. 141–46 in *Foreign Language Instructional Technology Conference Proceedings, 21–24 September, 1982.* Monterey, CA: Defense Language Institute, 1983.
17. Sanders, Ruth H., and Alton F. Sanders. A German essay processor, personal communication.
18. SMOOTHTALKER Speech System. Program for the Apple Macintosh Computer. Long Beach, CA: First Byte, Inc., 1985.
19. Underwood, John. "Simulated Conversation as a CAI Strategy." *Foreign Language Annals* 15 (1982):209–12.
20. _____. *Linguistics, Computers, and the Language Teacher: A Communicative Approach.* Rowley, MA:Newbury House, 1984.
21. _____, and Richard Bassein. Juegos Comunicativos: Spanish Games for Communicative Practice, Program for the Apple IIe Computer. New York: Random House, 1985.
22. Vernick, Judy, and Lori Levin. "Intelligent Grammar Tutoring in ESL." Paper presented at the 1986 TESOL Convention, Anaheim, California, March 1986.
23. Weizenbaum, Joseph. "ELIZA—A Computer Program for the Study of Natural Language Communication between Man and Machine." *Communications of the Association for Computing Machines,* 10 8(1967):474–80.
24. Winograd, Terry. *Understanding Natural Language.* New York: Academic Press, 1972.
25. _____. "A Procedural Model of Language Understanding," pp. 154–86 in

Roger Schank and Kenneth Colby, eds., *Computer Models of Thought and Language*. San Francisco: W. H. Freeman, 1973.

26. ――――. "Towards Convivial Computing," pp. 56–72 in Michael J. Dertouzos and Joel Moses, eds., *The Computer Age: A Twenty-Year View*. Cambridge, MA: MIT Press, 1979.

27. ――――. "Computer Software for Working with Language." *Scientific American*, 251,4(September 1984):131–45.

28. ZORK. Program for the IBM PC Computer. Cambridge, MA: Infocom, 1982.

9

Language Teaching Approaches, the Evaluation of CALL Software, and Design Implications

Philip L. Hubbard
Stanford University

Introduction

Evaluating software for computer-assisted language learning (CALL) is a formidable task, even for those who are relatively familiar with the field. Whether one carries out an evaluation informally for a local institution or writes more formally for published review, there are at least five parameters of the judgmental process that make the evaluation of courseware more difficult and challenging than that of conventional textbooks.

First, there is the sheer novelty of this infant field of instructional technology to contend with. Reviewers of textual materials generally have had many years of experience working with print madia as student and teacher. In contrast, software evaluators may be only recently computer literate, and the field is new enough that few can boast more than a few years of experience using computer materials in their classes; fewer still have ever experienced CALL from the students' perspective.

Second, there is usually no way to "skim" through the software as with a textbook and other print materials. With few exceptions, the evaluator must proceed relatively lockstep once a choice is made from the main

Philip L. Hubbard (Ph.D., University of California, San Diego) is Lecturer in Linguistics and English for Foreign Students and Coordinator for Summer Programs in ESL at Stanford, where he also teaches English for foreign students and EFL/ESL methodology. He is the founder of the Clearinghouse for ELS Public Domain Software at the Ohio University (Athens), and a member of TESOL and CALICO.

menu. This restriction makes it very difficult to obtain an overview of the lesson format and content as quickly as is possible with a textbook.

Third, the relative complexity in the placement of lesson components on a disk makes the review process laborious. The hierarchical structuring and branching routines typically found in some of the more complex programs may define a large number of possible paths through a given lesson, which makes it difficult to view all of the material that a student might access while using the disk.

Fourth, there are visual and auditory dimensions in computer software missing in print material and that require evaluation. In the visual dimension, while both a textbook and computer software may include text alone, text plus pictures, or diagrams and charts, only the computerized lesson can animate graphics and highlight aspects of the text in a dynamic way. And speech synthesis aside, there are the congratulatory and critical buzzes, beeps, and electronic melodies that require a judgment whether they actually enhance or detract from the lesson.

Finally, there are interactional aspects to consider. To what extent does the student control the lesson or vice versa? How "intelligently" does the program evaluate the student's input? How does the computer respond after having made that evaluation? A program—whether drill and practice, tutorial, or simulation—in a real sense acts as teacher; the evaluator must determine to what extent that "teacher" is able to aid the student in learning the target language.

The relative newness of CALL software has meant that most guidelines or checklists for software evaluation concentrate largely on the parameters mentioned above, along with the equally vital questions about what hardware is required to run a given piece of software. As useful as such evaluation forms may be, however, they typically fail to address the crucial questions related to *approach*, the essential foundation of all language instructional material. While the variables mentioned above are important to evaluate, the bottom line must be "How is this piece of software going to improve a student's proficiency in the target language?"

This chapter discusses a supplementary evelation form developed to aid in answering this question by looking directly at important aspects of language-teaching approaches, where "approach" is taken to mean the set of underlying principles that outline a set of conditions for successful language learning and that, in turn, often follow from a theory of language acquisition and provide the foundation for specific classroom methods and techniques (Anthony, 1). Thus, the first section in this chapter shows how a typical checklist fails to address the appropriate questions for language-teaching software. The second section defines three major categories of language-teaching approaches and suggests that the principles they encompass can be applied to software evaluation. The third section discusses the evaluation of software for its potential in teaching the student strategies for learning, and the fourth will consider the relationship between software, approach, and syllabus. The final section introduces the supplementary evaluation form and outlines a procedure for using it to evaluate CALL materials. The chapter concludes with some implications of these concepts for software design.

Problems with Existing Checklists

There are a number of published software evaluation checklists, but many, such as the MicroSIFT form produced by the International Council for Computers in Education (Marler, 31), have been designed for use with CAI materials in any field. Using them to review foreign language materials assumes that learning a second language is essentially the same as other types of learning when, in fact, it is not. However strongly psychologists, linguists, and language teachers may disagree on other issues, the overwhelming majority support the view that learning a second language differs in significant ways from learning anything else.

In addition to such general-use forms and questionnaires, other checklists that have been developed specifically for second and foreign language materials (Strei, 42, Decoo, 17, Hope et al., 23, and Curtin and Shinall, Chapter 10 in this volume) similarly do not focus on the relative fit of the software to instructional approach and require supplementation to extract meaningful judgments whether the materials are likely to accomplish their advertised ends. The checklist formulated by CALICO (currently under revision) is a case in point, as can be seen in Figure 1 (an abridgment by this author of the original in which contents irrelevant to language-teaching approach considerations have been omitted and the items renumbered for internal consistency).

  I. General Questions
    1. Is the courseware intended to be teacher dependent or teacher independent?
    2. Are the exercises mechanical, meaningful, or communicative?
 II. Pedagogical Considerations
    1. Are the courseware contents substantively correct?
    2. Are the explanations complete and adequate in number?
    3. Are there adequate examples?
    4. Are concepts presented well?
    5. Can the courseware be used to introduce material as well as reinforce it?
    6. Are there adequate application activities?
    7. Are there adequate evaluation activities?
    8. Are all instructional units of approximately the same length?
    9. Are all the instructional units at approximately the same level of difficulty?
  10. Is the purpose of the package well defined?

11. Does the package achieve its defined purpose?
12. Is the package motivational?
13. Is the level of difficulty found in the courseware appropriate to the target audience?
14. Is the courseware suitable to students with a wide range of ability levels?
15. Does the level of difficulty vary according to the demonstrated ability level of the student?

III. Adaptability to Computer Medium
1. Is the instructional program interactive?
2. Is it clearly individualized?
3. Are branching or help options provided for students who need remedial attention?
4. Does the student have more than one chance to answer the question correctly?
5. Are opportunities provided for student feedback?
6. Can the student return to the start at any time?
7. Can the student exit at any time?
8. Does the student control the rate of presentation?

Figure 1. Abridged Version of the CALICO Software Evaluation Form

While lack of space prevents looking at each item in Figure 1, a significant weakness throughout is the omission of the word *language*, which detracts significantly from the face validity of the instrument in evaluating language materials. The CALICO form thus is just as suitable for evaluating CAI materials in chemistry or mathematics as it is for judging language-teaching courseware. A second problem with the CALICO checklist is a bias toward what can be called an explicit learning approach, considered by some to be the dominant form of second-language teaching at both the high school and university levels, although perhaps not the most effective.

In summary, there are shortcomings in the majority of existing checklists for evaluating CALL software. This article will suggest guidelines to overcome these limitations, taking as a basis for intelligent evaluation of CALL courseware the need for the evaluator to have a clear understanding of the *approach* underlying the curriculum and the syllabus for which it is intended.

Three Categories of Approach

Over the years, a number of distinct approaches to second-language teaching have guided classroom efforts and materials to help students learn. Although the boundaries that distinguish them may not always be clear, three major categories of approach can be identified for discussion purposes. Unlike the case of a specific approach, however, none should be taken as corresponding directly to any particular theory; rather, they are simply convenient labels for discussing distinguishable trends in second-language learning and teaching. Some of the more recently proposed theoretical models of second-language learning—Krashen (26), Bialystok (6,7) Strevens (43), Swain (44)—find representation under all the headings, while others—stimulus-response theories underlying behaviorist approaches (e.g., Brooks, 8)—are more clearly limited to a single descriptor. Nevertheless, these three categories reflect useful distinctions for materials development and CALL software evaluation, since they reflect major principled components of specific theories and models of second-language acquisition (see also Chapter 7 by Doughty in this volume).

Behaviorist Approaches

A number of authors (Dalgish, 16, Ariew, 2, Underwood, 46, Baker, 4) have noted that much of current CALL software seems to be based on a stimulus-response theory of language learning. Whether one agrees with this type of approach or not, the characteristics that distinguish behaviorism from other approaches are worth noting so that they can be recognized when they appear in CALL courseware.

Historically, behaviorist approaches to language learning are based on the principle that a response, linguistic or otherwise, is learned behavior resulting from associating that response with a given stimulus. Through positive reinforcement for correct behavior and negative reinforcement for incorrect behavior, these responses become overlearned until they are automatic. The main difference between learning a language under a behaviorist approach and learning mathematics, for example, is that most of the methods derived from it (such as audiolingualism) also place heavy stress on learning about the second-language culture.

Larsen-Freeman (28) lists a number of principles underlying the audiolingual method. Considering just those most relevant to the computer medium, CALL software will be representative of a behaviorist approach to language teaching to the extent that it does the following:

1. presents vocabulary and structure appropriate to the learner's level
2. maintains the learner's attention to task
3. does not accept errors as correct answer
4. requires the learner to input the correct answer before proceeding
5. provides the learner with positive feedback for correct answers
6. provides sufficient material for mastery and overlearning to occur
7. reinforces patterns and vocabulary presented in a lesson

8. presents grammar rules or patterns inductively with no attempt at teaching explicit formulations of them

Explicit Learning Approaches

Explicit learning approaches, including the so-called cognitive approaches in second-language teaching trace their heritage to the grammar and grammar translation methods of the Middle Ages and Renaissance. The central notion of explicit learning is that the target language can be learned through a conscious knowledge of the meanings of its words and the rules of its grammar. Currently, there are several theoretical positions taken with respect to explicit learning. Some researchers (Ellis, 19; Bialystok, 6,7) maintain that explicit learning and practice of grammar rules can lead to the automatic processing necessary for fluent conversation in the target language. Others, including Krashen (26), maintain that explicit learning cannot lead to automatic processing and that conscious linguistic knowledge can only be utilized by the Monitor, a cognitive linguistic device that applies rules consciously in speech production and edits the output at a significantly slower rate than the automatic processing system.

A somewhat different position is taken by McLaughlin et al. (32), who propose an information-processing approach that distinguishes controlled from automatic processing but assumes that either can be conscious or unconscious. In short, McLaughlin et al. allow for explicit learning to become automatic under certain conditions. Even within Krashen's Monitor Theory, however, it is acknowledged that explicit learning can be utilized when time is not a significant factor, as in writing or intensive reading. Further support for explicit learning approaches in teaching comes from a review and reanalysis by Long (29) of data from twelve experiments in language learning. Long concluded that explicit instruction at least facilitates the development of language proficiency and is more effective than language exposure alone.

If explicit learning is aimed at both consciously learned rules and their appropriate application in comprehending and producing the target language, it is desirable for the learner to have access to as much relevant information about the rules as possible. Thus, even in a standard practice exercise, whether mechanical or meaningful, it is helpful for students to have the option of requesting assistance in the form of hints to lead them to a correct response as well as answers to questions like "Why is my answer wrong?" and "Why is this answer right?" Few teachers in a typical classroom situation fail to respond to such questions, yet many current computer programs presumably aimed at explicit learning do not make this kind of assistance available. A related issue is the importance of accepting a range of appropriate answers for certain exercise items. If the goal of the exercise is to move the student in the direction of native-speaker competence, then any learner language a native speaker would accept as correct in a given context also should be considered correct. Teachers typically accept a range of answers as correct in classroom or homework exercises (often accompanied by a comment about minor differences in meaning or register); not many CALL programs, however, are designed to accommodate this need.

Providing drill-and-practice material in explicit learning approaches that is meaningful, contextualized, and interesting to the students is a recent trend that parallels developments in communicative approaches (Madsen and Bowen, 30). In much the same vein, Oller (36, p. 49) advocates paying greater attention to "story-writing" principles in ESL teaching, suggesting that while teachers should maintain a commitment to the explicit learning of grammar, they should also look at the pragmatic factors that affect the meaningfulness and comprehensibility of discourses used for instructional purposes. Although the focus in explicit learning materials is still more on form than on language use, there are compelling arguments in support of this trend. An exercise that is meaningful requires the students to integrate grammatical form and lexical content, leading to a deeper level of psycholinguistic processing. An exercise that is appropriately contextualized (e.g., a coherent paragraph or a series of sentences relating to a common theme, a picture, etc.) will lead the students toward the pragmatic competence necessary to extend the rules or vocabulary items correctly to novel instances. Finally, material that is interesting is more likely to hold students' attention and motivate them to complete the exercise successfully and attempt others of a similar type.

A final point within the explicit learning paradigm that relates exclusively to CALL materials involves student control of the software. Higgins (21) has argued that student-controlled software will be far more effective than lockstep program-controlled learning. Research by Stevens (41) supports this view, although the optimal degree of student control will no doubt vary with the student's level and the task. A study by Hubbard et al. (25) also bears on this issue by pointing out that if students are given a significant amount of control without appropriate training in how to use the software, they may fail to utilize the powerful options available to them.

Translating the above considerations into evaluation criteria for CALL, software will be representative of explicit learning approaches to the extent that it does the following:

1. introduces or reviews grammar rules and word meanings in an understandable, learnable, and reasonably accurate form
2. provides effective practice so that (a) novel target-language input can be readily understood, and (b) the learner's understanding of rules leads to the production of grammatically acceptable spoken or written target-language discourse in novel situations

3. gives meaningful rather than mechanical practice
4. gives practice contextualized in a coherent discourse larger than a single sentence
5. provides hints of various types to help lead students to acceptable answers
6. accepts alternative correct answers within the given context
7. provides the student with explanation of correct answers
8. anticipates incorrect or inappropriate answers and explains why such answers are incorrect or inappropriate
9. maintains the student's interest throughout the exercise
10. allows an appropriate degree of student control

In short, software that follows the principles of explicit learning as outlined above should be essentially tutorial in its approach and based on paragraph-length, episodically related examples of realistic language rather than isolated sentences. In programming the lesson, the author must anticipate the kinds of information that would most help the student learn and retain the material and provide that information in a form that is accessible and understandable. Drill-and-practice software, especially the type whose exercises can be processed in a superficial way, is simply less likely to lead to the learning and retention of explicit rules and vocabulary than is software that requires a deeper level of cognitive processing.

Acquisition Approaches

While the learning/acquisition distinction has only been popularized recently through the work of Krashen (26) and Dulay, Burt, and Krashen (18), the idea that languages can be learned effectively without formal study of language structure and vocabulary has been with the field of second-language learning for some time. To some extent, the Direct Method and other implicit learning approaches are based on this idea. The current revival of the notion of natural language learning can be traced to Newmark (34) and Newmark and Reibel (35), who suggested that languages can be learned in a natural environment that holds meaningful and understandable "chunks" of language provided that the learner simply pays attention to the language as it is being used. Krashen (26) later refined these ideas into a theory of second-language learning and acquisition involving (1) the Monitor, mentioned in the previous section, for explicit learning and processing, (2) an Organizer, or Language Acquisition Device, and (3) an Affective Filter (Dulay, Burt, and Krashen, 18). The Organizer and Affective Filter are central to the acquisition portion of the overall model, as they are involved in the learner's unconscious analysis of strings of speech in the processing of speech input, the production of output, and the synthesis of new rules.

Krashen's model, though far from being universally accepted, has exerted a profound influence on second-language acquisition research in the past decade. It has also provided a theoretical foundation for a class of communicatively oriented approaches (Terrell, 45; Krashen and Terrell, 27; Winitz, 49). There is, in fact, a significant overlap between acquisition approaches and communicative approaches in general, even though the two are not synonymous. Specifically, it is possible to include communicative methodology within the umbrella of an explicit learning approach. As Brumfit (10, p. 37) has pointed out, however, a number of second-language acquisition researchers and language-teaching methodologists have assumed a dichotomy roughly parallel to the learning/acquisition division in Krashen's theory and, while they vary somewhat with respect to the role explicit learning might play in a communicative approach, the importance of acquisition in developing communicative competence is generally supported. For this reason, in the discussion that follows communicative approaches are subsumed under "acquisition." (See Doughty, Chapter 7 in this volume, for a further discussion of the acquisition/learning distinction.)

The first requirement for acquisition in Krashen's model is that the input (the language directed at the learner) be comprehensible, i.e., that its meaning can be determined by the learner from the communicative context and the linguistic information in the learner's acquired system at that point in the acquisition process. Given some linguistic input, the Affective Filter determines how much of this input makes its way to the Organizer for processing. Two significant variables in the Affective Filter are the learner's attitude and motivation. A positive self-image, a low level of anxiety, and a strong desire to learn the language (and engage in the communicative tasks necessary for acquisition) are among the criteria for keeping the Affective Filter at a low level, thus allowing maximum linguistic input into the Organizer. Finally, the learning environment and the types of learning tasks are assumed to have a significant effect on the Affective Filter.

Krashen's Organizer is reminiscent of the Language Acquisition Device that Chomsky (13) hypothesized for first-language acquisition. Input that has not been filtered out, or *intake* as Krashen calls it, is unconsciously analyzed by the Organizer, which also formulates rules (again unconsciously). While the internal operation of the Organizer remains a mystery, it is hypothesized to operate most effectively on linguistic structures that are just beyond the level already attained in the acquired grammar. Because of the implied developmental sequence in the acquisition of grammatical rules, it is also generally assumed that overt error correction will have no real value in acquisition and, in fact, may be detrimental, because correcting learner errors leads to anxiety and raises affective barriers.

Krashen's model focuses on the learner's linguistic input and does not require any production explicitly in order for acquisition of linguistic and communicative competence to occur. However, acquisition-based approaches generally put some emphasis on developing the learner's ability to produce as well as to understand novel utterances. Thus, a final point about acquisition approaches is that they allow the learner practice in producing comprehensible *output* in addition to processing input.

Although Krashen's model has had little influence on the development of CALL software, it is not the case that CALL specialists have ignored acquisition approaches altogether. Higgins and Johns (22), Dalgish (16), and Baltra (5) discuss the use of games and simulations as communicative activities and stress the value of learner–learner conversation in front of the screen. Having pairs and even larger groups of learners working together at a single screen allows the computer material to act as a catalyst to promote real communicative interaction between the participants. Underwood (46), another advocate of communicative CALL, discusses at length the need for developing software that is consistent with current linguistic and language-learning theory. His thirteen premises for communicative CALL have much in common with the evaluation criteria that are presented below. Unlike these evaluation criteria, however, many of Underwood's premises focus on what communicative CALL is *not*: "Communicative CALL will never try to do anything a book could do just as well" (p. 54), while some of his other premises are more consultatory: "Communicative CALL will use the target language exclusively" (p. 53).

Looking at the above factors in terms of computer courseware, and following Krashen's theoretical model with the addition of some insights from communicative methods, CALL software will be representative of an acquisition-oriented approach to the extent that it does the following:

1. provides meaningful communicative interaction between the learner and the computer
2. provides comprehensible input at a level just beyond that currently acquired by the learner
3. promotes a positive self-image in the learner
4. motivates the learner to use the software
5. motivates the learner to learn the language
6. provides a challenge but does not produce frustration or anxiety
7. does not include overt error correction
8. allows the learner the opportunity to produce comprehensible output
9. acts effectively as a catalyst to promote learner–learner interaction in the target language

Note that "meaningful communicative interaction" (number 1 above) does not necessarily imply that both the learner and the computer use language in an exchange. It is possible for the computer to react to input nonlinguistically (e.g., by moving text or graphics in response to the learner's command) and for the learner to react to the computer's target-language output nonlinguistically (e.g., by moving the cursor or a graphics figure with pointing devices, such as the cursor keys or a mouse, in response to the computer's command). In fact, the latter type of interaction is typical of beginners in delayed production approaches and methods such as the Natural Approach (Terrell, 45; Krashen and Terrell, 27), Total Physical Response (Asher, 3), and the Comprehension Approach (Winitz, 49).

This section has focused on three categories of approaches— behaviorist, explicit learning, and acquisition—which were defined broadly in the interest of comprehensiveness. These broad categories of definition are not meant to imply, however, that all approaches will fit directly under one heading; rather, a given approach may not share all of the principles of its closest superordinate category and may include other significant principles not mentioned above (such as whether the native language may be used at all in instruction). In practice, too, the individual teacher may quite consciously vary the approach, based on perceived student needs. For example, in second or foreign language classes or programs whose goals include grammatical accuracy as well as communicative competence (as is often the case with languages taught for academic or professional purposes), it is not uncommon to see a preference for acquisition approaches in conversation/discussion components and explicit learning approaches in reading/writing/grammar components. Often, there is variation based on the learner's level as well, with acquisition approaches favored for beginning levels and explicit learning approaches favored for more advanced ones. Nevertheless, the parameters listed above for these categories are useful aids in determining the language-teaching approach underlying given CALL software and, in turn, provide a means for judging a fundamental question in software evaluation: How well does the teaching approach manifested in the software match that of the teacher whose students will be using it?

Learner Strategy Orientation

An additional area of consideration in judging the probable effectiveness of foreign language software is the degree to which the materials may directly or indirectly promote the use of particular strategies in the learner, that is, procedures for learning, acquiring, or using the target language more easily and effectively. The concept of learner strategies is not limited directly to any particular category of approaches. In fact, it is possible for the learner to be taught or to develop strategies compatible with approaches in any of the three major categories mentioned above.

The idea of using strategies to enhance learning is not new. Learner strategies have received increasing attention from both researchers in second-language learning and materials developers in the past decade as part of the general trend toward focusing on the language learner, and several taxonomies have been proposed to describe them. Most, in one way or another, distinguish direct or cognitive learner strategies (those involving deliberate manipulation of material to enhance learning or retention) from indirect or metacognitive ones (those involving self-monitoring, self-assessment, and goal setting—Oxford-Carpenter, 37, p.1). Wenden (47) has added communication strategies (those used to facilitate information exchange) and global practice strategies (those that lead the learner to utilize the environment effectively for target language practice). Rather than attaching itself to any particular taxonomy, however, the discussion that follows will look at learner strategies from the viewpoint of some general principles that are particularly appropriate for the evaluation of strategy-oriented software.

In a sense, any structured or semistructured exercise, from pattern practice to open-ended role play, represents a strategy on the part of the teacher for aiding the student in gaining proficiency in the target language. But these are really *teaching* strategies. A *learner*-strategy orientation, on the other hand, involves focusing more on those strategies that the learner may come to employ consciously and control independently. For example, in teaching vocabulary with a learner-strategy orientation, the focus is not on learning individual lexical items; instead, the teacher introduces and provides meaningful practice in strategies for guessing the meaning of an unknown word (attending to context, deducing the part of speech, decomposing it into stem and derivational morphemes, etc.). In the first instance, for example, the student can be taught the strategy of looking ahead to the words that follow the unknown word for clues to its meaning, rather than simply ignoring it or stopping and reaching for the dictionary as soon as it is encountered. As this example illustrates, the teaching of strategies helps move the learner from being a passive recipient of linguistic input to becoming a more conscious and autonomous processor; in short, learner strategies shift much of the responsibility for successful learning from the teacher to the student (Wenden, 47, p. 5).

It is significant for CALL that many of the strategies that are useful in second-language learning are utilized by native speakers as well. This is because many learner strategies are aimed primarily at improving the individual's performance, rather than achieving linguistic competence. Thus, CALL software developed for native speakers to enhance their strategies for learning, particularly in the areas of reading and writing, may be quite helpful for advanced learners of a target language.

As with other strategy-oriented material, the focus for CALL software should be on strategies that can be learned consciously or induced in the learner, rather than on those that seem to be a universal by-product of second-language learning, e.g., overgeneralization and avoidance as discussed by Brown (9). Strategies to be taught may range from the very general, e.g., the fourteen major ones for "the good language learner" discussed by Rubin and Thompson (38)—learn to tolerate ambiguity, let context help you, learn formalized routines, etc.—to the very detailed and skill-specific, e.g., skimming a passage by reading the first sentence of each paragraph to gain a general idea of content (Grellet, 20).

There are several types of strategies that seem particularly well-suited to being introduced and practiced on the computer. In reading, for example, psycholinguistic research has pointed to the importance of top-down processing strategies, using information from skimming a passage, from its title and introduction, or from the reader's background knowledge of the subject to build an anticipation schema for its rhetorical structure and content (Coady, 14; Carrell and Eisterhold, 12). Experiments reported in Carrell (11) provide evidence that ESL learners even at the advanced level make less use of such strategies than do typical native English readers, and it is plausible to assume that this may be true of second and foreign language reading in general. In writing, there are production strategies such as writing dialogs, brainstorming, list making, and flexible outlining that many second-language learners are either unaware of or ignore (Spack, 40; Hubbard, 24). At the level of rhetorical structure, Scarcella (39) has shown that the reader orientation strategies of advanced ESL writers differ significantly from those of native writers, which suggests that strategies learned in the first language may not transfer to or be appropriate in a second.

Unlike the behaviorist, explicit learning, or acquisition approaches, there are no specific learning theories or models associated with learner strategies. Consequently, much of what follows is based on the writer's views of how to teach learner strategies effectively.

A number of factors must be considered in producing materials to teach learner strategies. A particular strategy will be effective to the degree that it fits both the learner's needs and his or her preferred learning style. If the strategy is being taught explicitly, as is generally the case, it must be presented in a comprehensible way and be accompanied by an explanation of the principles underlying it—without this, the learner is unlikely to be convinced of its value. Reinforcement tasks, then, should be designed so that they are accomplished more efficiently if a given strategy is used appropriately. In many cases, a variety of related strategies may be presented together with explanations of their respective strengths and weaknesses. In this instance the accompanying exercises will give the learner the opportunity to experiment and discover which strategies work best under specific conditions.

Based on the preceding considerations, CALL software will effectively promote the learning and use of learner strategies to the extent that it does the following:

1. introduces the learner to strategies that are useful and immediately usable

2. introduces the learner to strategies appropriate to the learner's level

3. explains the value of the strategies
4. provides meaningful practice in the use of the strategies
5. presents practice material in such a way that the task is more easily or successfully accomplished if the appropriate strategy or strategies are used
6. provides, when possible, a variety of strategies (or of techniques for utilizing a given strategy) for a given type of task suited to a range of learning styles
7. provides feedback on which strategies might have worked best for given tasks after the learner has attempted them

As research continues in the area of learner strategies, it is likely that more explicit methods and techniques will be developed to teach and to judge their relative effectiveness. In the meantime, the parameters mentioned above provide a usable evaluation metric for determining the potential effectiveness of strategy-oriented software.

The Syllabus and CALL Materials

The software evaluator, particularly one making decisions for his or her class or program rather than for published review, must determine to what extent the orientation and content of the software is compatible with the orientation, content, and sequencing of an institution-specific syllabus. Some of the parameters that áre useful to consider in answering that question are discussed below for four major syllabus types—structural, situational, notional–functional, and content-centered—recognized generally as typical in second or foreign language teaching.

Structural Syllabus

The focus of a structural syllabus is the grammar of the target language. Within a behaviorist or explicit learning approach, the grammar patterns or rules of the language are typically sequenced along continua of presumed ease of learning (easiest structures first) and to a lesser extent relative frequency (more common structures first). In either case, the structural focus of CALL software to be used as an integral part of a course must be at a level that is consistent with that prescribed by the syllabus. If the software is used on a voluntary basis by the students, then it may be appropriate to have material at a lower level for remedial purposes.

A learner-strategy orientation in CALL can be incorporated into a structural syllabus to the extent that the software is designed to introduce and practice general procedures for learning and using grammatical constructions. As reading is often a component of an explicit learning approach in a structural syllabus, software that focuses on appropriate reading strategies can also fit into this combination.

The structural syllabus per se is not really compatible with an acquisition approach, although it is possible to have genuine communicative exercises, either on the computer itself or involving the learners in conversation with the computer acting as a catalyst, which lend themselves naturally to promoting the use of a particular grammatical construction (e.g., giving instructions would promote the use of imperative forms).

Situational Syllabus

In a situational syllabus, the focus is on introducing the learners to situations they are likely to encounter in using the target language (ordering a meal, cashing a check) and helping them to build frames of reference for communicating appropriately. In practice, a situational syllabus is often integrated with a structural or notional–functional syllabus. However, the central focus in a true situational syllabus is on the relevant vocabulary and the interchanges between the participants within a prototypical context, ideally leading the learner to an understanding of the expectations, both linguistic and nonlinguistic, of target language speakers. Regardless of the approach, CALL software being reviewed for use within a situational syllabus should demonstrate content and situations which the learner is likely to encounter in real life; ideally, it should be sequenced to reinforce or complement the situations the learner is exposed to in the text and classroom.

When a behaviorist approach is applied to a situational syllabus, the goal is presumably to drill the learner in prototypical situations and variants with a similar communicative structure. CALL software that involves this type of drill, particularly if it allows for the repetition necessary for habit formation, would be consistent with this combination.

If an explicit learning approach is linked to a situational syllabus, CALL software consistent with the combination would need to provide lists of vocabulary to be learned, examples of appropriate interchanges, and a discussion of what the structural and sociolinguistic elements of the interchanges are, along with practice in initiating the conversation and responding appropriately. Bearing in mind earlier comments about the tutorial nature of good explicit-learning software, hints and explanatory feedback should also be provided. An appropriately programmed interactive videodisc containing a common situation, such as learning the language and behavioral protocols of going to a restaurant, would be an example of explicit learning within a situational syllabus.

An acquisition approach can be maintained in a situational syllabus by using CALL software whose content provides comprehensible input in the given situations and that allows the learner to interact with the computer and/or other learners. Simulations of common situations, for example, could provide both communicative language practice and information about target culture expectations, e.g., getting from the airport to a specific location in a strange city.

Learner-strategy software within a situational approach is also a possibility. In this case, the focus of the software is on strategies for acquiring information about the given situation by observing or asking native speakers for assistance, and on strategies for identifying and repairing miscommunication in an acceptable manner according to the target culture standards of behavior.

Notional-Functional Syllabus

Strictly speaking, a notional syllabus divides the target language into semantic categories (greeting, apology, anger, etc.) while a functional syllabus focuses on language use (asking, expressing feelings, responding, etc.). In practice, they are generally combined into a syllabus built around using language within particular semantic categories—asking for assistance, expressing anger, responding to an apology, etc. (Wilkins, 48). While it is possible to realize a behaviorist or explicit learning approach within a notional/functional syllabus, the focus on real language use that lies at the root of this syllabus orientation makes it much more compatible with acquisition approaches.

CALL software that allows for real communicative interaction between the learner and computer or between two or more learners in front of the computer will be in line with an acquisition approach in a notional-functional syllabus to the extent that it meets the criteria for acquisition-oriented software in general and provides practice in using the notions/functions called for by the syllabus at the level it is being used. Software that reviews notions/functions from earlier lessons can provide acceptable material toward this end as well, as long as the lessons remain challenging enough to engage the learners' interest. However, a reviewer should be wary of software that might assume that the learners have mastered a particular notion/function (e.g., making polite requests) that in fact they do not control, even if the grammar and vocabulary are familiar to them.

Learner strategies relate well to a notional-functional syllabus, since some of the notions/functions typically taught (asking for clarification, restating, etc.) can be viewed as communicative strategies as well. The type of CALL software that would be relevant is similar to that mentioned above for the situational syllabus, i.e., that which focuses on strategies that aid the learners in acquiring information, comprehending it, and making themselves understood.

Content-Centered Syllabus

In a true content-centered syllabus, language is not the focus; rather, it is the tool the student learns to manipulate to get at information about the subject matter of the course (Mohan, 33). To a limited extent, content-centered courses have been around for years in the form of foreign language classes whose material relates to teaching about the target culture. Typically, however, such courses have tended to have structural sequencing as the overriding consideration; that is, content-centered courses simply inject content into a structural syllabus. More recently, building on the model of bilingual transition programs where certain subjects are taught in the child's second language, content-centered courses focusing on other topics have appeared in second and foreign language teaching (Curtain, 15), particularly in English for academic programs and "language" for business classes in the United States. Structural, situational, and notional-functional aspects of the language may still be considered within this more recent view of content-centered language teaching, but they are of secondary importance.

Like the notional-functional syllabus, the content-centered syllabus is founded on the assumption that meaningful, natural use of language in a realistic communicative setting will lead to increased proficiency in the target language (Mohan 33, p. 1). Thus, the content-centered syllabus is not really compatible with the drill-and-practice focus of behaviorist approaches or the language-analysis orientation of explicit learning approaches. It is, however, quite compatible with acquisition approaches and a learner-strategy orientation.

Within an acquisition approach, there are three important considerations in evaluating content-centered CALL software. The first, which is an important consideration for the course as a whole, is to be sure that the subject matter is linked to the needs and/or interests of the learners so that they are motivated to use it. The second consideration is to determine to what extent the content of the software is consistent with that of the rest of the course. If too much of the content is already familiar, learners will be less motivated to attend to it; on the other hand, if the concepts are too challenging or too dependent on unfamiliar background information, they may become frustrated. Finally, the linguistic level must be appropriate for the learners' current degree of proficiency. If the vocabulary and structure are too simple, then very little language acquisition may occur, even though the content may be mastered. Similarly, if there are too many unknown words or unfamiliar constructions, then the input may not be comprehensible enough to allow for much acquisition, and again, frustration may result.

Learner strategies that are most valuable to introduce and practice in a content-centered course, in addition to those mentioned above for a notional-functional syllabus, are those that involve more efficient language production and comprehension. CALL software that promotes the use of reading-comprehension strategies is particularly appropriate, as is software that focuses on strategies for organizing compositions, assuming the overall curriculum and course requirements include a writing component.

In summary, the focus of this section has been on the criteria for evaluating software vis à vis its relative consistency with respect to the course or program syllabus and its orientation. The three most important criteria seem to be the following:

1. the approach manifested by the software is compatible with that of the syllabus type
2. the level and sequencing of the linguistic content is appropriate for the course as determined by the syllabus
3. the subject-matter content is appropriate for the goals of the course or program as determined by the syllabus and the presumed knowledge base of the learners

The degree to which the software meets these criteria will aid the evaluator in determining whether the CALL materials can be integrated effectively into the syllabus as basic or supplementary material.

A Supplementary Evaluation Form for Language Teaching Approaches

This final section of this chapter presents a three-part supplementary evaluation form for CALL software (Figure 2) that takes into account the characteristics of the three types of approaches and the learner-strategy considerations presented above, and describes a procedure for using it. Users adopting this form for in-house evaluation are encouraged to adapt and simplify it, selecting those categories considered most relevant and ignoring the rest. As the evaluation criteria represent to some extent the author's interpretation of each approach, it is also possible that an evaluator will want to expand or revise the form on the basis of a different interpretation of these central principles.

It is also important to realize that a teacher using this form may not find his or her teaching approach described or encapsulated within any single category. The direct method, for example, as described by Larsen-Freeman (28), includes characteristics of behaviorist approaches (with respect to pointing out and correcting errors as they occur) and acquisition approaches (with respect to providing comprehensible input and promoting learner–learner interaction). Thus, teachers who do not embrace a particular method exclusively are even more likely to find their assumptions about language learning included under more than one category—and this is in itself instructive, for it demonstrates a fundamental eclecticism that many subscribe to. For the same reasons, using this supplementary form to evaluate CALL software is likely to demonstrate clearly that the approach underlying the software itself reflects characteristics of more than one category. Thus, using the form will reveal (1) the approach in which a given piece of software may find its greatest correspondence and most efficient use, and (2) a pattern of response across all categories that describe the approach subscribed to by the teacher.

It is unusual to find CALL software that rates highly in *all* the areas within a given category. Thus, the evaluation form will also provide information about less-than-ideal but nevertheless usable correlations between content of extant software and its intended purpose. Finally, the Supplementary Evaluation Form focuses *only* on the language-teaching aspects of the software, and it should therefore be used in conjunction with other forms or checklists such as those described in the first section of the chapter. Part I of the form holds principles that describe the three categories of approach—behaviorist, explicit, acquisition; Part II encompasses descriptors common to learner strategies; Part III is a short questionnaire for other pedagogical considerations.

I. *APPROACH CHECKLIST*

PRINCIPLE	DEGREE?	HOW WELL DONE?	COMMENTS

Behaviorist Approaches

	PRINCIPLE	DEGREE?	HOW WELL DONE?	COMMENTS
1.	Presents vocabulary and structure appropriate to the learner's level	0 1 2 3 CJ	1 2 3 4 5 CJ	
2.	Maintains the learner's attention on the task	0 1 2 3 CJ	1 2 3 4 5 CJ	
3.	Will not accept errors as correct answers	0 1 2 3 CJ	1 2 3 4 5 CJ	
4.	Requires the learner to input correct answer before proceeding	0 1 2 3 CJ	1 2 3 4 5 CJ	
5.	Provides the learner with positive feedback for correct answers	0 1 2 3 CJ	1 2 3 4 5 CJ	
6.	Provides sufficient material for mastery and overlearning to occur	0 1 2 3 CJ	1 2 3 4 5 CJ	
7.	Subsequently reinforces patterns and vocabulary presented in earlier lessons	0 1 2 3 CJ	1 2 3 4 5 CJ	
8.	Presents grammar patterns inductively without attempting to teach formulations of rules	0 1 2 3 CJ	1 2 3 4 5 CJ	

Explicit Learning Approaches

1. Introduces or reviews grammar rules and word meanings in an understandable, learnable, and reasonably accurate form   0 1 2 3 CJ   1 2 3 4 5 CJ
2. Provides effective practice so that (a) novel target-language input can be readily understood and (b) the learner's understanding of the rules studied leads to the production of grammatically correct spoken or written target-language forms   0 1 2 3 CJ   1 2 3 4 5 CJ
3. Gives meaningful rather than mechanical practice   0 1 2 3 CJ   1 2 3 4 5 CJ
4. Gives practice contextualized in a coherent discourse larger than a sentence   0 1 2 3 CJ   1 2 3 4 5 CJ
5. Provides hints of various types to help lead students to correct answers   0 1 2 3 CJ   1 2 3 4 5 CJ
6. Accepts alternative correct answers   0 1 2 3 CJ   1 2 3 4 5 CJ
7. Provides explanations for why correct answers are correct   0 1 2 3 CJ   1 2 3 4 5 CJ
8. Anticipates incorrect answers and provides explanations of them   0 1 2 3 CJ   1 2 3 4 5 CJ
9. Maintains the learner's interest throughout the exercise   0 1 2 3 CJ   1 2 3 4 5 CJ
10. Allows an appropriate degree of student control   0 1 2 3 CJ   1 2 3 4 5 CJ

CJ = cannot judge   0 = not at all   1 = poorly
                                 3 = to a great   5 = excellently
                                 extent

PRINCIPLE	DEGREE?	HOW WELL DONE?	COMMENTS

Acquisition Approaches

1. Provides meaningful communicative interaction between the student and the computer   0 1 2 3 CJ   1 2 3 4 5 CJ
2. Provides comprehensible input at a level just beyond that currently acquired by the learner   0 1 2 3 CJ   1 2 3 4 5 CJ

3.	Promotes a positive self-image in the learner	0 1 2 3 CJ	1 2 3 4 5 CJ
4.	Motivates the learner to use it	0 1 2 3 CJ	1 2 3 4 5 CJ
5.	Motivates the learner to acquire the language	0 1 2 3 CJ	1 2 3 4 5 CJ
6.	Provides a challenge but does not produce frustration or anxiety	0 1 2 3 CJ	1 2 3 4 5 CJ
7.	Does not include overt error correction	0 1 2 3 CJ	1 2 3 4 5 CJ
8.	Allows the learner the opportunity to produce comprehensible output	0 1 2 3 CJ	1 2 3 4 5 CJ
9.	Acts effectively as a catalyst to promote learner–learner interaction in the target language	0 1 2 3 CJ	1 2 3 4 5 CJ

II. *LEARNER STRATEGY CHECKLIST*

1.	Introduces the learner to strategies that are useful and immediately usable	0 1 2 3 CJ	1 2 3 4 5 CJ
2.	Introduces the learner to strategies appropriate to the learner's level	0 1 2 3 CJ	1 2 3 4 5 CJ
3.	Explains the value of the strategies	0 1 2 3 CJ	1 2 3 4 5 CJ
4.	Provides meaningful practice in the use of the strategies	0 1 2 3 CJ	1 2 3 4 5 CJ
5.	Presents practice material in such a way that the task is more easily or successfully accomplished if the appropriate strategy or strategies are used	0 1 2 3 CJ	1 2 3 4 5 CJ
6.	Provides an appropriate variety of strategies (or of techniques for utilizing a given strategy) for a given type of task suited to a range of learning styles	0 1 2 3 CJ	1 2 3 4 5 CJ
7.	Provides feedback on which strategies might have worked best for given tasks after the student has attempted them	0 1 2 3 CJ	1 2 3 4 5 CJ

CJ = cannot judge   0 = not at all   1 = poorly
                       3 = to a great   5 = excellently
                       extent

III. *OTHER PEDAGOGICAL CONSIDERATIONS*

1. Based on your own interpretation of the ratings, what approach or approaches does this courseware most clearly represent?
2. How well does the software fit into the syllabus for the class or program for which it is being evaluated?
   a. Is the approach manifested by the software compatible with that of the syllabus?
   b. Are the level and sequencing of linguistic content appropriate for the course as determined by the syllabus?
   c. Is the subject-matter content appropriate for the goals of the course or program as determined by the syllabus and for the presumed knowledge base of the learners?
3. Briefly describe the methods and techniques used; comment on how successfully they have been adapted to the computer medium.

Figure 2. Supplementary Evaluation Form for Language Teaching Considerations

In the first two sections of the form (Approach and Learner Strategy), a two-part, scaled-response format replaces the simple yes/no format characteristic of the CALICO checklist and many others. The first part (Column 1) is a purely quantitative measure, scaled from 0 to 3, and represents the degree to which a certain criterion is met, with 0 meaning "not at all" and 3 meaning "to a great extent." The second part (Column 2) is meant to be a qualitative measure, scaled from 1 to 5, and represents a judgment on the part of the evaluator on how *well* the criterion is met, with 1 meaning "poorly" and 5, "excellently." Under both, the abbreviation CJ stands for "cannot judge." The expanded response scale offers these advantages: First, the scales provide more information than a binary format. Second, the "how well done?" column provides a way for judging the effectiveness rather than the mere presence of an option. For example, it is quite possible to have hints and explanations in explicit learning software that are copious but not particularly helpful, and this form is designed to indicate that information explicitly.

Going through the evaluation form will reveal that in come cases the judgments in the second part are unnecessary. For example, if the reviewer circles "0" for an item under the "Degree" column, then there is no sense in rating how well it was done. Further, for certain items, e.g., whether the material "motivates the learner to use it" (Acquisition Approaches, item 4), the rating in the "Degree" column should correspond closely to the rating under "How Well Done" simply because of the type of information requested. Note also that because scales alone may be misleading, there is a short space for comments after each item.

The third section of the form, Other Pedagogical Considerations, provides for a more open-ended response in three areas. The first question simply asks the evaluator to make a judgment about what approach the courseware under review represents most clearly. Note that because the principles may differ in importance to a given approach or to a practitioner of that approach, simply averaging the numbers in sections I and II is unlikely to offer a reliable numerical index that defines approach. Rather, the rater will have to determine the answer to this question through a careful inspection of the categories themselves and an assessment of the relative weight of each item. Question 2 in section III covers the relationship between the software and the syllabus as outlined in the previous section. Question 3 asks for a brief description of the methods and techniques the software uses and an evaluation of how well they have been adapted to the computer.

It should be noted that this supplementary form is designed for CALL software that includes language content and is inappropriate without significant changes for evaluating word-processing programs and the like. Finally, there are judgments requested that may be duplicated in other parts of a more general checklist. This is a minor annoyance, however, and perhaps not much of a price to pay for seeing the information specific to a language-teaching approach represented in a more readily interpretable fashion.

A Procedure for Using the Evaluation Form

As mentioned in the opening section of this chapter, evaluating software for second-language instruction is a challenging task. The paragraphs that follow offer a procedure to aid an evaluator in completing that task successfully; its goal is to lead the evaluator to an informed decision about adopting a given piece of software.

Before beginning the evaluation process, it is necessary to acquire a general evaluation form like that in Figure 1, to which some version of Figure 2 above should be appended. The base form should include at least questions about the skill area, intended level, and hardware requirements, as well as whether the software requires or allows for student collaboration (see Wyatt, Chapter 4 in this volume), etc. As suggested earlier, the evaluator may also wish to adapt the Supplementary Evaluation Form in Figure 2 so that it includes only those areas deemed relevant for the class or program for which the software is being considered. For instance, if the software is to be used in a class taught strictly within a given approach, then the evaluator may not feel it is necessary to rate the fit of the software with other approaches and simply eliminate those categories. When the instructional focus encompasses a wider variety of approaches, the evaluator will need to use the entire checklist.

The actual evaluation process involves five steps, moving from a cursory level to a very detailed and critical review. As the goal is not necessarily to complete the form but to decide on whether to adopt a given piece of software, the evaluation procedure should normally stop at any point where the evaluator becomes convinced that the software is *not* appropriate for his or her class or program.

The first step is to examine the available documentation. The evaluator looks for general information such as the following:

1. language skill area and approximate level
2. form and content of the language material
3. types of student response required (multiple choice, completion, etc.)
4. types of feedback to the student available from the program
5. procedures for monitoring student progress and consequent adaptation of the lesson sequencing
6. record-keeping options available to the teacher

The next step is to skim through selected parts of the disk for additional information in the areas just mentioned and to get a sense of screen layout, clarity of instructions, and ease of use. A good strategy is to look at parts of at least three lessons taken from the beginning, middle, and end of the lesson sequence (if one exists). In multiple-disk packages this may mean looking at one lesson on each of three disks.

The third step is to take an in-depth look at one or more lessons (or parts of lessons if they are long). If more than one exercise type is available, then a sampling should be taken of each. At this stage, all the available user options should be explored. Hints and help options should be tried, and both correct and incorrect answers should be attempted with the evaluator noting the computer's responses and judging their appropriateness for the presumed users. It is at this time that many of the questions on the Supplementary Evaluation Form can be answered with a fair degree of reliability, and if the evaluator's time is an important consideration, a decision to adopt or reject the software can often be made. The information gathered from this and the previous step is also useful for determining whether the students will be able to use the software in its present form or will need additional documentation or instruction.

The final two steps are taken when additional information is either needed or desired: The fourth step is to move through the entire program from start to finish, essentially following the same procedure as in step three. The fifth step, which may be accomplished without going through the fourth, is to field-test the software on one or more students in the target audience. Any software that rates highly after these final two steps can be given a sound recommendation.

Conclusion

This chapter has stressed the importance of considering teaching approach in the evaluation of CALL software and has presented a Supplementary Evaluation Form to that end as well as a procedure for implementing it. The supplementary form provides teachers with access to the kind of information that allows for a more confident decision whether a given piece of software is consonant with their assumptions about language learning, with the needs of students in their foreign language classes, and with the scope and sequence of their syllabus. While the focus of this chapter has been on the individual teacher's evaluation of CALL materials, there are two additional areas in which the concepts discussed above also find relevance: software reviews and software design.

If the evaluation parameters suggested in Figure 2 are valuable to individuals evaluating software for their own use, they are unquestionably important to reviewers. Due to time factors, the complexity of the evaluation process, and the difficulty in acquiring software for that process, published reviews play a vital role in the initial stage of deciding whether to consider given software for adoption or purchase. In some cases, for expedience, published reviews may even comprise the *only* information outside of the publisher's description that a buyer has access to prior to purchasing a software package. Thus, evaluators who publish software reviews need to address the sorts of questions found in the Supplementary Evaluation Form whether they use the actual form or not. In addition, journals and newsletters that publish reviews of CALL software could encourage the use of a checklist similar to that in Figure 2, or at base develop some guidelines for reviewers as a part of their editorial policy to ensure that *some* information concerning language-teaching approach is made explicit in the review proper.

The implications of focusing on language-teaching approach as the organizing principle in software design are also potentially quite significant. There are a number of specific recommendations that can be made to software authors and publishers, all of which stem from taking the principles listed in the Supplementary Evaluation Form as *design criteria.*

First, in the earliest stages of the design process, individual software developers and development teams should describe the language-teaching approach to be targeted; that is, determine the overall lesson structure and the role that graphics, sound, screen layout, etc., will play. By definition, this means that the author or one or more members of the designing team should have a solid background in contemporary second-language acquisition theory and research as well as a fair amount of teaching experience with the target audience. Too often, it seems, software has been authored on the basis of general CAI design principles alone or on insufficient language-teaching experience, with the result that a very limited and haphazard set of language-teaching principles is applied.

A second implication of widespread adoption of evaluation forms that include the type of information presented in Figure 2, especially in published reviews, is the potential to have a significant impact on commercial software packages. As was noted at the outset, current checklists and guidelines do not address specifically the kinds of evaluation parameters found in the Supplementary Evaluation Form. This fact suggests that potential buyers do not consider the areas described therein to be of much importance, whereas checklists that include approach and strategy-specific parameters contain the message that these parameters *are* important. This could have two possible results. First, the publishers themselves may develop design criteria that include approach considerations, both for language software that they create directly and CALL software solicited from outside professionals. Second, once it is clear that evaluators and users consider this type of information important, publishers may become more consistent about including it in promotional brochures and in the documentation accompanying the software.

This chapter has described a rationale and a procedure to distinguish CALL software from other forms of CAI by something besides its subject-matter content. It is clear that many CALL practitioners, reviewers, and authors need to pay more attention to second-language acquisition and to teaching methodology in order to *apply* the insights from those fields appropriately in CALL software design, evaluation, and use. CALL is already on the cutting edge of technology: it can also be on the cutting edge of methodology. In order to achieve this, it is necessary to start with the concept that second-language learning is essentially *different* from other types of learning and that, consequently, the criteria for judging the pedagogical soundness of instructional courseware for mathematics, chemistry, or history are not sufficient for judging software for second-language instruction.

References, Language Teaching Approaches, the Evaluation of CALL Software, and Design Implications

1. Anthony, Edward M. "Approach, Method, and Technique." *English Language Teaching* 17 (1963):63–67.
2. Ariew, Robert. "Computer-Assisted Foreign Language Materials: Advantages and Limitations." *CALICO JOURNAL* 2, 1 (1984):43–47.
3. Asher, James J. "The Total Physical Response Approach to Second Language Learning." *The Modern Language Journal* 53 (1969):3–17.
4. Baker, Robert L. "Foreign Language Software: The State of the Art, or Pick a Card, Any (Flash) Card." *CALICO Journal* 2, 2 (1984):6–10,27.
5. Baltra, Armando, "An EFL Classroom in a Mystery House." *TESOL Newsletter* 18, 6 (1984):15.
6. Bialystok, Ellen. "A Theoretical Model of Second Language Learning." *Language Learning* 28, 1 (1978):69–83.
7. _____. "On the Relationship between Knowing and Using Forms." *Applied Linguistics* 3, 3 (1982):181–206.
8. Brooks, Nelson, *Language and Language Learning.* Orlando, FL: Harcourt Brace Jovanovich, 1980.
9. Brown, H. Douglas. *Principles of Language Learning and Teaching.* Englewood Cliffs, NJ: Prentice-Hall, 1980.
10. Brumfit, Christopher. *Communicative Methodology in Language Teaching: The Roles of Fluency and Accuracy.* New York: Cambridge University Press, 1984.
11. Carrell, Patricia L. "Three Components of Background Knowledge in Reading Comprehension." *Language Learning* 33, 2 (1983):183–207.

12. _____, and Joan C. Eisterhold. "Schema Theory and ESL Reading Pedagogy." *TESOL Quarterly* 17, 4 (1983):553–73.
13. Chomsky, Noam. *Topics in the Theory of Generative Grammar.* The Hague: Mouton, 1969.
14. Coady, James. "A Psycholinguistic Model of the ESL Reader," pp.5–12 in Ronald Mackay, Bruce Barkman, and R. R. Jordan, eds., *Reading in a Second Language.* Rowley, MA: Newbury House, 1979.
15. Curtain, Helen A. "Integrating Content and Language Instruction." *ERIC/ CLL News Bulletin* 9, 2 (1986):1,10–11.
16. Dalgish, Gerard M. *Microcomputers and Teaching English as a Second Language: Issues and Some CUNY Applications.* New York: Instructional Resource Center, City University of New York, 1984.
17. Decoo, Wilfred. "An Application of Didactic Criteria to Courseware Evaluation." *CALICO Journal* 2, 2 (1984):42–46.
18. Dulay, Heidi, Marina Burt, and Stephen Krashen. *Language Two.* New York: Oxford University Press, 1982.
19. Ellis, Rod. "A Variable Competence Model of Second Language Acquisition." *International Review of Applied Linguistics and Language Teaching* 23, 1 (1985):47–59.
20. Grellet, Françoise. *Developing Reading Skills: A Practical Guide to Reading Comprehension Exercises.* New York: Cambridge University Press, 1981.
21. Higgins, John. "Can Computers Teach?" *CALICO Journal* 1, 2 (1983):4–6.
22. _____, and Tim Johns. *Computers in Language Learning.* Reading, MA: Addison-Wesley, 1984.
23. Hope, Geoffrey R., Heimy F. Taylor, and James P. Pusack. *Using Computers in Teaching Foreign Languages.* Language and Education: Theory and Practice, no.57. Orlando, FL: Harcourt Brace Jovanovich, 1984.
24. Hubbard, Philip. "Alternative Outlining Techniques for ESL Composition." *CATESOL Occasional Papers* 10 (1984):59–68.
25. _____, James Coady, John Graney, Kouider Mokhtari, and Jeff Magoto. "Report on a Pilot Study of the Relationship of High Frequency Vocabulary Knowledge and Reading Proficiency in ESL Readers." *Ohio University Working Papers in Linguistics and Language Teaching* 8 (1986):48–57.
26. Krashen, Stephen D. *Second Language Acquisition and Second Language Learning.* New York: Pergamon Press, 1981.
27. _____, and Tracy D. Terrell. *The Natural Approach: Language Acquisition in the Classroom.* San Francisco: Alemany Press, 1983.
28. Larsen-Freeman, Diane. *Techniques and Principles in Language Teaching.* New York: Oxford University Press, 1986.
29. Long, Michael H. "Does Second Language Instruction Make a Difference? A Review of Research." *TESOL Quarterly* 17, 3 (1983):359–82.
30. Madsen, Harold S., and J. Donald Bowen. *Adaptation in Language Teaching.* Rowley, MA: Newbury House, 1978.
31. Marler, Jerilyn, ed. *Evaluator's Guide for Microcomputer-Based Instructional Packages.* Eugene, OR: International Council for Computers in Education, 1982.
32. McLaughlin, Barry, Tammi Rossman, and Beverly McLeod. "Second Language Learning: An Information Processing Perspective." *Language Learning* 33, 2 (1983):135–58.
33. Mohan, Bernard A. "Language and Content Learning: Finding a Common Ground." *ERIC/CLL News Bulletin* 9, 2 (1986):1,8–9.
34. Newmark, Leonard. "How Not to Interfere with Language Learning." *International Journal of American Linguistics* 32, 1–2 (1966):77–83.

35. _____, and David A. Reibel. "Necessity and Sufficiency in Language Learning." *International Review of Applied Linguistics in Language Teaching* 6, 2 (1968):145–64.
36. Oller, John W. "Story Writing Principles and ESL Teaching." *TESOL Quarterly* 17, 1 (1983):39–53.
37. Oxford-Carpenter, Rebecca. "Second Language Learning Strategies: What the Research Has to Say." *ERIC/CLL Bulletin* 9, 1 (1986):1–4.
38. Rubin, Joan, and Irene Thompson. *How to Be a More Successful Language Learner.* Boston: Heinle & Heinle, 1982.
39. Scarcella, Robin C. "How Writers Orient Their Readers in Expository Essays: A Comparative Study of Native and Non-native English Writers." *TESOL Quarterly* 18, 4 (1984):671–88.
40. Spack, Ruth. "Invention Strategies and the ESL College Composition Student." *TESOL Quarterly* 18, 4 (1984):649–70.
41. Stevens, Vance. "Implications of Research and Theory Concerning the Influence of Choice and Control on the Effectiveness of CALL." *CALICO Journal* 2, 1 (1984):28–33.
42. Strei, Gerry. "Format for the Evaluation of Courseware Used in Computer-Assisted Language Instruction (CALI)." *CALICO Journal* 1, 2 (1983):43–46.
43. Strevens, Peter. *Teaching English as an International Language: From Practice to Principle.* Oxford, England: Pergamon Press, 1980.
44. Swain, Merrill. "Future Directions in Second Language Research," pp. 15-28 in Carol A. Henning, ed. *Proceedings of the Los Angeles Second Language Research Forum.* Los Angeles: University of California at Los Angeles, 1977.
45. Terrell, Tracy D. "A Natural Approach to Second Language Acquisition and Learning." *The Modern Language Journal* 61 (1977):325–36.
46. Underwood, John A. *Linguistics, Computers, and the Language Teacher: A Communicative Approach.* Rowley, MA: Newbury House, 1984.
47. Wenden, Anita L. "Learner Strategies." *TESOL Newsletter* 19, 5 (1985):1,4–7.
48. Wilkins, David A. *Notional Syllabuses.* New York: Oxford University Press, 1976.
49. Winitz, Harris, ed. *The Comprehension Approach to Foreign Language Instruction.* Rowley, MA: Newbury House, 1981.

10

Teacher Training for CALL and Its Implications

Constance O. Curtin
University High School, Champaign-Urbana, Illinois
Stanley L. Shinall
University of Illinois

Introduction

The purposes of this chapter are to provide a rationale for the inclusion of training in computer-assisted instruction (CAI) in teacher education programs at both preservice and inservice levels and to suggest by example what the nature of teacher training in computer-assisted language learning (CALL) should be. Every era that witnesses a technological breakthrough or ideological advance lends itself to a descriptive label that attempts to capture its essence. In the middle of the 1980s one hears of the Communication Age, the Communication Revolution, the Technological Revolution, and the Information Explosion. Industry has the lead in the development of hardware and software. Education follows slowly on its

Constance O. Curtin (Ph.D. in Chemistry, Columbia University, MAT in Russian, University of Illinois) is a teacher of Russian at University High School in Champaign-Urbana, Illinois, and a Research Associate in computer-assisted instruction with microcomputers and on large systems such as PLATO. She is a member of the American Association for Advancement of Slavic Studies, the American Council for Teaching of Russian, NEA, and CALICO and is past president of the Illinois Chapter of AATSEEL. She is the author of *Russian for Review* and *The Russian Alphabet Program* for the microcomputer published by COMPress.

Stanley L. Shinall (Ph.D., University of Illinois) is Assistant Professor of French and Coordinator of Undergraduate Instruction in the French Department at the University of Illinois, Urbana-Champaign, where he is also the Foreign Language Area Coordinator for the Council on Teacher Education and a member of the faculty at the University High School. He is an assistant editor for pedagogy for the *French Review* and the author of the *French Review Packets*, microcomputer software published by COMPress. His professional affiliations include ACTFL, AATF, and CALICO.

heels. Library card catalogs are being replaced by computer files; word processors are replacing office typewriters. Secondary schools increasingly include "computer science" or "computer literacy" among requirements for graduation; some postsecondary schools place a microcomputer in the hands of every student. We are in the middle of a technological revolution. To ignore advances in technology is to be left behind. How to train teachers to make informed use of this technology is a major challenge for trainers and the focus of this writing.

This chapter is organized as follows: (1) the need for an understanding of the potential applications of CALL in the learning process; (2) the need for teacher training in CALL as reflected in the literature; (3) training teachers in theory and technical knowledge; (4) the kinds of CAI and CALL currently available; and (5) questions raised by CALL, proposed answers to those questions, and a suggested agenda for teacher training in CALL now and in the future.

What Can Teachers Expect from CALL?

What can foreign language teachers find in the literature to help them select and integrate CALL into their curriculum? The literature on the topic, grounded in such diverse areas as psychology, educational psychology, linguistics, and psycholinguistics, is rich in implications, but the abundance of publications easily overwhelms preservice teacher trainees as well as classroom teachers. Moreover, there is little research based upon long-range studies in CALL that reflects the rapid changes in technology and available software. The picture is further complicated by conflicting evidence on the effect of CAI on achievement in different disciplines (often mathematics or sciences) with students of different age and class levels (frequently from elementary school or postsecondary programs). Furthermore, the nature of the hardware, the lesson design, and the degree to which CAI has been involved have varied dramatically. It is not surprising that foreign language teachers have difficulty finding CALL applications in the research.

Methods and the Medium

In 1983 Clark (6)reviewed the research on and the use of media (including CAI) in educational settings and concluded that the evidence provided by media-based attempts to determine the components of effective instructional methods was questionable. Clark found that the investigation and formulation of theories of media attributes (what the intrinsic capabilities of media are believed to be) may be of use in instructional design, but they do not contribute to an understanding of the conditions effective methods must meet in order for learning to take place. Clark suggested that future research focus on characteristics of methods used in instruction and related variables such as task, learner aptitude, and what the learner thinks he or she can get from the medium used in instruction. Clark found that high-ability students preferred more structured and directive methods and media, because they viewed them as a shortcut to success, but in fact such students were insufficiently challenged. On the other hand, low-ability students preferred less structured and more discovery-oriented methods and media, not wanting to expend the energy required in more directive methods, from which they anticipated poor results. Unstructured approaches for the latter students seemed to offer an escape in the crowd; in other words, students could remain passive, although they might otherwise have performed better with more structure. Clark concluded that where media are employed in teaching, the methods used in the media are probably decisive for student achievement, while learner expectations affect their preference for the type of media. In short, students think that specific kinds of media are related to specific learning outcomes, and teachers need to keep those student expectations in mind when integrating CAI into instructional programs. Indeed, the integration of a media component into a curriculum is a critical training consideration; most software now available is prepared with the assumption of either prior or concurrent study. Student aptitude, attitude, and learning strategies are thus important variables in the selection of software for different purposes as well as for the choice of media for presentation.

Cognitive Development

A brief review of models of language learning and the role of aptitude is useful in informing teachers about where CAI might play a role in education. Since most commercially prepared CAI software is designed for beginning levels of instruction, it is important to consider language-learning theory applicable to age groups at the middle-school or secondary-school level, the target populations of most teacher-education programs in foreign language. However, some understanding of what seems to be happening at even earlier age levels prepares us to plan better. In 1981, Walsh and Diller (38) described research done on cognitive development from birth and concluded that young children are able to learn two languages simultaneously with a native accent in each because sound-mastery is a lower-level brain function at work long before higher-level functions develop. Later stages of cognitive development that occur after puberty are more pertinent to the integration within the learner of higher-order linguistic processes (semantic processing, word-object relationships, grammatical sensitivity, and grammatical reasoning), which in turn explains why postsecondary curricula are able to introduce greater amounts of grammar and vocabulary in a given period than can be accomplished in elementary school programs. Heavy emphasis on grammar-demanding analytical skills is inappropriate at the elementary school level where emphasis on practical vocabulary and routine function is called for. The fact that the integration of sound into CALL programs—that is, voice recognition—is still primitive will preclude its discussion here, although sound or more precisely phonology plays an important role in language learning/acquisition. There are some promising possibilities on the horizon, such as interactive video and voice synthesizer/micro matches (see Marty and Hart, 21), that encompass various instructional aspects of interactive audio.

Aptitude

In extensive research, Carroll (3 and 4) has addressed the question of aptitude from the viewpoint of foreign languages. He does not downplay the importance of motivation and attitude as factors in the success of a learner, but states that foreign language aptitude "seems to consist of some special cognitive talent or group of talents that is independent of intelligence, and operates independently of the motivations and attitudes of the learner" (4, p. 94). Carroll breaks down these talents into four areas: phonetic coding, grammatical sensitivity, rote learning, and inductive reasoning. The instrument devised to evaluate these talents is the Carroll and Sapon *Modern Language Aptitude Test* or *MLAT* (1959), a widely used test for learners from grade 9 through adult. The *MLAT-Elementary* (Carroll and Sapon [1967]) is an adaptation of the MLAT designed for learners in the 3rd through the 6th grade. The *Pimsleur Language Aptitude Battery* or *PLAB* (Pimsleur, 1966) is particularly applicable to learners at the junior high school level. The PLAB contains six subtests to measure phonetic coding, verbal intelligence, and auditory ability and also provides for a measure of motivation, while the MLAT uses its five subtests to measure phonetic coding ability, grammatical sensitivity, and rote memory. Carroll states that weakness in any of these areas may be counterbalanced by instructional strategies or perhaps, in some cases, by time on task (Carroll's definition of aptitude). In short, learners with high aptitude may be expected to learn at a faster rate through CALL than those with low aptitude, although the latter may profit too from the motivational aspects that contact with the medium may afford.

Wesche (39) matched attitude and aptitude profiles with instructional modes among adult learners of French in the Public Service Commission of Canada. Aptitude test subscores, information gathered by trained staff through interview, and other means were used to place students appropriately. The core instructional method, Dialogue Canada, was inductive, utilized audiovisual material, and was laddered in its sequencing of structural difficulties. Two alternative instructional modes were designed for students whose profiles suggested that the core program might be inappropriate, one Analytical, the other Functional. Both were built around the core program, but incorporated special patterns and activities to help capitalize upon the learning strengths of participants as well as to compensate for weaknesses.

The kinds of alternative instruction reported by Wesche, particularly those involving media, suggest hypotheses about the types of CALL programs to help learners who demonstrate particular deficiencies in aptitude or motivation and thus may be useful to a general range of students, as follows:

Low Auditory Ability. Programs with audio must have very clearly articulated voices speaking slowly. Presentation of the text on screen may be helpful. There should be provision for student control of pacing and repetition.

Low Phonetic Sensitivity. There is a similar need for control over pacing and repetition to practice sound/symbol correspondences. Programs that present graphics and simulations with text and offer a multisensory presentation help, too, as do tutorials and drills with attention to spelling to help fix written forms in memory.

Low Grammatical Sensitivity. Programs that point out patterns in syntax, grammatical functions, and analogies between first and second languages should incorporate explanations related to concrete examples and employ more functional than analytical language.

Poor Memory. Authoring programs with capabilities to allow the user to input needed vocabulary will help teachers modify drills for specific purposes. Students with poor memory benefit from contextualization, pictorials, and simulations. Programs that show and contrast simulated elements of the language that tend to be easily confused constitute another approach of possible benefit to the lower-aptitude learner with CALL.

It would be reassuring to know that the use of such CALL materials together with other classroom strategies would guarantee student success. More probable is that they provide opportunities closer to the "optimum" conditions that may help to compensate for lower aptitude.

Attitude

Positive learner attitudes toward second-language learning have long been felt to contribute importantly to learner success. Therefore it is important to consider aptitude, attitude, and motivating factors as well: self-image, peer attitudes, and cultural attitudes toward the target language, the learning environment, and the teacher, whether the actual teacher or the medium of instruction, including the computer. Clark (6, p. 456) reported instances of students attributing more fairness and impartiality to CAI than to their teachers, although some highly analytical students did not care for the limitations of restrictive responses in the CAI programs. In addition to aptitude and attitude, there are other individual variables to consider in structuring CALL programs, including how the learner perceives and what strategies the student employs in a learning task.

Learner Characteristics

A recent example of research into learner perception—of interest both for software selection and for program design—is that conducted by Mellgren (24), who found that, in the programs she developed for students of Spanish, field-independent learners (those who demonstrate an ability to perceive meaningful parts of a whole and not be distracted by nonessential elements) were most responsive to CALL. Similarly, Krashen (18) has pointed to studies that indicate a relationship between field independence and the development of second-language proficiency in older children.

Learner Strategies

An excellent source for investigating learner strategies is the research by McLaughlin (23), who claims that, in all likelihood, learners use two kinds of strategies when they learn a second language, both of which form hypotheses, as the grammar of the language is internalized. One set of strategies is found in virtually all learners and involves such things as simplifying, generalizing, imitating with simple and uncomplicated structures, and avoiding the unfamiliar or complicated. The second set tends to be idiosyncratic. The learner attempts to apply formal rules, uses rote memorization, guesses from context, looks for recurrent patterns, attempts to find opportunities to speak or hear the language, and goes to others for help. McLaughlin makes a case for using pedagogical rules in instruction by claiming that rule-guided practice may in fact facilitate storage in long-term memory, encourage retention over time, and aid automatic use of stored language patterns.

Seliger (31) also finds benefit in the use of pedagogical rules to encourage learners to manipulate and to understand the language by concentrating on specifics. Formal rules, according to Seliger, preclude the students' testing of false hypotheses and encourage creativity by aiding learners to construct their own grammars more efficiently.

McLaughlin and Seliger see formalized rules as tools to aid the student;

that is, as facilitators in the internalizing of input with a view to more efficiently informed and confident output. In short, it is important to consider learner aptitude, strategies, and learning styles for their relevance to software development.

Proficiency Development

Higgs and Clifford (12) counsel that early correction of learner errors in the beginning stages of instruction is not only desirable but crucial to attaining high levels of proficiency. Their concern is based upon studies that led them to report that inattention to accuracy encourages and rewards communication at the expense of form and, in some instances, "fossilizes" the learner at a low level of proficiency. For this reason Higgs and Clifford recommend careful consideration of instructional goals, even to the point of multiple tracking. They advocate that feedback on accuracy of production be incorporated into teaching strategies. By extension, decisions about the creation and selection of software should be shaped by the nature of corrective and other feedback deemed appropriate to curricular goals. While achievement and proficiency are not identical, the academic curriculum has generally emphasized achievement. Often oral proficiency has been either an expected concurrent development or sacrificed to a degree. How to have both without ignoring either is a critical problem. The judicious use of CALL may be one of the keys that will unlock the door to future success in both areas. Formal instruction in the language may be largely via computers with class time given over to activities for interpersonal communication and the development of oral proficiency.

Research Summary

The foregoing considerations of aptitude, attitude, learner characteristics, strategies, and proficiency have implications for both the learner and the curriculum. Let us now consider applications of this information in a training course that integrates technology and software in the learning process of teacher trainees. Because it is unlikely that computers will ever be expected to replace teachers under normal conditions, teacher education programs can help teachers to determine how best the computer may serve them and their students. The teacher education curriculum provides an opportunity to examine CALL software and investigate the purpose, the nature of feedback, the suitability for the level of instruction, and whether the design of the program is responsive to learner strategies. Training should include an investigation of the match between student needs and technological capabilities of the medium, while recognizing that software at present does not match every deficiency or every individual learning style or strategy. There is, however, much promise. Interactive CALL with audio may make a significant impact on the student's phonetic coding ability, particularly with random access. Learners with little "grammatical sensitivity" can be led through stages to observe structures and language in action (see Garrett, Chapter 7 in this volume). In addition, the question of time on task can be investigated directly (Hawley and Rosenholz, 9), and more effective use of time has been one of the benefits noted from CALL used by foreign language learners (Curtin et al., 8). CALL can help learners see relationships between words and functions (for example, building word families, examining affixes and inflectional forms). Finally, teachers should be exposed to the potential usefulness of simulation and the promise of interactive videotape and videodisc for the nonverbal aspects of communication.

To date most attention to CALL has focused on its function as a support medium and its capacity to occupy part of the class in a meaningful task while the teacher concentrates on verbal activities with other learners. The profession has yet to see how effective CALL will be if and when more attention is given to developing programs for larger blocks of the curriculum.

Training Needs

What needs are perceived by the profession for training preservice and inservice teachers in CALL? What has been done in professional programs and by others to respond to these needs? In 1983, Renney and Dupuis (30) cited studies in the 1970s in which recent graduates in education were asked to identify areas in which they felt inadequately prepared by their professional training experience. One was the use of media and instructional equipment in the classroom. Marty (20) in 1981 had already pointed to the crucial importance of involving foreign language teachers in the use and applications of computer technology. McCoy and Weible (22) have since warned of the possible disaster that could arise from a sudden urgent need to implement the use of CALL but with foreign language teachers unqualified to use it. Results of a national survey conducted by Stolurow and Cubillos (34) stress the need felt by foreign language teachers for training in CALL.

Institutional Response

Imig (16), also writing in 1983, stated that, generally speaking, schools of education were training teachers in educational technology and that some

20 percent required courses in technology and computer literacy for graduation while another 35 percent provided elective courses in those areas. Has the picture changed? Wright (40) reports that in 1983–1984 nine out of ten college or university schools of education in the United States provided some access to computers, but this training was of a quite diverse nature: computer courses, applied computer courses, and noncredit inservice training. Each merits closer examination.

Computer Courses.   Wright's survey defined computer courses as those devoting 80 percent or more class time to learning about computers themselves or to instructional applications of computers. Wright reports that roughly half of the schools responding to the inquiry offered computer courses to undergraduates in education while two thirds offered such courses to graduates.

Applied Computer Courses.   The second category, "methods" curricula with a computer component, often involved more than one course defined by a criterion that 15 percent course time or less was devoted to computers. Wright found that over 40 percent of the schools with courses in computers also offered a course in instructional uses of the medium, but only one quarter offered instruction in programming; a mere 13 percent provided an overview of hardware or software or touched upon computer-managed instruction, defined as "computers as tools for teachers or students." Yet only one school of education in four required applied computer courses in teacher training programs for secondary education in fields other than computer science, science, or mathematics.

Inservice Training.   The third type of instruction surveyed was noncredit inservice courses made available by schools of education through workshops, conferences, and seminars. Of the responding schools, almost half provided some training in this area, although instruction time varied from four to forty hours in length.

Curricula with a computer training component were considerably more prevalent than applied computer courses at the time of Wright's survey. Approximately half (52 percent) of the institutions offered courses in programming; 47 percent provided an introduction to computers; 31 percent gave courses for teachers and students in computers as tools; 28 percent provided an overview of software or hardware.

Wright's survey also asked respondents to rank-order various plans for initiating or for increasing a computer training program at their institutions within the next two years. Only 25 percent gave high priority to initiating or increasing inservice training programs while 46 percent gave that interest definitely low priority.

Finally, the institutions surveyed were asked questions regarding problems in initiating or expanding extant programs. Problem areas cited were: inadequate software (45 percent); inadequate hardware (34 percent); difficulties of integrating CAI into existing courses (26 percent);

lack of trained faculty (42 percent); and insufficient educational research (16 percent).

It is clear that institutions preparing teachers are making efforts to meet the challenge of technology, but the population targeted for instruction is narrowly defined for the most part, and the type of training uneven. It remains unclear whether training programs incorporating CALL will be mandated for all preservice teachers or whether offerings will be elective. Will programs include instruction in the use of hardware and software components? It is improbable that inservice workshops of only a few hours or days can prepare teachers adequately to select or to use software. Longer and more intensive training is required. An excellent model in this regard is the series of summer workshops and training sessions initiated by CALICO (Computer Assisted Language Learning and Instruction Consortium) held at Brigham Young University (1985) and Duke University (1986). Among others, topics treated have included materials development, lesson design, authoring, networking, graphics, voice, and interactive video. Such curricula, taught by specialists in CALL and foreign language, provide precisely the kind of training needed by teachers unable to obtain institutional training during the academic year.

Noninstitutional Response

There are, of course, inservice training possibilities other than those provided by institutions or professional societies. Stedman (32) called for the evaluation and prompt sharing of innovative teaching practices and recently developed, evaluated educational materials. Stedman places some of this responsibility in the hands of state agencies, claiming that institutions simply are not prepared to handle the volume of demand. His appeal is not alone. An investigation by Fisher (10) found that teachers are excited, not threatened, by new technology. They typically oversubscribe courses designed to introduce them to computer technology. He also noted that if educators and other interested parties fail to demonstrate the full potential that computer-related technology offers to education, companies that produce software will succeed in marketing substandard products because of insufficient critical evaluation to demand quality vis-à-vis pedagogical standards. Fisher also feared that a failure of sufficiently prepared and interested parties to capitalize on the benefits of technology would result in the postponement or even the loss of those benefits. He also considered that the "ordinary" way of training teachers in educational institutions was insufficient for the need at hand. In addition, Fisher emphasized the inability of local school districts to undertake research and development efforts by themselves. Pointing to the existence in some states of agencies such as the Minnesota Education Computer Consortium, he designated the need for federal support in research and development. The uneven distribution of state resources required such consideration.

Many states are attempting to meet the demand through consortia of the type described in Minnesota. Regional offices of state agencies commonly offer noncredit workshops or training sessions in the evenings or on weekends. Rarely, however, are the trainers prepared to deal with specific disciplines, but rather are most qualified to explain computer programming in a general sense. As grateful as teachers may be for this otherwise unavailable training, unless discipline-specific considerations are given, the full potential of CAI instruction may not be realized. The same criticism may be leveled at workshops or training programs sponsored by corporations, specifically by producers of hardware, and related professional organizations. While informative, these sessions usually are directed by individuals more expert in programming than in pedagogy. The training is not necessarily fulfilling, especially if discipline-specific applications are missing. Moreover, such training is often expensive, and in districts with little money available for specialized training, foreign language teachers are frequently not considered priority faculty nor their curriculum most in need of such instruction.

Teacher Concerns

In 1982, Brickel and Paul (2) reported the results of a survey in which, among other things, inservice teachers were asked to identify the three topics of greatest concern and those most needed as inservice topics for the future. Among the most common responses was the need for guidance in developing and teaching innovative curricula, including the use of self-instructional material. Some 40 percent of the respondents were teaching multilevel classes (more than one level in the same class hour or more than one language in the same class). For these teachers, help in developing multilevel instruction approaches was a clear priority. Brickel and Paul also found that 40 to 50 percent of the teachers surveyed attended annual state or regional conferences, and 65 percent attended local professional meetings. Only 20 percent attended national professional conferences, while another 20 percent attended national meetings every several years. Of the respondents, 70 percent reported reading professional journals and newsletters at least monthly.

Information about the quality of software and how to implement it into the curriculum is published in the professional literature and, through its pages, is most likely to reach inservice teachers. Nevertheless, reading about CALL is scarcely enough contact with its technology and application to give practitioners the confidence needed to make an impact on their curriculum with the new media. A much better and thorough long-range tactic is to reach teachers in their preservice training as described below.

What approach is the most economical in time and content to ensure sufficient exposure and training? A preservice course suggests itself to provide an introduction to the psychology of language learning along with a technical understanding of program capabilities, software evaluation, and suggestions for implementation that are responsive both to learner need and to the demands of the learning environment. The authors have implemented such a course at a field site, permitting academic hands-on training and field experience with secondary school students using CALL. The scope and content of this preservice course is exemplified in the following section, and is offered not as a prescriptive blueprint for a teacher training course in CALL but as an example of a successful curricular approach to computers in language teaching that incorporates information and experience that contributes to the knowledgeable use of the medium.

Technical Knowledge

What technical knowledge do foreign language teachers need to acquire in a CAI course in order to use CALL with confidence? Those who teach like to feel in control of the tools they use as well as the subject matter. Since many foreign language teachers have had almost nothing to do with computers, considerable anxiety may be generated by their lack of technical background. The topics that follow constitute a suggested outline for a course designed to prepare teachers to feel comfortable with the new medium.

History

A good place to start a CAI course is with the history of the machine itself, which allows teachers to understand the natural progression from the 17th century calculator of Blaise Pascal through Leibniz's multiplier and the fundamental ideas of Charles Babbage to the earliest computers. The connection between Lord Byron's daughter, who programmed for one of the earliest counting machines, and ADA, the modern computing language named for her, provides a link from the humanities to the microcomputer that sets a positive tone for foreign language teachers in a new technical area. A summary of early history can be found in Clark and Lambrech (5). The computer is a new tool for arts and letters bringing aid and comfort to the humanist much as the arrival of the printing press enabled scholars to reach out to one another and to a larger public.

CAI Terminology

Interaction with students is another area in which teachers are accustomed to feeling in control of the means of communication, both in the foreign language and in English. New vocabulary must be acquired and used in order to converse knowledgeably with students who are interested in programming on the computer. If new CAI terms are presented to teachers as steppingstones to assist them in understanding the computer, this will facilitate learning to use it. The principal terms can be demonstrated or used in meaningful contexts as the teachers work with programs. Recent glossaries of computer technology terms are helpful, such as those compiled by Hope et al. (15), Jones (17), and by Pusack in Chapter 1 of this volume.

Programming Languages

The more popular programming languages, for example, LOGO, BASIC, FORTRAN, TUTOR, Pascal, and PILOT, can be differentiated by identifying and describing them. Teachers who later decide to create lessons will have a basis for deciding which programming language to use. Moreover, knowing what some of these languages can do can assist in judging software. One difficulty with some CAI material is that the computer language in which it is written is not flexible enough to accommodate a variety of possible student responses. On the other hand, a lesson loaded with intricate branching, elaborate help sequences, gratuitous comments, and graphics unrelated to the lesson content might be the result of an irresistible urge on the part of the programmer to show off the power of the programming language and, in the long run, may or may not make a contribution to learning. In addition, a discussion of what is meant by machine and assembly languages or compiled and interpreted BASIC will go a long way towards familiarizing teachers with what their own students are talking about and what popular computer magazine articles on the subject are referring to.

Hardware

An overview of the techniques used for running programs on the microcomputers in common use in the schools today will encourage teachers to try new machines and programs. The Tandy, Commodore, APPLE, and IBM families of microcomputers are used in many high schools and universities. Each has unique routines to turn the equipment on and off and to load and run programs. Each has its own maintenance and checking systems. Even a quick look at a program for word processing will reassure and enlighten those teachers who have not yet used the microcomputer in this way. Hands-on experience with as many of the machines and programs as possible is essential to instill confidence.

Databases

The use of organized collections of data called computer databases is growing in schools. Preservice teachers can profitably explore a simple database system because all teachers must become familiar with the system in their school. And in social studies and English, for example, where literature searches are common (and in foreign language, to a growing extent, when the students research topics relating to the culture of the language studied) teachers must know how to assist students to set up their own databases. Since prospective teachers do not know what facilities and help will be available to them later in their schools, they will find practice with an uncomplicated database particularly valuable.

Hard Disk and Networking

Similarly, an acquaintance with hard-disk management can permit teachers to interact comfortably with networking systems, which are used increasingly in the larger schools. The problems of setting up indices (to find material of specific interest), of backing up the system to ensure against inadvertent loss of programs, of loading material into the computer system for the whole school, not just foreign language programs, are best tackled before teachers are faced with the care and maintenance of such powerful hardware in their parent institution. Effective use depends upon a basic understanding of the advantages and potential trouble spots of a hard disk with or without networking.

Programming

An important part of teacher training on the technical side is acquiring a feeling for what programming is all about. In a series of reader surveys in *Classroom Computer Learning* (29), teachers have asked for a more detailed look at how CAI materials are constructed. Experience indicates that among the programming languages available now, PILOT is a good place to start. A good working description of the language can be found in a recent publication by Conlon (7). (The versions of PILOT used at the University of Illinois in the training program described below are: SuperPILOT, Cupertino, California: The Apple Company; and PC

PILOT, Boca Raton, Florida: International Business Machines, from PC PILOT, Bellingham, Washington: Washington Computer Services, 1985.)

PILOT furnishes a nice blend of simplicity of form, usability, flexibility, and relatively low cost. Simplicity of form means that it is easier to comprehend and faster to learn than some other languages for teachers who do not expect to become professional programmers. Usability refers to its general ability to allow the creation of a great variety of teaching programs, drills, tutorials, simulations, problem-solving lessons, and games. And, for foreign languages in particular, character sets are readily drawn, made accessible through the keyboard, and made available to the user of the computer lessons according to the requirements of the lesson content as planned by the teacher/programmer. Graphics (illustrations, backgrounds, animations, simulations) can be created and connected easily to the lessons. One version of PILOT for the IBM, PC PILOT, will permit the use of a variety of graphics packages beyond the one provided in the package. SuperPILOT for the Apple provides a superb graphics package that can be used immediately by teachers new to programming. PILOT's flexibility is evidenced by the choices available to the programmer for answer judging. The MATCH command allows the teacher/programmer to accept a wide variety of responses on the part of the learner, yet restrictions on responses are possible when necessary. Alternatively, when exact matches are required, which is often the case with CALL materials, PILOT can be written using numerical and string variables. A recent workshop conducted by University High School, University of Illinois, revealed that foreign language teachers who were absolute novices in CAI could learn to create a PILOT lesson, free it from programming and factual errors, test it with a few users, and demonstrate it within two weeks. The most primitive lesson contained a few similar drills with randomization, a character set differing from English, illustrations, and explanations. All but a few of the teacher/programmers accomplished even more, creating a variety of lesson segments, some with unique and innovative routines for interaction with student users.

Undergraduate teacher-trainees in a recent one-semester CAI course also at University High School each prepared one drill using SuperPILOT on the APPLE microcomputer. In this exercise, the trainee created at least one graphic, employed a foreign character set, and developed a series of questions in the second language of their training. No two drills were alike. Some drew attractive scenes and related the questions to the visual material. Others used cultural differences as their theme. One revealed a wry sense of humor that came through successfully in the computer material. In the words of one trainee, this part of the course was "mindblowing."

In addition to working with one system, teachers also need to know that additional excellent programming assistance is available. For example, at the University of Iowa, Pusack (28) has created DASHER, software that allows authors to insert their own material. The software automatically sets in motion a judger that marks errors in the answer, instantly alerting the student to their position and nature, a strategy designed to capitalize on the advantage of immediate feedback (error detection) and nonjudgmental correction (anxiety reduction). The teacher/programmer can build with DASHER a wide variety of exercises including transformation, substitution, fill-in-the-blank, true–false, multiple choice, vocabulary building, translation, and other drills.

For teachers who wish to program in BASIC on a more long-term basis, an authoring aid titled EnBASIC by Tenczar, Smith, and Avner (36) allows extremely flexible sentence judging combined with a precise answer markup system and easy handling of character sets. At present, graphics for programs in EnBASIC must be accomplished either by placing drawings on character sets (attaching sections of a picture to letters of the alphabet) or through independent graphics packages (for example, the *Graphics Magician* brought out by Penguin Software) with the associated increased need for programming knowledge. A very advanced authoring language for the microcomputer is "TenCORE" by Tenczar et al. (35), which is set up for both IBM and APPLE microcomputers.

There are also a number of authoring languages that allow teacher/programmers to insert their own problems into a prearranged computer program in addition to the authoring languages already mentioned. However, after the initial novelty of preparing lessons on the computer wears off, some authoring systems may turn out to be somewhat confining. Teacher/programmers may be limited to using a few exercise formats rather than creating new ones. On the other hand, for a teacher who would like to add CAI-mediated exercises to the curriculum quickly, it is helpful to know that these systems exist. More elaborate systems are being developed that may become more flexible and attractive to use as time goes on. For a discussion of this topic consult Holmes (13).

That all teachers will want to do their own programming is highly unlikely. On the other hand, the belief that it is not worthwhile to provide any training in programming, since overburdened teachers do not have time to write software is an oversimplification. The best teachers already spend a great deal of time preparing innovative class activities. Those who are attracted to using and later preparing CAI for themselves should have access to the necessary training. (See Otto and Pusak, 26.) Teachers who may direct students in writing CAI/CALL lessons for the class need to know what can reasonably be accomplished by computer and what is too time consuming or can be done just as well by another method. At the very least, the teacher's intellectual curiosity is satisfied and a better basis for judging commercial software is established.

Current CAI/CALL Materials ⎯⎯⎯⎯⎯⎯⎯⎯⎯⎯

What kinds of CALL exist today that must be taken into consideration by foreign language teachers and by those who train teachers in this field? CAI and CALL may be divided into five basic types for purposes of clarification (although effective CAI materials generally exist in combination): tutorial, drill, simulations, problem solving, and games.

Tutorial

Tutorial programs include initial topic presentation and review. They may present facts, raw data, or problems, then clarify, outline, explain, and discuss them. They may detail an outline for skill development from step 1 through to step n. They may present, analyze, or synthesize ideas, concepts, or theories, making deductions and drawing conclusions from them.

Drill

Drill programs offer extensive practice, either on a single concept or a series of problems that require massed practice. Drill-based materials assist students in retrieving the practiced items more rapidly at a point when they are needed later for conversation or writing. Drills are developed as practice aids to help students express themselves more freely and confidently, especially in a highly inflected second language. Supplementary interactive CALL drills take place at a lower stress level than in typical teacher/student classroom exchanges. Guided instruction keeps more distractible students on task and is therefore more efficient for them. Remedial drills and "make-up for missed work" are primary areas where CALL practice can help the student catch up with the class.

Simulations

Simulations via CAI/CALL are limited only by the scope and imagination of teachers and students. Students can interact with computer programs on a background of illustrations or with the simulation itself or they can build screen displays to show their growing control of the second language. For example, students could be asked to route oil tankers from production points to final destination keeping in mind the political and physical forces that would interfere with such a route, answering questions in the target language as they develop proposed trade routes. Culture such as history (perhaps a series of maps portraying changes of borders/rulers with interactive practice and optional discussion) or art and architecture typical of one group of people (illustrated, discussed, connected to the people's history, politics, and economic changes) are samples of what can be taught effectively through simulation. Language can be taught or reinforced along with cultural knowledge, with varying emphases depending on the student's level of proficiency and control of the second language. Situations in the foreign culture (e.g., the restaurant or the market) can be portrayed even through illustrations as simple as stick figures made to converse in idiomatic language to which the students are expected to respond. Everyday customs, habits, or details of lifestyles can be brought to life through simulations that include animation as well as static drawings and background illustrations. Language suitable to business, science, and agriculture can be taught, used, and practiced in those contexts with graphic illustrations.

Problem Solving

Problem solving applies as much to foreign language as to mathematics. In a Russian grammar example, first a form can be learned such as the perfective aspect of a verb, then a contrasting form such as the imperfective aspect, followed by the use of an auxiliary to express the imperfective future. These forms can then be asked for, presented as contrasting verbal forms in contextualized sentences and followed by verbs in a variety of contexts. In well-constructed CALL software, students are asked to use these forms as they learn them in order to respond to a series of simulated real-life situations. In another example, contrasting grammar usage between the second language and English can be pinpointed on the screen through interactive CALL programs. The student can be led stepwise in a series of contrasts between troublesome differences in grammar. In a Russian example again, the difference between "I have a book" in English and "A book is of/by me" in Russian might require a series of student responses indicating that the difference has been understood. The small screen, the focus, and the call for response all concentrate the student's attention on the problem at hand.

Problem solving can also include a wide variety of situations in which the student takes newly acquired knowledge in several areas and synthesizes the correct responses in novel situations. If the emphasis is on cultural differences rather than language, problem solving can also require adaptive responses to certain behaviors expressed either in the second language or in English. As an example, the student is asked about a figure gesturing on the screen. Does the gesture indicate "goodbye," "hello," or "watch for thieves"?

Games

Games can run the gamut between those that concentrate on the recreational aspects of the activity and those that are similar to simulations or drills with scoring added. The ideal game is one that exercises a wide range of the student's vocabulary and language usage while incorporating challenge (variable difficulty levels), chance, dexterity, mystery (fantasy, curiosity), and speed (Malone, 19). In better games, the activity that makes for success should be an integral part of a learning process. For example, if students had to learn certain key words, "key" and "lock" in French, and then had to use them correctly to advance through a simulated house (in order to find a treasure—an adventure game) then the use of these words would be natural (the students unlock a door). The students would improve their French and "win" in a direct and positive correlation. Unfortunately, in most games of this nature, the time spent in "unlocking the door" makes learning the words "unlock" and "key" very inefficient. Idiomatic and correct use of the verb as well as recalling the noun is not required in current games of this kind, possibly because it slows the game too much. Games, then, are compromises between how much time and effort is given to active time on task in the foreign language and how much is spent on the mechanics of the game. More recreational games can be used as rewards for completing other activities, and games predicated on a great deal of studied learning can be fitted into the curriculum on a more regular basis.

Combinations

After discussion and demonstration of various types of software, it should be apparent to the teacher learning about CALL that combinations of types will enhance the educational process. Tutorials are much more effective when accompanied by practice on each point interspersed with explanation. Or tutorials can be worked into student interaction with simulations. A series of drills on various points of grammar or culture can be integrated to develop a problem-solving exercise. Students can learn to solve various language problems by working through simulated foreign situations. For example, a shopper appears on the screen in an open-air market and asks the price of certain foods in the target language. A choice of possible replies by the merchant is presented under the picture. The student picks a reply and sees its consequences on the screen. Games can consist of gamelike drills or simulated interactions with foreign language speakers. They can also consist of general problems to be solved using reasoning, skill, dexterity, and intuition in a game format.

Instructional Concerns _____

Another major area that must receive careful consideration by teachers who are involved in CALL use or development falls within the sphere of pedagogy. How does computer-assisted instruction relate to the problems of teaching in general? What general instructional concepts must the foreign language teacher consider when planning to judge or write CALL? Because the medium is so new, insufficient thought has sometimes been directed to pedagogical considerations when judging or developing CAI. A pioneering discussion can be found in Steinberg (33) who summarizes the roles the teacher/author/programmer must assume when creating software. These same factors must be discussed in some form in any course offered in teacher training for CAI. They include expertise in content, learning theory, lesson design, computer programming, and evaluation. If these roles are treated as general educational concerns for any teacher involved in CAI, associated instructional questions will lead to the logical development of criteria for judging software.

Content

A primary concern for foreign languages is accuracy of content. Preteachers especially need to learn to be critical of published CALL materials. Semantic, lexical, and syntactic accuracy in the foreign language must be considered along with cultural authenticity. A native speaker should be consulted when a dubious point arises. The software should demonstrate grammatical accuracy, modern expressions, and up-to-date style. Authentic cultural surroundings are a must. John and Wendy pictured sitting in an American-style fast-food establishment speaking Spanish does little to broaden the students' cultural awareness of the rest of the world, no matter how far the hamburgers are supposed to have traveled.

Learning Theory

A second major area of instructional concern in training teachers for CALL lies in learning theory, especially with regard to motivation. Highly motivated students of foreign language want to achieve proficiency. Well-constructed CALL materials can motivate students toward that goal. To allow students to use software that is repetitive, error-filled, slow-moving, unillustrated, and poorly planned, and which provides little chance for student input is a serious misuse of CALL and dampens motivation. On the other hand, a positive learning experience makes it clear to students that their skills are increasing and that their proficiency can improve.

Rewards that lead to higher motivation should be provided to help the learner achieve a feeling of progress and personal enjoyment in working through a variety of computer programs.

The endless patience of the computer and the privacy of the CAI learning situation are two factors thought to reduce anxiety in learners. Preservice teachers should be warned to avoid programs that use critical remarks about students in feedback even in jest. Audio cues of an unpleasant nature should be used infrequently and with caution. Force-timed routines should be avoided along with forced repetition of exercises. (See Holmes and Kidd [14] for a discussion of learner control.) Students using CALL should always have a sense of where they are in each exercise and in the overall lesson scheme. They should never be left without recourse to help when unable to answer a question. Except in the most obvious situation, i.e., a choice between *a* and *b,* the correct answer must ultimately be available to them no matter what format is chosen for display.

Teachers new to CAI should learn to look for programs that offer students variety. This increases motivation for learning, because the students get a feeling of being in control. Higgins and Johns (11) recommend leaving choices (which drill, what repetition, what path and rate of learning) to the student whenever possible, whether the materials reflect an extensive serious approach or recreational learning. A discussion of the effect of individual differences on instructional variables and the necessity for the development of more student control as the student moves through a CAI lesson can be found in a recent article by Tennyson and Park (37), who counsel that fast-moving students should be able to move ahead, take on extra activities, or repeat selected areas of their own choosing at will. Slower students similarly need to proceed at their own pace and to review at leisure. Students should be challenged but feel in control, inspired but not anxious, stimulated but not tense, active but not driven, helped but not harassed by CAI.

Teachers need to take a good look at the population each software program is intended to reach. A CALL program must be directed to the level of the users. Relevant questions to consider are: What is the students' preparation? What is their reading level in English? What level of language sophistication have they reached? What general age is targeted? Instruction should proceed from the simple to the more complex, but it should begin at the students' current level, and the student should be prepared for the next step. Obviously grade school pupils have interests different from those of college students. Even the directions to the user must differ in addressing these two groups and those in-between. There should be serious programs and those in a lighter vein. However, fun for children might bore the young adult and subtlety may be lost on the very young.

Learners vary in their physical receptiveness to the study of foreign languages, that is, whether they are eye- or ear-minded. A few students feel much more at home with the spoken language. They enjoy, understand more directly, and prefer instruction through listening; they do not feel too uncomfortable even when making mistakes in speaking. Other students feel strongly that they must see the written word before they can retain it, and are particularly sensitive to mistakes in their speech. A few would prefer to substitute learning about the culture for learning the language itself. Most students have a mixture of such feelings. Teachers attempt to satisfy the needs of all by providing a mix of instruction in the four skills with large doses of higher culture and everyday life abroad. Owing to the extra, private time afforded to listening and comprehending the second language, the language laboratory appeals variously to students who enjoy learning by ear and to those who have trouble listening and understanding. CALL programs as offered today attract the students who want at least part of their instruction to be eye-based. In addition, the most recent, heavily illustrated CALL lessons appeal to those for whom a picture is worth a thousand words.

Design, Execution, and Evaluation

In the following discussion of computer lesson design, programming techniques, and student evaluation, a series of open questions will be proposed for consideration by teachers using or developing CALL. Rather than prescriptive answers to these problems, the value of posing such questions in a CAI course lies in the fact that they stimulate teachers toward thinking about these problems. The answers depend on the conditions under which the teachers work with computers, on the student body they teach, on the goals they and their students have set, and on the demands of administrators and parents. As teachers answer the questions individually, they will be guided to develop criteria that are generally applicable to CALL. Suggested criteria to this end are appended to this chapter. (See also a discussion on this topic by Wyatt and Hubbard, chapters 4 and 9, respectively, in this volume.)

Lesson Design.   A practical concern that must be discussed with teachers learning about CALL is lesson design. What sequencing and/or branching should be used? Is there forced branching that depends on a scoring algorithm or is the decision left to the student? How long are the lesson subsections? What are the options for repetition and review? What testing is done and when? Which are optional exercises and which are required? Are the lessons discovery-based (inductive) or do they depend upon reasoning from general principles (deductive)?

Screen design poses other problems. How much should be presented on one screen? The amount may depend upon the context and what is to be taught. What graphics are necessary for clarity? What illustrations improve the lesson? What pictures attract the student? What decoration has been added? Are color and sound used, and how? Is sound optional? Are timed activities included and are they optional? Answers to these questions should indicate that the CALL author has taken into account what is being taught in relationship to what audience or user the effects are intended to reach.

Decisions about lesson design also depend partially on content and learning theory. What to present and how to motivate the learner heavily influence the arrangement of the lesson. As an example, many changes of pace and activity, bright colors, explanations worded in language suited to the less-mature, less-sophisticated, less-prepared student are expected in materials intended for young children.

Technique. Technical programming problems are particularly worrisome for novice teacher/programmers, since they present entirely new questions rather than familiar ones in a new context. What kind of answer-judging techniques are used for lessons in CALL? Are they open-ended? For instance, can students enter a somewhat personalized rendition of the answer to a question as long as they include at least the sought-after key portion of a correct answer in the response? Are only grammatically correct responses accepted? Whether open-ended or exact, are synonyms admissible and provided for? How do the answer-judging routines handle spelling mistakes? Is there a possibility of changing the spelling conventions according to the instructional situation? For example, the spelling requirements for English might be less stringent when that is not the focus of the lesson. Are foreign character sets clear and easy to read? Can English and the foreign language be mixed at will? Are uppercase and lowercase used and easy for students to access? Are the graphics drawn compatible with the screens available in most schools? How are data managed if the CALL in question gives the option of storing/collecting data? What data are valuable? How easily can the teacher collect data? In what form are the data presented? (As totals? In graphs?) What clearing of student data on the disks is the teacher required to do in order for the students to add new data?

Evaluation. How does the software being considered evaluate student performance? Is there forced branching to review material if the scores are sufficiently low, or are there suggestions for review provided for the student? Each teacher must consider carefully whether to use software for student self-testing or for gathering test scores. If evaluation of student performance is done, how does the teacher collect the data? Are tests taken without teacher supervision to carry the same weight as supervised evaluation?

Criteria for Software Evaluation. Once teachers studying CALL have been alerted that content, learning theory, lesson design, computer programming, and evaluative techniques are critical in judging computer software, they can form evaluative criteria to review sample software. An adaptation of the general criteria for evaluation of CAI suggested by Peters and Eddins (27) can be found in the Appendix. Examples follow:

A. Language-based criteria
   1. Is the lesson content correct?
   2. Is the language used authentic culturally?
   3. Is colloquial language used?
B. User-based criteria
   1. Is a specific audience of student users addressed?
   2. Are the computer responses to student input nonjudgmental and encouraging?
   3. Is the program flexible enough to provide for individual differences in student responses?
C. Instruction-based criteria
   1. Are the lesson segments integrated and sequenced logically with flexible branching?
   2. Is the material arranged interactively, requiring thoughtful replies from the students?
   3. Are the responses from the computer program meaningful and helpful?

These are only a few of the criteria in each category, many of which the teachers discover for themselves. With the aid of these criteria, teachers can be led to make evaluative decisions about software on the market now.

Critiques

How can teachers be taught to judge software? One of the best ways to teach evaluation is to ask foreign language teachers to try out as much software as possible interspersed with lectures about CALL covering the topics discussed earlier in this chapter. Following an initial evaluation of sample CALL courseware (which deliberately covers poor as well as good examples) teachers investigate student reaction to samples of programs. Listening to what students say as they work with CALL materials can lead to a genuine understanding of the process the students are going through as well as provide an in-depth and critical look at the software. What seems attractive and clear to teachers may baffle students. Some programs that appear unsophisticated to teachers can be popular with students if they have a gamelike appearance.

In the light of student reaction, issues in learning theory present themselves with renewed force. Is the student–machine interaction a barrier to learning or is it more or less transparent? Do the students feel comfortable with the mechanics of the program so that they can concentrate on learning or are they distracted by confusing directions or unexpected branching? Is there help when the student really needs it, or is the help unnecessary and unused while genuine problems are neglected? Only a student sampling CALL software can tell the teacher how it feels to learn in this way.

Training in the School

As well as evaluating CALL in the light of student reaction, the teachers in a training program typically plan and lead CALL sessions integrated with the curriculum. A variety of activities build competence in this area. Teachers (1) write goals and objectives for various software programs, (2) block out a plan for using CALL in the classroom, in the laboratory, and as homework, (3) demonstrate the capability to lead a class through a CALL lesson, (4) work with small groups while supervising others working at the computer, (5) give demonstrations using a large screen either in the classroom or the microcomputer center followed by practice monitoring the entire class, listening and giving help when needed, and (6) supervise individual students who are reviewing or taking tests at a student microcomputer station or playing language games as reward for good work.

Culture and Daily Life

The potential of CALL to deepen student understanding and involvement with foreign culture and to enrich and enliven foreign language instruction is so great that training programs should give much attention to this aspect. On the small screen, students can see changes in geography connected with political and economic events in the history of a particular group of people. They can interact in the second language with simulations that will bring culture to life, e.g., connecting the art of a particular culture with its language in a lively and attractive way invites the student to learn in a fashion that cannot fail to arouse interest. The simulation may be a pale copy of real life, but considering the little time most students can spend abroad, these simulated activities provide some part of an in-country, cross-cultural experience and help prepare them for the real thing. Geography, history, politics, economics, art, and architecture lend themselves especially to CALL presentations and need not be target-culture specific as long as the programs reflect the target language in question.

The customs and culture of daily life in foreign countries are equally good candidates for CALL lessons. Through drawings, tracings, or maps for example, the students can view ordinary life abroad, the bus trip, the hotel, or the circus to name a few possibilities. They can translate what appears on the screen, perhaps a conversation or narration, or choose the correct response (in the second language) or from a variety of correct responses that lead to differing story lines. Games involving choices between culturally authentic responses and those that are correct in our culture but not in another can mix fun with learning.

Specialized language in daily use about weather or occupations can be introduced with drawings or in games on the small screen. The vocabulary of the professions can be illustrated similarly as it is introduced and used in simulated contexts. All this is looking ahead, but the teachers in training now may provide models of these types of programs as future authors of software.

The Future

No course for pre- and inservice teachers would be complete without a look ahead. Changes occur so rapidly in the computer field that the future may be upon us and our students before we finish exploring the implications of today. Illuminating remarks are to be found in papers by Meredith (25) and Wyatt (41).

A positive development that opens new dimensions for CALL is videotape and videodisc material interfaced with CAI programs. These media provide a moving picture with sound in a combination attractive to students. One drawback is that the amount of material to be worked with is fixed; changes cannot be made in the original type or disk. This problem will be overcome partially when costs go down and much more material is available. Unfortunately, creating the accompanying CALL software takes a great deal of time and therefore effective instruction will come slowly. Videotape is less costly, but the result is limited to back-and-forth access, while videodisc provides random-access but is more costly. See a discussion of this topic in McCoy and Weible (22).

The integration of sound with CALL presents a problem with several possible solutions, each of which has severe drawbacks. Simulated speech is currently not good enough to be used for second-language teaching. Voice digitalization takes too much memory to be practical. The use of a tape recorder under computer control has synchronization problems and loss of random-access capability; interactive videodisc technology overcomes some of these drawbacks but is still in its infancy. Consult a summary of these problems by Ariew (1).

In a discussion of the future of CALL the field of artificial intelligence (AI) cannot be neglected. Until now, theories of AI have not had much impact on CALL. Ideas about teaching the computer enough rules and facts so that it can respond to students in a manner similar to a human have been only moderately successful. However, teaching the computer to "think" reveals some of the processes people go through and should eventually be valuable to teachers. Teachers and teacher candidates should be introduced to CALL/AI (See Chapter 8 by Underwood in this volume) and encouraged to continue following this research in their reading. More important even than what the computer might do by itself is what teachers can do with such a useful ally. The computer can extend the capabilities of a search for knowledge in numerous ways by handling raw data, carrying out directed syntheses, or providing graphic representations of theories or assemblages of facts. A useful discussion of this topic can be found in Higgins and Johns (11).

Conclusion

This chapter has revealed that educators in general and the foreign language profession in particular sense the necessity for teacher training in CALL. The most economical and practical method of training is through preservice programs, since it is not easy to reach teachers in the field. However, training institutions need to expand outreach and inservice programs as well. Professional foreign language organizations must also continue to serve the practicing teacher with preconference workshops and conference sessions in order to share and disseminate innovations and applications in CALL.

Criticism of current CALL must not dissuade teachers from its use. In the future, CALL can be used to explore modalities other than those useful in providing formal understanding of a second language. However, the profession cannot postpone using CALL just because the medium and its materials do not do the ultimate now. Teachers must be trained to evaluate software available today in terms of its technical capabilities and merits, its content, and curricular goals. Cognitive development, aptitude, and learner attitude, attributes, and strategies all help determine the appropriateness of software for thoughtfully planned integration into the curriculum. Second-language educators must be prepared to move with the times, trying new CALL techniques as they become available. They also must be encouraged to ask for new tools as they learn about them in the literature.

Curricular suggestions for training teachers outlined in this chapter are summarized in the following outline of a syllabus for an introduction to CALL:

Technical knowledge	Instructional concerns
History	Content
CAI terminology	Learning theory
Programming languages	Design execution and evaluation
Hardware	Lesson design
Databases	Technique
Hard disk and networking	Student evaluation
Programming with hands-on experience	Criteria for software evaluation

CAI/CALL	Student critiques of software
Tutorial	Training in the school
Drill	Emphasis on culture and daily life
Simulations	for CALL software
Problem solving	The future
Games	
Combinations	

In summary, curricular suggestions for a CALL course for teachers include familiarity with the history of microcomputers, with technology, and with educational concerns touching the use of CALL. Consideration is given to learner needs and professional objectives in the use of this new medium. A rationale is provided for the selection of CALL for school use through suggested criteria. Practical experience with students in school using CALL reassures and encourages beginning teachers to use this tool. Hands-on experience preparing CALL programs deepens insight into both the constraints and possibilities of the medium. A brief look at future developments sets the stage for teacher self-education. The chance to enhance one's teaching using a new, powerful assistant has arrived for those who are willing to take on the challenge. The inservice course for teacher training described here will make it easier for teachers to approach this new medium, the microcomputer, and to participate in the opportunities of the Communication Age opening before us all.

References, Teacher Training for CALL and Its Implications

1. Ariew, Robert. "Computer-Assisted Foreign Language Materials: Advantages and Limitations." *CALICO Journal* 2, 1 (1984):43–47.
2. Brickel, Henry M., and Regina H. Paul. "Ready for the '80's? A Look at Foreign Language Teachers and Teaching at the Start of the Decade." *Foreign Language Annals* 15 (1982):169–84.
3. Carroll, John B. "Characteristics of Successful Language Learners," pp. 1–7 in Marina K. Burt, Heidi Dulay, and Mary Finocchiaro, eds., *Viewpoints on English as a Second Language*. New York: Regents, 1977.
4. _____. "Twenty-Five Years of Research on Foreign Language Aptitude," pp. 83–118 in Karl C. Diller, ed., *Individual Differences and Universals in Language Learning Aptitude*. Rowley, MA: Newbury House, 1981.
5. Clark, James F., and Judith J. Lambrech. *Information Processing Concepts, Principles and Procedures*. Cincinnati: Southwestern, 1985.
6. Clark, Richard E. "Reconsidering Research on Learning from Media." *Review of Educational Research* 53, 4 (1983):445–59.
7. Conlon, Tom. *PILOT—The Language and How to Use It*. Englewood Cliffs, Prentice Hall, 1984.

8. Curtin, Constance, Allen Avner, and Nolen Provenzano. "Computer-Based Analysis of Individual Learning Characteristics," pp.201–13 in Robert S. Hart, ed., *The PLATO System and Language Study*. Studies in Language Learning, vol. 3. Urbana, IL: Language Learning Laboratory, University of Illinois, 1981.

9. Hawley, Willis D., and Susan J. Rosenholtz. "Effective Teaching," *Peabody Journal of Education*. 61, 4 (Summer 1984):15–52.

10. Fisher, Francis D. "Computer-Assisted Education: What's Not Happening?" *Journal of Computer-Based Instruction* 9, 1 (Summer 1982):19–27.

11. Higgins, John, and Tim Johns. *Computers in Language Learning*. Reading, MA, Addison-Wesley, 1984.

12. Higgs, Theodore V., and Ray Clifford. "The Push toward Communication," pp. 57–79 in Theodore V. Higgs, ed., *Curriculum, Competence, and the Foreign Language Teacher*. The ACTFL Foreign Language Education Series. Lincolnwood, IL: National Textbook Company, 1982.

13. Holmes, Glyn. "Creating CAL Courseware: Some Possibilities." *System* 11, 1 (1983):21–32.

14. _____, and Marilyn E. Kidd. "Serving Learner Needs: From Teletype to Micro." *System* 9, 2 (1981):125–32.

15. Hope, Geoffrey R., Heimy F. Taylor, and James P. Pusack. "Glossary of Computer Technology." *Die Unterrichtspraxis* 17, 1 (1984):3–7.

16. Imig, Donald C. "Oversight on Teacher Education." Report given at the Hearing before the Subcommittee on Postsecondary Education of the Committee on Education and Labor, House of Representatives, 98th Congress, First Session, November 1983.

17. Jones, Randall. "A CALI Glossary for Beginners." *CALICO Journal* 1, 1 (1983):15–17.

18. Krashen, Stephen D. "Aptitude and Attitude in Relation to Second Language Acquisition and Learning," pp. 155–75 in Karl C. Diller, ed., *Individual Differences and Universals in Language Learning Aptitude*. Rowley, MA: Newbury House, 1981.

19. Malone, Thomas W. *What Makes Things Fun to Learn?* Stamford, CT: Xerox Corporation, 1980.

20. Marty, Fernand. "Reflections on the Use of Computers in Second-Language Learning," pp. 25–53 in Robert S. Hart, ed., *The PLATO System and Language Study*. Studies in Language Learning, vol. 3. Urbana, IL: Language Learning Laboratory, University of Illinois at Urbana-Champaign, 1981.

21. _____, and Robert S. Hart. *Computer Programs to Transcribe French Text into Speech: Problems and Suggested Solutions*. Technical Report no. LLL-T-6-85. Urbana, IL: Language Learning Laboratory, University of Illinois at Urbana-Champaign, 1985.

22. McCoy, Ingeborg H., and David M. Weible. "Foreign Languages and the New Media: The Videodisc and the Microcomputer," pp. 105–52 in Charles J. James, ed., *Practical Applications of Research in Foreign Language Teaching*. The ACTFL Foreign Language Education Series. Lincolnwood, IL: National Textbook Company, 1983.

23. McLaughlin, Barry. "The Monitor Model: Some Methodological Considerations." *Language Learning* 28, 2 (1979):309–32.

24. Mellgren, Millie Park. "The Effect of Supplemental Computer Instruction on Achievement in Spanish." Ph.D. dissertation. University of Nebraska (Lincoln), 1984.

25. Meredith, R. Alan. "Materials and Equipment: The New Generation." *The Modern Language Journal* 67 (1983):425–30.

26. Otto, Sue E. K., and James P. Pusack. "Stringing Us Along: Programming for

Foreign Language CAI." *CALICO Journal* 1, 2 (1983):26–33,47.
27. Peters, G. David, and John M. Eddins. *A Planning Guide to Successful Computer Instruction.* Champaign, IL: Electronic Courseware Systems, 1981.
28. Pusack, James P. *DASHER: An Answer Processor for Language Study.* Oakdale, IA: CONDUIT, 1983 [Foreign Language Authoring System].
29. Readers' Surveys," *Classroom Computer Learning.* September, 1985:79; October, 1985:37; January, 1986:30–33; March, 1986:53.
30. Renney, James E., and Victor L. Dupuis. "An Analysis of the Perceived Needs and Proficiencies of Preservice Teachers for Program Evaluation." Final Report. University Park, Pennsylvania State University, 1983. [EDRS: ED 237 482.]
31. Seliger, Herbert W. "On the Nature and Function of Language Rules in Language Teaching." *TESOL Quarterly* 13, 3 (1979):359–68.
32. Stedman, Donald J. *Improving Teacher Education: Academic Program Review.* Southern Regional Education Board, Atlanta, 1980. [EDRS: ED 205 467.]
33. Steinberg, Esther. R. *Teaching Computers to Teach.* Hillsdale, Lawrence Erlbaum, 1984.
34. Stolurow, Lawrence M., and Enrique M. Cubillos. *Needs and Development Opportunities for Educational Software for Foreign Language Instruction in Schools,* Iowa City, IA: Center for Educational Experimentation, Development, and Evaluation, University of Iowa, June 1983. [EDRS: ED 242204].
35. Tenczar, Paul et al. *TenCORE Language Authoring System.* Champaign, IL: Computer Teaching Corporation, 1984.
36. _____, Stanley Smith, and Allen Avner. *EnBASIC.* Wentworth, COMPress, 1984 [Foreign Language Authoring System].
37. Tennyson, Robert, and Okchoon Park. "Computer-Based Adaptive Instructional Systems: A Review of Empirically Based Models." *Machine-Mediated Learning* 1, 2 (1984):129–53.
38. Walsh, Terence M., and Karl C. Diller. "Neurolinguistic Considerations on the Optimum Age for Second Language Learning," pp. 3–21 in Karl C. Diller, ed., *Individual Differences and Universals in Language Learning Aptitude.* Rowley, MA: Newbury House, 1981.
39. Wesche, Marjorie Bingham. "Language Aptitude Measures in Streaming, Matching Students with Methods, and Diagnosis of Learning Problems," pp. 119–54 in Karl C. Diller, ed., *Individual Differences and Universals in Language Learning Aptitude.* Rowley, MA: Newbury House, 1981.
40. Wright, Douglas A. "Teacher Preparation in the Use of Computers." Bulletin of the Office of Educational Research and Improvement. Washington, DC: United States Office of Education, 1986.
41. Wyatt, David H. "Computer-Assisted Language Instruction: Present State and Future Prospects." *System* 11, 1 (1983):3–11.

Appendix

Criteria for the Evaluation of CALL Software

1. Is the lesson content correct?
2. Is the language colloquial and modern?
3. Is the material authentic culturally?
4. Is a specific audience of student users addressed?
5. Is help available for the students should they need it?
6. Is the lesson engaging for the student? Are the exercises varied and inventive? Are games or gamelike activities included?
7. Do the students feel successful and rewarded?
8. Are the computer responses nonjudgmental and encouraging?
9. Is there room for individual differences in student responses including multiple correct answers?
10. Is there some degree of student control over the path and pace of instruction including repetition and review?
11. Are the lesson segments integrated and sequenced logically with flexible branching?
12. Do the methods of presentation suit the lesson to be taught? Are they inductive or deductive? Is color or sound used? Are timed exercises used appropriately?
13. Is the material interactive, requiring thoughtful replies from the students? Are the responses from the computer program meaningful and helpful?
14. Are generally accepted teaching practices followed? For example, does the material progress from easy to more difficult steps? Does the material build on what the student already knows? Are there clear directions? Are there uncrowded pages?
15. Does the lesson have specific goals: skills measured by test or checklist, or knowledge gained measured by test or task?
16. Do the students succeed as measured by independent testing?
17. Is there adequate documentation? Are there suggestions for school use?

Index to Persons Cited

Index to
Topics and Programs Cited

NTC PROFESSIONAL MATERIALS

ACTFL Review

Published annually in conjunction with the American Council on the Teaching of Foreign Languages

Modern Media in Foreign Language Education: Theory and Implementation, *ed. Smith*. Vol. 18 (1987)

Defining and Developing Proficiency: Guidelines, Implementations, and Concepts, *ed. Byrnes*. Vol. 17 (1986)

Foreign Language Proficiency in the Classroom and Beyond, *ed. James*. Vol. 16 (1984)

Teaching for Proficiency, the Organizing Principle, *ed. Higgs*. Vol. 15 (1983)

Practical Applications of Research in Foreign Language Teaching, *ed. James*. Vol. 14 (1982)

Curriculum, Competence, and the Foreign Language Teacher, *ed. Higgs*. Vol. 13 (1981)

Action for the '80s: A Political, Professional, and Public Program for Foreign Language Education, *ed. Phillips*. Vol. 12 (1980)

The New Imperative; Expanding the Horizons of Foreign Language Education, *ed. Phillips*. Vol. 11 (1979)

Building on Experience—Building for Success, *ed. Phillips*. Vol. 10 (1978)

The Language Connection: From the Classroom to the World, *ed. Phillips*. Vol. 9 (1977)

An Integrative Approach to Foreign Language Teaching: Choosing Among the Options, *eds. Jarvis and Omaggio*. Vol. 8 (1976)

Perspective: A New Freedom, *ed. Jarvis*. Vol. 7 (1975)

The Challenge of Communication, *ed. Jarvis*. Vol. 6 (1974)

Foreign Language Education: A Reappraisal, *eds. Lange and James*. Vol. 4 (1972)

Foreign Language Education: An Overview, *ed. Birkmaier* Vol. 1 (1969)

Professional Resources

3 5282 00141 1357

A TESOL Professional Anthology: Culture

A TESOL Professional Anthology: Grammar and Composition

A TESOL Professional Anthology: Listening, Speaking, and Reading

ABC's of Languages and Linguistics

Award-Winning Foreign Language Programs: Prescriptions for Success, *Sims and Hammond*

Complete Guide to Exploratory Foreign Language Programs, *Kennedy and de Lorenzo*

Individualized Foreign Language Instruction, *Grittner and LaLeike*

Living in Latin America: A Case Study in Cross-Cultural Communication, *Gorden*

Oral Communication Testing, *Linder*

Practical Handbook to Foreign Language Elementary Programs, *Lipton*

Teaching Culture: Strategies for Intercultural Communication, *Seelye*

Teaching French: A Practical Guide, *Rivers*

Teaching German: A Practical Guide, *Rivers, et al.*

Teaching Spanish: A Practical Guide, *Rivers, et al.*

Transcription and Transliteration, *Wellisch*

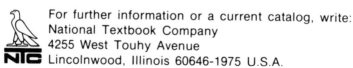

For further information or a current catalog, write:
National Textbook Company
4255 West Touhy Avenue
Lincolnwood, Illinois 60646-1975 U.S.A.